Managing the
Corporate Dream

Restructuring for Long-Term Success

Managing the Corporate Dream

Restructuring for Long-Term Success

William R. Torbert
Graduate School of Management
Boston College

DOW JONES-IRWIN
Homewood, Illinois 60430

© William R. Torbert, 1987

All rights reserved. No part of this publication may be reproduced, stored in a retrieval system, or transmitted, in any form or by any means, electronic, mechanical, photocopying, recording, or otherwise, without the prior written permission of the copyright holder.

This publication is designed to provide accurate and authoritative information in regard to the subject matter covered. It is sold with the understanding that the publisher is not engaged in rendering legal, accounting, or other professional service. If legal advice or other expert assistance is required, the services of a competent professional person should be sought.

From a Declaration of Principles jointly adopted by a Committee of the American Bar Association and a Committee of Publishers.

ISBN 0-87094-922-5

Library of Congress Catalog Card No. 86–72274

Printed in the United States of America

1 2 3 4 5 6 7 8 9 0 K 4 3 2 1 0 9 8 7

To my sons Michael,
Patrick, and Benjamin,
who have made it all impossible—
and delightful

ACKNOWLEDGMENTS

Is it inevitable that a book about restructuring should itself have been restructured as many times as this one has? Perhaps, but whatever the answer, the fact that this book has changed so much since its conception means that many people have influenced it profoundly, yet none can be blamed for the unforeseeable outcome.

My own influence on the outcome has frequently seemed limited to accepting the influence of others, so I certainly do not wish to be blamed for the result. But I suppose that since my name is on the cover, I must at least agree to serve as a locus for whatever commentary there may be.

Early in this book's development, I was most grateful for the at once confronting and supportive feedback of Tony Athos, Barry Bluestone, Jennifer Cassettari, Michael Cassettari, David Ellerman, Sergio Foguel, Jim Gips, Rosabeth Kanter, Bob Kegan, Lou Pondy, Emily Souvaine, and Joe Spieler. Bob Kegan actually influenced this book long before the first word was put on paper, for it is his dynamic version of developmental theory that I have studied most carefully over the past decade. The reader will find his work cited at various points in the book (see especially Appendix A). In addition to his formal work, I have had the good fortune to know Bob as a friend and to experience him discovering the different logics that different people bring to situations. I have learned from him by osmosis and can feel his influence not only on my thinking but on my day-to-day managing and my consulting.

Later versions of the manuscript received close readings and detailed, helpful suggestions from Marcy Crary, Paula Duffy, Alice Holstein, Viviane Robinson, and Marlene Veldwisch. Throughout the project, Jean Bartunek, Ivan Brown, Francine Crystal, Fred Grubb, Bob Krim, Richard Nielsen, Sev Bruyn, and John Van Tassel provided continuing colleagueship, discussion, and commentary. Individual chapters received helpful critiques from George Aragon, Tom Dunn, Walter Klein, Meryl Louis, and Marcia Millon.

Other colleagues have become my research associates over the years in the various empirical studies underlying this book. Suzanne Cook-Greuter, Dal Fisher, and Keith Merron have participated in much of the research. It would simply never have been done without them. Cindy Bromenschenkel, Nancy Cassard, Patty Costigan, Barbara Garrey, Elaine Kiuber, Charlie Moore, Kathryn Pierce, Peter Roberts, Marianne Votta, and Tom Wells all served as formal or informal research assistants at various points in the research and writing.

At a point after I had given up the search for the right agent, Salay Smith came to the rescue and led me toward Helen Rees. Helen is empathic, committed, enthusiastic, and effective. From my limited point of view, Helen is perfect. Thank you, Helen.

A practicing manager, such as a dean of a graduate school of management, should not have time to write in the first place. I certainly would not have had time to write had not Jack Lewis generously agreed to take my place while I took a sabbatical. Even that would not have sufficed, however, were it not for the extraordinary competence and professionalism of my administrative secretary, Priscilla Sliney, who has gracefully managed whatever was necessary in my presence and my absences over the past five years.

I am especially grateful to all the managers who participated in the various phases of the research that underlies this book and who in many cases gave their permission for case studies they wrote to be used, anonymously, in this text and other papers describing the research. In particular, I have been sustained throughout this project by the unusual commitment and cooperation of the many Boston College MBA students who have served as second-year consultants within the program and who have later become ongoing members of an alumni group dedicated to continuing on-the-job learning about the subtleties of managerial practice.

Jack Neuhauser, my boss, is militantly antitheoretical in his managerial practice, teaches the virtues of waiting and unobtrusive action by example, disarms potential opposition and self-importance through humor and disillusioning candor, and in general, functions in what to this neophyte appears for all the world to be a Zen master-like manner in the midst of the American executive scene. Like the ancient tree in Chuang-Tsu's story, he survives, and provides a service that benefits all in his neighborhood, by appearing useless. Certainly, he is centrally responsible for the pleasures of my work over the past eight years and for the blossoming of the Boston College School of Management.

William R. Torbert

Managing is the art of making dreams come true.

Done properly, managing is the broadest yet most precise, the most unrealistically demanding yet simultaneously the most practical, the most straightforwardly humane yet also the most mysterious and paradoxical of all the social arts.

But how rarely is managing done properly! More often than not, the dream does not come true as planned. Why not?

Some managers insulate themselves within narrow dreams of what they are supposed to do and how their organization is supposed to work. Their dreams insulate them from the dreams of others, from what is really going on, and from taking responsibility for the consequences of their own actions. Such narrow dreams never come true. Either they are shattered and the dreamer is rudely awakened, or else they slowly constrict the success and the awareness of the dreamer.

Other managers take pride in their "realism," sometimes harsh, sometimes benign. They imagine that they hold no dreams at all. They imagine that they calculate and manipulate objective quantities of raw materials, money, technology, and human resources. In fact, they live in a dream as well, cut off from the source of their own vitality. They live enclosed within the tattered dream of "pure objectivity," from which the physical sciences began to awaken three quarters of a century ago.

Making dreams come true is the most demanding and paradoxical of human processes because to do so requires that one wake up, repeatedly, without losing the dream. Different awakenings are required at different stages of making the dream come true. In economic and organizational terms, the entrepreneur fired by a dream must first awaken from mere dreaming enough to transform his or her intuitive vision into a politically and financially viable strategy that attracts the investment of others. Many ventures do not attract sufficient investments and fail at this early point.

If the entrepreneur succeeds in attracting investments, he or she must next awaken from mere strategizing enough to transform the strategy into an actual operating entity. Many well-capitalized ventures do not get quality products or services out the door and into an attractive market position on time, and fail at this point.

But, even if the new venture initially succeeds operationally (in the sense of generating net revenues, winning an election, conquering territory, gaining converts, etc.), it may nevertheless fail at this point because that which it operationalizes may contradict the original dream rather than make it come true. This form of failure is, of course, not directly visible, is easily confused with success, and is the cause of much misery and injustice.

Imagine a young professional—whether engineer, accountant, lawyer, doctor, consultant, or architect—who has apprenticed at a large firm and is now starting his or her own small business. Let us say it is an architect who wishes to build flexible structures for midsized, fast-growing businesses. The dream is to integrate aesthetics and functionality, to develop an ongoing relationship with clients, and to build unique structures that truly meet and change with clients' needs, while symbolizing their evolving identity.

But the architect's family must eat. So in the early months, he accepts whatever commissions come his way. A year later, his office has twice outgrown itself and the company is a startling success in economic terms, but his life is a pressure cooker and his business is remodeling private residences. He is not doing what he dreamed of doing. He is not managing the corporate dream. He experiences the incongruity between dream and actuality as anguish.

This is part of a true story. We will return to learn its outcome in Chapter 5 when we consider this stage of organizing in greater detail.

The important point for this introduction is simply that as

dreams are transformed into tangible realities, they are frequently deformed or forgotten. On a much larger scale than the young professional, the Coca-Cola Company became uncertain several years ago as to what the "real thing" really was. After much market research, it replaced its old soft drink formula with a new one. Within weeks, the company began to realize it had lost something more central to its success than it had realized. Individuals and social systems rarely recoup as quickly as the Coca-Cola Company managed to do. On a still larger social scale, we know that in 1789 the French revolutionary dream of liberty, equality, and fraternity was transformed in short order into the actuality of the Reign of Terror and the guillotine. In 1917, the Russian revolutionary dream of a democratic, proletarian socialism was transformed in short order into the actuality of the autocracy of Lenin and Stalin—far more totalitarian than the autocracy of the tsars who preceded them.

As dreams are transformed into actualities, they are reinterpreted and reenacted again and again in new circumstances, as the foregoing examples begin to suggest. Each reinterpretation and reenactment must be different in order to speak to the different circumstances. Yet each action must nevertheless be consistent with the dream, or else an acknowledgment of deviation and a reaffirmation of the dream. When Coca-Cola managed to reintroduce its original formula as "Coca-Cola Classic" while continuing to market its new formula as well, this paradoxical response met the challenge of managing the corporate dream at that point in Coca-Cola's history and the history of the soft drink industry.

THIS BOOK'S THEMES

This book describes how managers and organizations evolve as they seek to make their personal and corporate dreams come true. Each stage of evolution represents a complete and internally consistent interpretation of the dream, an interpretation appropriate to a particular era in the project of making a dream come true, but an interpretation that easily substitutes itself for the underlying dream.[1] Consequently, managers and organizations easily become stuck at a particular stage of development. Transformations between stages are commonly resisted because they are periods without clear guidance, periods when strategies, structures, and the very meaning of concrete events go out of focus. Yet, repeated, timely unfocusing and refocusing, destructuring and restructuring is necessary if a manager or an organization is to become successful in the first place and then remain so over the long term.

The contemporary world of the late 1980s demands, as never before, managers who can guide teams and organizations through fundamental tranformations by becoming clearer about, rather than losing, a guiding dream. At the simplest technological level, product life cycles in the electronic information and communications industries have become drastically foreshortened. Products frequently move from *conception* to *capitalization* to *introduction* to *maturity* to *senescence* all within less than five years. Since each of these stages represents a fundamental change in focus and priorities, this fast pace of change virtually eliminates the notion of stable state management. A manager either leads the organization through these fundamental changes by equally fundamental changes in his or her own style at the appropriate times, or else he or she does not last. Many managers today do not last.

Somewhat more generally, recent research on the CEOs of fast-growing midsized companies shows that their outstanding characteristic is their ability to transform their leadership role at each successive stage in the company's development.[2] They move from being *idea generators*, to being *doers*, to *managing doers*, to *strategizing and managing organizationwide change*. Other entrepreneurial CEOs are fired when their company outgrows them, or else they have the sixth sense to sell the company just before disaster hits.

Large, mature companies must transform too. Even those labeled "excellent" are frequently incapable of transforming themselves when market conditions change suddenly, when they are acquired and expected to play a new role vis-à-vis their new "parent," or when they reach a size that their previous systems can no longer support. The result is a short-lived dream of excellence. A full third of the companies that Peters and Waterman classified as excellent in their 1982 book *In Search of Excellence* no longer met their criteria for excellence two years later![3]

This book uses the words "restructuring" and "transforming" interchangeably to refer to periods of fundamental personal or organizational change from one stage of development to the next. In the 1980s, the word "restructuring" has been popularized as referring more narrowly to legal and financial changes in ownership—to mergers, acquisitions, defenses against unfriendly takeover threats, leveraged management buyouts, or worker buyouts through Employee Stock Option Plans (ESOPs). During the 1980s, companies have been restructuring, in this narrower sense, faster than a snake sheds skins. These changes of identity are beginning to be understood, not as a onetime phenomenon for a given company but as a continuing condition of business. The argument of this book is that financial and legal restructuring will only be an economically productive venture when it in fact helps the organization(s) to transform to the appropriate next stage of development, becoming more attuned to the corporate dream.

The issue of how to transform and simultaneously become more attuned to a corporate dream confronts U.S. businesses on a still wider, global scale today. The long and deep recession of 1980–82, capping the stagflation of the 1970s, threw a glaring light on the inefficiencies in American management, especially in contrast to the Japanese. For the first time in the 20th century, Americans found themselves in the position of looking abroad for lessons in management. Effective management had seemed America's special genius. Suddenly, the Japanese seemed to be making the dream come true better than we. It was very disorienting and disturbing.

At the same time, the Japanese success highlighted the fact that most markets were now global rather than national. This change in the playing field was catching most American businesses by surprise. They scrambled to reorient their strategies to the reality of world companies in global competition. For example, when the most significant competitors of a U.S. company are actually in Austria and Australia, then strategies which worked vis-à-vis one's domestic competitors may turn out to be putting one at a disadvantage globally. Moreover, since the rules of the economic game are significantly different in different countries, no single global strategy will suffice. Company managers must learn how to formulate an abstract but meaningful global vision or mission and how to translate that passionate mission into multiple country strategies. A global company must become a federation of self-managing subsidiaries, each testing its relationship to an overarching corporate dream. This is a fundamentally different managerial "game" from mandating a single strategy from above and treating the issue of dream or mission as nothing more than public window dressing.

Not only must organizations transform their strategies as they develop, or as their environment changes, but managers must be capable of transforming their own leadership strategies depending upon the person or organizational unit they are dealing with. If a large company buys a new venture in order to infuse capital into the new venture and entrepreneurial products and spirit into itself, the CEO and the vice president for finance of the parent company had better relate differently to the new venture than to the parent company. Otherwise, they will simply destroy the entrepreneurial environment. This negative scenario has happened so frequently in the past decade that today the hottest new strategy is for major corporations to take *minority* positions in small companies so as *not* to control them, so as not (inadvertently) to kill them off. Obviously, CEOs of major corporations have not, in general, been good at transforming their own leadership strategies to match the organizational unit with which they are dealing.

In the face of fundamental, transforming changes such as those of the early 1980s, managers can no longer assume that they know what actions are efficient, effective, or legitimate. Hungry for coherent descriptions of what is happening to them, for hope that someone is doing it right, and for advice about how to recover their balance, managers have recently made a slew of business books into best-sellers. Not surprisingly, the "one-minute" recipes for "excellence" that they have found in popular business books are often simplistic. A simple answer is always to be preferred to a complex answer, all else being equal. But, as managers have already discovered from experience, the simple answers will not do. One minute's worth of intense managing will not resolve knots tied by years of bad habits or inattention. Descriptions of excellent companies do not help in any direct way to make one's own company excellent. For any stable system, it is fairly simple to observe and deduce what actions are efficient, effective, and legitimate. For us today, the question is: what actions are efficient, effective, and legitimate in a world of rapid transformations?

This book describes a rare quality of action, here named **action inquiry,** that can generate efficiency, effectiveness, legitimacy, and restructuring all at once.[4] Action inquiry can diagnose and relate effectively to each stage of development, and encourages timely, nonviolent transformations from stage to stage. Action inquiry is the paradoxical process referred to earlier of repeatedly waking up (and waking others up) without forgetting the guiding dream. It involves a constant testing back and forth among dream, strategy, action, and outcome to discover whether they are consistent with one another and where changes can improve effectiveness. Each dilemma is treated as requiring a fresh effort to be aware, to be attuned, and to act creatively. Every slothful molecule in us resists this effort and makes us eager targets for the perennial brisk trade in easy answers.

Because action inquiry emerges as a necessary and desirable approach to managing only as persons reach relatively late stages of personal development, after less demanding approaches have been tried and found wanting, it is introduced here in the latter half of the book. The claim is that only those managers who awaken to the point where they can make dreams come true in their own lives become fully capable of exercising action inquiry. Therefore, only such managers can lead larger groups, organizations, or nations through the developmental transformations that make corporate dreams come true. Only such managers can be said truly to be managing the corporate dream.

This book offers a *complex* developmental theory, along with a mode of practice—action inquiry—that is *difficult* to master. It argues that this complexity and this difficulty appropriately reflect the actual complexity of reality and the actual difficulty of managing well. Instead of promising a "quick fix" (and in reality providing a "fast fade"), this book introduces a theory and a mode of managerial practice worthy of a lifetime of exploration and refinement.

The reader should not expect that this theory and practice will function like a magic wand eliminating all difficulties. This theory cannot be verified once and for all in some external way and therafter be implemented in a rote, mechanical fashion. Quite the reverse, each practitioner must retravel the path of development and rediscover the taste of action inquiry for himself or herself, by verifying why it is essential to him or her. Moreover, the more the paradoxical dream and practice of action inquiry is mastered, the more it will highlight the complexities and difficulties in each new situation, so that one is less likely to pretend they are not there, less likely to stumble over them blindly, less likely to blame someone else for unanticipated problems, and more likely to transform such problems into timely opportunities. In other words, the more this theory and practice are mastered, the more they highlight the need for a fresh awareness in each new situation.

THE BOOK'S STRUCTURE

The book as a whole, with its many organizational and managerial cases, is dedicated to illustrating both the theory of developmental stages and the practice of action inquiry. Although some of the more intimate inside views of managers are masked to protect confidentiality, many of the episodes concern figures and companies already very much in the public domain—the two Thomas Watsons and IBM, Fred Smith and the early years of Federal Express, Harold Geneen of ITT, Secretary of State Henry Kissinger, venture capitalist Arthur Rock, corporate raiders Irwin Jacobs, Sam Zell, and T. Boone Pickens, and others.[5]

The first section of the book examines the first three stages of organizational and personal development. Organizations are generally not yet concretely visible at the first two stages—do not yet consist of a plant and employees. Managers at the first two stages are also rare, since these are stages that persons usually move through before adulthood. Nevertheless, how organizations and persons are guided through these early stages of development will deeply influence their later success.

The second section of the book examines the fourth, fifth, and sixth stages of organizational and personal development. Most organizations and managers function at the fourth or fifth stage of development. Many mature organizations and executives today are reaching towards the sixth stage of development, though few envision—much less achieve—the process of continuing inquiry and timely, flexible action characteristic of this stage. Only at the sixth stage do organizations and executives be-

---

The First Six Stages of Development

Organizations	*Persons*
1. Conception	1. The Impulsive Manager
2. Investments	2. The Opportunist
3. Incorporation	3. The Diplomat
4. Experiments	4. The Technician
5. Systematic Productivity	5. The Achiever
6. Collaborative Inquiry	6. The Strategist

---

gin to recognize the importance of history and timing for effective initiatives. Only at this stage do they begin to accept that organizations and managers can frame reality in radically different ways (and that each frame may be appropriate to a particular stage of development). Only at this stage do they begin to act in ways that help other managers and organizations to restructure.

One might expect that each managerial style would be most successful at the corresponding stage of organizational development. For example, the **Investments** stage of organizing parallels the **Opportunistic** style of management. At this stage, an incipient organization's most crucial priority is attracting the initial investments necessary to open its doors for business. Consequently, one might expect an **Opportunistic** manager to be the most successful kind of manager at this organizing stage, since he or she is focused on spotting and seizing external resources.

As a carefully directed subordinate, the **Opportunistic** manager may indeed be successful at this stage. But because persons at the **Opportunistic** stage of development have a rigidly externalized perspective, with a very short time horizon—a perspective that most people outgrow by their early teenage years—the **Opportunistic** manager will not function effectively in an executive leadership role. For an organization's leadership is responsible, not just for meeting the external demands of a given stage of organizing, but for meeting them in a way that develops enduring legitimacy for the organization and sets the stage for further transformations. A manager at the sixth stage of development (or at still later stages sketched briefly in the Postscript) is able to act opportunistically at the appropriate moment rather than always being opportunistic. Such a manager has mastered the logic of opportunism rather than being enslaved by it like the **Opportunist.** Such a manager will better meet the demands of leading an organization into, through, and beyond the **Investments** stage.

In this way but in greater detail, each chapter on a given managerial style suggests its relationship with the corresponding organizational stage, its limits when executive leadership is required, and the organizational conditions which can encourage development to a later style.

Section Three describes the discovery and practice of action inquiry. These chapters offer two kinds of illustration—(1) of individual managers beginning to exercise action inquiry in their own immediate work and (2) of interventions that help whole companies transform from one stage to another. The chapters on action inquiry offer examples of incredibly precise action. Readers may wonder what it is necessary to *become* in order to *act* so precisely. You may wonder whether it is possible to cultivate a quality of attention so active, so motivated, so precise, and so obedient to a higher order that it can, right in the midst of the hurly-burly, transform debt into equity, cut through the Gordian knots into which situations twist themselves, and parlay incipient chaos into new organization. To develop this kind of attention, this kind of precision, and this kind of power requires not just a little more discipline than most of us currently exercise, but rather further developmental transformations.

NOTES

1. Chapter 2 provides an overview of the stages of development, and Appendix A describes the underlying theory of development in more detail.

2. This research was conducted by McKinsey & Co. on CEOs of companies that had more than doubled in size over the previous five years and is described by J. Albertine and A. Levitt, "How Entrepreneurial Winners in Mid-sized High-Growth Companies Satisfy Their Appetite for Daring," in *Management Review*, December 1984.

3. "OOPS! Who's Excellent Now?" *Business Week* (cover story, November 5, 1984). According to the article, at least 14 of 43 companies cited as excellent by T. Peters and R. Waterman, *In Search of Excellence* (New York: Harper & Row, 1982) had stumbled badly by late 1984.

4. Ordinarily, we try to divide action from inquiry—the "real world" from the "ivory tower"—in order to preserve the strength of our action and the

objectivity of our inquiry. But we cannot, in fact, accomplish this, either in everyday business or in the purest of the physical sciences. Every inquiry we make is an action, whether we recognize it as such or not. And every conclusion we reach about the significance of the actions of others represents an inference of questionable validity, whether we recognize it as such or not. Indeed, all information—even scientific or philosophical—is simultaneously an action, influencing where our attention goes and what we give authority; and all action is simultaneously information communicating some meaning, whether intended or not. Recognizing this, action inquiry shapes itself so as simultaneously: (1) to learn about the developing situations, (2) to accomplish whatever task appears to have priority, and (3) to invite collaborative transformations (rather than resisting change altogether or imposing it unilaterally). How action inquiry accomplishes all these aims at once is the object of illustrations in the later chapters of this book.

The way in which all language, even when intended to be purely descriptive, functions as action, and what this implies about both science and politics, is explored with virtuosity in three books related to the thought of Ludwig Wittgenstein: first, his own *Philosophical Investigations*, Wright and Anscombe (eds.), Anscombe (trans.), (Oxford: Basil Blackwell, 1953); next, H. Pitkin, *Wittgenstein and Justice* (Berkeley: University of California Press, 1972); then A. Janik and S. Toulmin, *Wittgenstein's Vienna* (New York: Simon and Schuster, 1973). One version of the implications of these ideas for the conduct of social science and social action is found in C. Argyris, R. Putnam, and D. Smith, *Action Science: Concepts, Methods, and Skills for Research and Intervention* (San Francisco: Jossey-Bass, 1985). This author's discussion of these issues is found in "Doing Rawls' Justice" in *Harvard Educational Review* 44, no. 4 (November 1974), pp. 459–60 in "On the Possibility of Revolution within the Boundaries of Propriety" in *Humanitas* 12 (February 1976), pp. 111–46; in several chapters in P. Reason, and J. Rowan (eds.), *Human Inquiry: A Sourcebook of New Paradigm Research* (London: Wiley, 1981); and in "Executive Mind, Timely Action," *ReVision* 4, no. 1, (1983), pp. 1–23.

5. Appendix A describes the methods used to collect the cases and assign them to particular stages of development.

CONTENTS

**SECTION III   Action Inquiry: An Approach to
Transforming Managers and Organizations**

Early Stages of Social Organizing and Managerial Learning

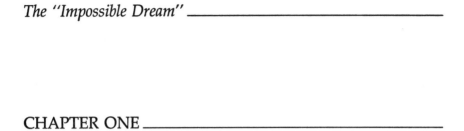

Conceiving an Organization

When does an organizing process begin? When and how is an organization conceived? As simple as these questions sound, the answers are remarkably complex and elusive. We can look first at the history of IBM for an illustration of the issues at stake.

IBM (International Business Machines) was legally incorporated as such in 1924. But in no other sense would one argue that IBM was conceived at that time.

The company had existed at CTR (Computing-Tabulating-Recording) since 1910, when Charles Flint, "the father of trusts," bought and combined three previously independent companies. And Thomas Watson, Sr., whose name is now indelibly linked with that of IBM, had been president of CTR since 1915 and was president of one of its three subsidiary companies, Tabulating Machine, before that. But neither 1910 nor 1915 represent the dates when the organization was conceived, for the tabulating machine that started it all and the man who invented it and started his own company to make and lease the machine went much further back than that.

Herman Hollerith went to work in Washington, D.C., after finishing college in 1879. There he learned that the crude tabulating devices then available were inadequate for the nation's burgeoning census needs. It would take nearly the entire decade to complete the 1880 census, and unless new machinery were invented, the 1890 census would not be tabulated before the 1900 census was taken. In 1882, Hollerith became an instructor at MIT. There he tried and eliminated several approaches to improving the tabulating process. He achieved the critical insight during a vacation train trip to the West, when he saw how conductors created "punch photographs" of passengers on their tickets so that they could not exchange them. He left MIT and took a variety of jobs while working mainly in his laboratory.

Hollerith received his first patent in 1884, and the machine had a successful trial in the Baltimore census in 1886. In 1890, his machines were matched in a test against two others, proved superior, and won him the 1890 national census contract. Austria, Canada, and Italy followed suit in the next two years. Hollerith incorporated in 1896. He initially subcontracted keyboard punch production to Pratt & Whitney and production of the electrical apparatus to Western Electric. But after receiving the 1900 census contract, he created his own manufacturing shop. He leased the machines, designed new types of cards that were commercially useful, and found himself making much of his money off the cards themselves which could only be used once. Over 100 million cards were used in the U.S. census of 1890 alone.

Hollerith took pride in the fact that he had no sales force— all his clients came to him. By 1908, he had over 30 commercial clients and a large backlog of orders. But he now had large manufacturing expenses and competitors as well. When he lost the 1910 census contract, he sold the company to Flint and became chief engineer of CTR.

With this brief sketch of the founding of IBM, we can begin to appreciate the complexity of determining when and how an organization is conceived. Was IBM conceived in 1879 when Herman Hollerith first recognized an unmet need? In 1882 on his vacation train trip? In 1884 when he received his first patent? In 1890 when his tabulating machine first went into production? In 1896 when he incorporated? In 1910 when CTR was created? In 1913 when Thomas Watson joined CTR? In 1915 when Watson became president of CTR? In 1924 when CTR became IBM? Or, since the IBM we know today is a computer company, should we say that IBM was conceived in the late 1940s when it first entered the computer business?

This trail of questions illustrates that organizational conception is a seed within a seed within a seed. Any single stage of development resolves into a whole history of development when observed more closely. Looking back over the past century of IBM's history, however, the entire period of Hollerith's innovation, right up to the merger in 1910, looks like the **Conception** period of the firm. The very qualities of which Hollerith was proudest—his lack of sales force and his "sole proprietor" mentality—blocked others from making major **Investments,** both financial and managerial, in the firm and thus prevented it from growing beyond Hollerith until he sold it.

But if we look more narrowly at Hollerith's company between 1879 and 1910, it appears to have moved through four stages:

1. **Conception,** 1879–1884, when he developed a patentable invention to meet a need.
2. **Investments,** 1884–1890, when first Hollerith, then the city of Baltimore, and finally the U.S. Census Bureau invested attention and money in the new tabulating machine.
3. **Incorporation,** 1890–1900, when the company developed a regular production process and became legally incorporated.
4. **Experiments,** 1900–1910, when Hollerith developed new cards and his own plant and production process.

If, on the other hand, we look not just at Hollerith's company, nor even just at IBM, but more broadly at the Information Era that is currently emerging from the Industrial Era, the entire first century of IBM may count as one of the **Conception** stage seeds of the new social era.

It is not important, either practically or theoretically, to establish a precise boundary between different stages. Any such precise boundary would inevitably be somewhat arbitrary. What is important, both in practical and theoretical terms, is that all the stages of one organizing process may nest within a single stage of some longer term organizing process.

We will return to IBM in each of the chapters on organizational development to see how its history illustrates the shape and significance of each of the stages in the organizing process.[1] Having seen how complex it is to determine *when* an organization is conceived, we can now turn to other questions about the **Conception** stage of organizing, such as how it occurs and what are the critical issues.

Both biologically and socially, **Conception** seems the most incidental and accidental of the stages of organizing. A casual and passing encounter—a twinkle in the parents' eyes—can be enough to engender a child or an organization. For example, a consulting firm called Stirring Occasions—that helps clients clarify what kind of parties they wish to give, then organizes the setting, staffing, costuming, catering, and entertaining—was conceived by a dozen people over a potluck dinner one night and started by them on a part-time basis while they initially retained their previous jobs.

Yet, however casual the occasion, the circumstances of **Conception** will critically influence the future of the organizing process. The twinkle in the parents' eyes can be more or less intelligent, more or less profoundly felt, and more or less linked to the resources and vision necessary for the later development of the newly conceived entity. The founding of Stirring Occasions, for example, was even more propitious than it was casual. The organization required no initial capital to start up. Its tasks corresponded closely to the skills and interests of the founding members. Perhaps most significant, some of the central practical, strategic, and spiritual dilemmas implicit in this corporate dream were discussed during the first evening, increasing the appeal of the project to those present rather than provoking anxiety. For example, the group realized that parties can be infinitely individualized, and that for many people, the objective at parties is to move beyond preprogrammed behavior toward spontaneity. Did this mean that the firm could not hope to be profitable because it could not prepackage its services in any way? Or might there be a general program for individualizing parties and developing spontaneity? Was there a way of walking the ethical tightrope whereon one simultaneously caters professionally to the client's aims yet avoids manipulative, exploitative, and coarse behavior? These questions, interweaving financial, marketing, political, and ethical issues, energized the group rather than defeated it. Had the organization avoided these difficult questions at the outset, it might well have been defeated by them later.

When the original **Conception** includes within itself a vision of mature social or spiritual functioning, then the vision can inspire and draw the organization forward to later stages of development. Consider the very name of the Guardian Angels, an organization that trains community youths, who might themselves otherwise be the source of trouble, to patrol their community. This is by nature a volatile organization and one that has been very controversial in certain communities, but the name "Guardian Angels" blends martial and religious imagery into a mythic vision of adult, spiritual responsibility that itself raises questions about whether members' actions live up to their mission, and thereby promotes their individual development.

Unlike children, organizations may have almost any number of parents, and these may be more or less compatible with one another as time goes on and more or less committed to the ongoing development of the organization. For example, the government bureaucrats who founded the National Institute for Education (NIE) did so primarily because they believed they could not reform an existing bureaucracy (the Bureau for Research in the Office of Education) and because they believed that Congress was more likely to appropriate the necessary funding to a new agency. Although NIE was supposed to parallel the much respected National Institutes for Health (NIH) in providing direction for research in education, the question of what constitutes good educational research is more difficult to answer than what constitutes good medical research. Those who conceived NIE had no clear and strong vision in response to this question and no commitment to the organization beyond the planning prior to its funding. Ironically, but not surprisingly, NIE's most distinguished contribution to date has been to serve as a case study of how *not* to start an organization.[2]

When, by contrast, great inventors like Thomas Edison or Edwin Land conceive of a new product, they continue to fuel and renew the initial **Conception** with whole subsequent generation of related inventions, so that the companies they inspire (General Electric and Polaroid, in these two cases) come to be animated by the excitement of continuous creation.

Negative or escapist motives for conceiving a new organization go a long way toward ensuring its eventual failure. Many individuals decide to become entrepreneurs and start their own businesses because they dislike their current boss or the atmosphere of their current company. Through sheer lack of business experience or of deep friendship, they imagine they will create a sunny, conflict-free environment in which each gets to "do his own thing." But no worthy creative human relationship or enterprise has ever been accomplished without conflict. And persistence, sacrifice, and continual ingenuity are all required to make a venture flourish.

At one day-long seminar sponsored by the Small Business Administration to brief budding entrepreneurs about small business planning, accounting, financing, and legal issues, the main speaker spent the entire morning providing information within the frame of trying to convince the roomful of aspirants *not* to pursue their dream. "You don't know what you're doing," he pounded into them, as he cited statistics on small business failures, described the difficulties of securing financing, and regaled them with stories of coronaries, incensed creditors, and embittered families. At first, the audience laughed heartily at his flamboyant approach and his "reverse psychology." But gradually they quieted as they realized he was also sincere. At the end he said, "I care about you, and I hope I have discouraged you from taking this step. If I have, don't feel badly about it. Just think: if you had continued on this foolhardy path, you would almost certainly look back on this morning as the least difficult and most amusing of all your experiences! Be smart: stop while you're ahead." If the advice indeed deterred anyone, it is safe to say that it is just as well, for it no doubt represented the least of the obstacles they would have had to overcome. But, of course, fewer people in the United States than in any other country take that advice each year.

The issue of negative, or unrealistic, motives for starting a new organization does not exist only at the level of isolated individuals. Huge companies can start new divisions—particularly New Ventures divisions—for equally negative and ill-fated reasons. In recent years, numerous large companies have started New Ventures divisions because top executives saw that their existing products were in mature markets that were not going to continue to grow and that their existing divisions were not producing any innovations. Note that these are negative reasons for starting the new organization. Although senior management frequently has sufficient control over resources to capitalize such new divisions handsomely, other divisions regard the capital as "stolen" from them, and subtly (or blatantly) refuse to cooperate. Moreover, like the case of NIE, the management of such New Ventures divisions are frequently handed a mandate to generate, say, two new marketable products a year, but with no vision to guide them and the rest of the company in determining what products are likely to generate the most synergy and thus the most profits for the company as a whole.

After two unproductive years, one *Fortune* 100 company decided to have its New Ventures division host a two-day conference of 24 of its top 30 executives worldwide, in order to include them in the planning for new products and thus get them more deeply committed to the division. But by then it was too late. So politicized had the matter become that 6 of the 24 managed to beg off from attending despite considerable pressure from the CEO to do so. Another six spent most of the conference running to phones to deal with "crises" in their own divisions. After the conference, as before, the New Ventures division survived solely through the support of the CEO.

There is no time limit on how long an organization may remain in the **Conception** stage, and this for several reasons. First, the entire prehistory of the organization influences its beginning. Second, **Conception** is an event that is both biologically and socially invisible to the naked eye. One establishes that it occurred only in retrospect, when an organization is literally (and sometimes legally) incorporated by having members and a space and resources devoted to it. Hence, it is not easy to tell when the beginning begins. Third, what counts as the beginning differs depending on the historical scale one's view seeks to encompass, as we saw in the case of Herman Hollerith and IBM.

Characteristics of the Conception Stage of Organizing*

---

1. Dreams, fantasies, visions about creating something new to fill a need not now adequately addressed.
2. Interplay, often conflict, among multiple "parents"—individuals, organizations, ideologies.
3. Informal conversations, occasional related projects with friends or work associates, working models to test and revise ideas and to show their relation to current products or services.

(*concluded*)
4. In cases where government, foundation, or venture financing will be sought, a grant application, project proposal, or business plan is developed.
5. Critical issues: timeliness and mythic proportions of the vision: does the vision relate to social needs that are both current and profound? Does the vision relate to participant motivations that will survive developmental transformations? Is the vision positive or escapist?

---

*Only a few, quite abstract characteristics are offered for each stage of organizational development because the effort is to offer only characteristics that are valid across many, if not all, types of social organizing.

NOTES

1. R. Sobel, *IBM: Colossus in Transition* (Toronto: Bantam, 1983).

2. L. Sproull, S. Weiner, and D. Wolf, *Organizing an Anarchy: Belief, Bureaucracy, and Politics in the National Institute of Education* (Chicago: The University of Chicago Press, 1978).

CHAPTER TWO _____

The Impulsive Manager: A Contradiction in Terms

The case of Herman Hollerith and the founding of IBM illustrates the cunning—or is it perhaps the vagary?—of history. The dreams and impulses of one rather stodgy man, Herman Hollerith, initiated an organizing process that ultimately far transcended his capabilities for leadership and even his capacity for vision. But whatever Hollerith's limitations as a leader, his enduring commitment to championing his invention makes it clear that his style was anything but short term and merely impulsive.

Some sort of dream or impulse is clearly necessary to initiate any action, let alone a whole organization. But that does not mean that those who start organizations are controlled by their impulses. A toddler is impulsive, tearing up plants, testing the limits of voice with sudden bloodcurdling screams, throwing toys at people, imperiously jealous and totally attention demanding. Most children transform beyond the Impulsive stage of development by the time they are eight or nine years old.

A quick glance at some major careers in business can, however, make them appear remarkably impulsive. Take Bill Poduska, an engineer and MIT professor. First, he jumped ship before his tenure decision at MIT to cofound a computer company. Then, he jumped ship again to found his own company.

And then, when that company faced its first economic adversity and had to make some layoffs, Poduska jumped ship yet again and set about forming yet a third company. One might think venture capitalists would keep a man with such a record at arm's length.

But Poduska's first company was Prime Computer, which rode the new single board technology of the early 1970s to enormous success. When Poduska left Prime, his wealth made it unnecessary for him ever to work again. He left, however, not on a whim, not merely to play, and not out of dissatisfaction, but because he was nurturing the concept of a company that would build integrated work stations based on the latest technological breakthroughs. Apollo Computer was the result, the first company into its market niche, a company that introduced new products each of its first five years, a company that repaid its venture investors at a ratio of 125:1 during that time. Poduska's return on his personal, not-inconsiderable financial investment was a mild 1,000:1 in the same time period.

Poduska left Apollo, not because of the company's brief contraction, but because he was nurturing another new dream based on another technological breakthrough. He had begun planning his departure well before the contraction. He hired Tom Vanderslice, formerly president of GTE, as his president and CEO, with the understanding that Vanderslice would guide Apollo to mature, large-company status. Indeed, Vanderslice and Poduska had discussed an entirely new choreography for helping entrepreneurial ventures develop. The idea is that Vanderslice and Poduska may eventually become chairmen of one another's boards of directors, with Poduska selling his newest enterprise to Apollo when it reaches its drive to maturity. They realize that there will be many impediments to making this dream come true, but they are holding it lightly, as a joint dream.[1]

In short, Poduska's moves have been anything but impulsive, negative, or escapist—all prescriptions for failure of a new venture, as we saw in the previous chapter. His moves to date have been based on timely commercialization of scientific/technological breakthroughs. Moreover, his most recent departure, from Apollo, has been choreographed with exquisite care and may itself result in a new prototype for relationships between large, mature companies and new ventures. As noted in the introduction, American business badly needs new models for such relationships.

THE STAGES OF MANAGERIAL DEVELOPMENT

An adult who has never developed beyond being dominated by impulses is not a manager or leader or entrepreneur, for all these roles demand the organization of actions across time. Dream or impulse must be delayed—as Poduska delayed leaving Apollo while developing a unique succession scenario—in order to increase the probability of the dream's realization.

Indeed, adults who are dominated by impulses are relatively rare, especially in everyday life. They are frequently institutionalized in prisons or mental hospitals. They cannot manage their own lives well and cannot establish relationships, let alone lead others. Three different studies of managers, using developmental measures, found no managers at the Impulsive stage of development, as shown in the table below.[2]

Using this table as our guide, we can gain a brief, preliminary impression of how managers at each stage of development view the world. As already indicated by the comments on the **Impulsive** stage, each stage is characterized by the "logic" that

		Study 2:	
	Study 1:	Junior and	Study 3:
	First-Line	Middle	Senior
Samples and	Supervisors	Managers	Managers
Number:	(37)	(177)	(66)
Developmental positions:			
Impulsive	0	0	0
Opportunist	0	5	0
Diplomat	24	9	6
Technician	68	43.5	47
Achiever	8	40	33
Strategist	0	2.5	14
Magician	0	0	0
	100%	100%	100%

Distribution of Managers by Developmental Position in Three Empirical Studies

controls it, the logic to which it is subject. In each transformation to a later stage, what was subject becomes object. The world-view or logic that the person *was* (controlled by) becomes a variable or capacity that the person *has* (control of).[3] Thus, managers at later stages of development can understand the logic of managers at earlier stages (though in the press of business they may not pause to do so). On the other hand, managers at earlier stages tend to reinterpret later stage logics and actions into their own terms (sometimes concluding that such actions are "unrealistic" or "don't make sense").

As the table shows, not only are *no* managers found at the **Impulsive** stage, but very few are found at the next stage, here called the **Opportunistic** stage. This is not surprising because 7- to 12-year-old children typically inhabit the **Opportunistic** stage. At this stage, persons gain control over their impulses and become capable of manipulating the external world. The logic to which this stage is subject is that things are made to work by manipulating them unilaterally or by making the most advantageous trades possible. Children at this stage treat other people as part of the external world (son to parent: "You've *got* to take me bowling. It's your job."). The **Opportunistic** manager has usually added considerable polish to his or her manipulations, but still views the world as never more than a one-against-all jungle fight.

Young teenagers typically inhabit the next, **Diplomatic** stage, but, as the table shows, a substantial number of managers, especially at the lower levels of management, still inhabit this stage. At this stage, persons become capable of appreciating others' preferences as well as their own, and become capable of exercising control over their own behavior as well as the outside world. They exercise their new selfhood by conforming to group norms. (How conformity can represent an *exercise* of selfhood is frequently obscure to persons at other stages of development, since from their perspective conforming for its own sake represents a *sacrifice* of selfhood.) William Whyte's *The Organization Man* and David Riesman's description of the "other-directed" man in *The Lonely Crowd* are two classic descriptions of the **Diplomatic** managerial style. Loyalty and group harmony are the highest goods for the **Diplomat,** public conflict and loss of face the great evils.

Later teenage years are frequently the time for a transformation from the **Diplomat** stage to the **Technician** stage of development. In between identifying with others at the **Diplomat** stage and identifying with one's own self-created system at the later **Achiever** stage, the **Technician** identifies with an external system that is supposedly internally coherent, such as a well-defined military hierarchy, car engines, computer programming, or logical positivism. The managerial style emanating from this identification with expertise is that of Mr. or Ms. Fix-It. Mr. or Ms. Fix-It knows subordinates' jobs better than they do and demands perfection. For such a manager, details are not merely important, God is in the details. All three studies represented in the table found the largest porportion of managers at this stage of development.

At the **Achiever** stage, the person achieves what we ordinarily call "one's own identity." The salesman no longer *is* his quarterly sales figure. The engineer no longer *is* her engineering expertise. The person becomes a goal-oriented system that takes responsibility for actual goal accomplishment, rather than excusing nonperformance by claiming "Nobody told me to do that" or "That case doesn't fit our system." Such a goal-oriented person seeks out feedback about whether he or she is accomplishing the predefined goals and behaves differently if necessary to achieve the goals. Managers at this stage are not *controlled by* a single, internally consistent logic as at the previous stage, but rather *use* multiple logics. Bill Poduska, for example, seems equally at home with the logics of engineering, finance, market research, and interpersonal relations. Such managers are committed to achieving results in a complex real world characterized by the collision of many types of logic, many scales of social system, and many different temporal rhythms. The table shows the second largest proportion of managers beyond the supervisory level at this stage.

Few managers today seek out or reach later stages of development. The table shows a significant proportion of managers at the **Strategist** stage (14 percent) only at the senior management level. And it shows no managers at what this book calls the **Magician** stage. Indeed, these later stages represent a frontier for developmental theory itself—a frontier at which the theory itself is most speculative and most controversial.[4] Because these stages are less apt to be familiar, single sentence sketches here would be more confusing than illuminating. Chapter 12 on the **Strategist** and the chapters thereafter introduce these rare and unusually effective transformational leaders.

NO MANAGERS ARE IMPULSIVE?

Despite the statistics in our table showing no managers at the **Impulsive** stage, it is anything but unusual for subordinates to describe their managers as almost randomly impulsive. "Everything's an emergency for my boss," says one junior manager. "And I mean everything. In the morning he tells me to interrupt an ongoing project for a new matter. At noon, he's suddenly on my back about some third issue. And before the day is done, he's a good bet to call off the morning emergency, act like I invented it, and set still another priority instead." If the senior manager being described here is not in fact ruled by the logic of his impulses, what may account for this apparent randomness and impulsiveness?

There are several possible reasons other than being at the **Impulsive** stage of development why a manager may act frequently in what appears to be an impulsive fashion. One reason is that the manager may be at the **Diplomatic** stage of development, to be described more fully in Chapter 6.

Because **Diplomatic** managers measure their own effectiveness in terms of meeting others' needs and others' expectations of performance, they are easily influenced by others' priorities. If different stakeholders (e.g., suppliers, clients, peers, superiors, etc.) have different and conflicting agendas, the **Diplomatic** manager feels in conflict, bending to the most recent influence attempt, often appearing randomly impulsive to subordinates who are not fully aware of the pressures being exerted on the manager.

A second reason why a manager may act frequently in what appears to be an impulsive fashion is that his or her organizational unit may be a focal point for many different developmental processes at the unit, firm and industry levels that are not well equilibrated with one another. For example, the internal consulting group for a high-technology manufacturing company may simultaneously be expected: (1) to help various organizational clients handle particular technical or marketing problems;

(2) to chart a major organizational restructuring for top management; and (3) to assess the organizational implications of new state-of-the-art scientific developments that may affect the industry. The restructuring of the whole firm may be secret, but the manager of the consulting group may know that it renders obsolete some of the particular technical and marketing problems now being addressed by her subordinates. Consequently, she may pull people off these projects without explanation. At the same time, new state-of-the-art developments that will affect the whole industry may be rendering aspects of the organizational restructuring obsolete or unwise, just as a political consensus is emerging within top management in favor of them. So, the consulting group manager may drag her feet on the organizational restructuring, in order to give top management the chance to digest the implications of the new technology.

Under these conditions, subordinates may find themselves with frequent unexplained stop-and-start orders that appear random and therefore impulsive. Over time, of course, an effective manager will attempt to fill subordinates in on directives that could not initially be explained. But in most high-technology companies, transfers to new projects, promotions, and company-to-company job-hopping are frequent occurrences, so a given manager or subordinate may depart before explanations are rendered.

A third reason why a manager may appear impulsive and changeable without being at the **Impulsive** stage of development is that he or she may be entering new and unexplored physical, social, or spiritual territory. Such a manager is in a position analogous to the toddler—testing its capacities as it develops the most rudimentary of skills, attacked by unmanageable pain as its teeth emerge, and frustrated by its inability to speak even after it begins to understand. Whether the manager is opening a subsidiary in a country the language and customs of which are unfamiliar, or is on the verge of moving from middle management into the not-always-friendly fraternity of top management, or is recognizing that his or her career has reached a plateau, the manager is at the beginning of a new project. So whatever his or her overall stage of development may be, such a manager is at the **Conception** or **Impulsive** stage of this new work project or life era.

Managers who have a single criterion of effective timing and performance—such as those at the **Technician** stage of development—are likely to respond impatiently and impulsively at the **Conception** stage of a new project. Consciously, they will simply be treating the new project or the new era of their lives as though it is a continuation of previous experience, with familiar criteria of success. Unconsciously, they will know they are somehow doubly off track (once because they don't really know what is up and secondly because they are acting as though they do). Consequently, they are likely to be more fearful and jumpy than usual and to act more impulsively, especially as their usual moves do not bear the usual results.

In sum, we see that there are many reasons, all consistent with a developmental perspective, why a manager may appear impulsive without *being* **Impulsive.** To appreciate which of these factors is operative at a given time, other participants must be capable of detaching themselves from their immediate impulses and interests. Such detachment is necessary in order to observe more steadily and impartially what is occurring. It is also necessary in order to ask the "impulsive" manager in a timely and effective fashion why he or she is acting impulsively. And such detachment is necessary if one is to recognize, and then attune one's action to support, the developmental thrust of the various social systems that are determining the significance of the event.

Each developmental transformation from one managerial style to the next can be understood as a detachment from an additional set of elements in the social world. Detachment brings the set of elements into view and makes it, for the first time, manageable. Without detachment, there is no such process as management. This is why an impulsive style of management is a contradiction in terms.

TRANSITION

In the previous two chapters, we have examined the earliest stage of organizational and personal development. In the next two chapters, we turn to the second stage of development.

At the second stage of development, the focus is on gathering and deploying the resources necessary to make the initial dream come true. On the organizational scale, we speak of these resources as **Investments.** On the personal scale, we speak of managers who focus primarily on accumulating and deploying tangible resources as **Opportunists.**

NOTES

1. The material on Poduska and Vanderslice is drawn from personal conversations during their day as Visiting Executives at the Boston College MBA program, November 20, 1985.

2. The table is taken from, and more fully described in K. Merron, D. Fisher, and W. Torbert, "Meaning-Making and Management Action" (paper delivered at the Academy of Management, August 1986). All three empirical studies use Jane Loevinger's measure of ego development (see J. Loevinger and R. Wessler, *Measuring Ego Development*, Vols. 1 and 2 [San Francisco: Jossey-Bass, 1978]). The names for the stages are ones we have developed as most descriptive of our data on managers (each major developmental theorist gives the stages a slightly different set of names).

3. Robert Kegan in *The Evolving Self* (Cambridge, Mass.: Harvard University Press, 1982) is responsible for this elegant way of describing development. His emphasis on the dynamic process of development has been critical to this author's understanding of both individual and organizational development.

4. See K. Wilber, *The Atman Project: A Transpersonal View of Human Development* (Wheaton, Ill.: Quest Books, 1980); and E. Langer and C. Alexander, eds., *Beyond Formal Operations* (New York: Oxford University Press, 1984).

Investing in a Dream

Once a new organization is conceived, it will remain a figment of the imagination unless a variety of parties invest time, energy, intelligence, and money up front, when there can be no assurance, no matter how complete the business plan, that the organization will succeed.

Like the stage of **Conception,** the stage of **Investments** seems almost too obvious to mention. Who does not know that you need capital in order to get started? But this is precisely the first mistake that persons and corporations and governments commonly make as they enter what they intuitively know to be the **Investments** stage: They tend to assume that the primary and central issue at this stage is the acquisition of money and other external resources for the nascent organization. Quite the contrary: Money and other tangible investments, though obviously necessary in most cases, are the least important of the investments necessary.

Mark McCormack, founder and CEO of the International Management Group, began representing sports figures in the early 1960s with $500 and Arnold Palmer as a client. Needless to say, the name "Arnold Palmer"—that is, Palmer's willingness to "invest" in McCormack's career—was a much more significant aspect of the initial stake than the $500. Had McCormack started with $50,000 and Arnold Palmer, Palmer would still be a much

more significant aspect part of the initial investment. As Mc-
Cormack puts it,

> There is a whole industry of venture capitalists who do nothing
> but fund new businesses. But the mere existence of this industry
> has created a kind of entrepreneurial myth—that there are all these
> people standing in line waiting for the opportunity to give you
> money and that you just haven't met any of them yet . . .
>
> Many new businesses never get off the ground, not because they
> were bad ideas, not because the people were wrong, but because
> the fund-raising efforts failed. Yet many of these new ventures, I
> believe, didn't actually require the capital the participants con-
> vinced themselves that they did.[1]

The primary investment necessary to give a new organization a fighting chance is, as we have already seen in Chapter 1,
the commitment of those starting it to its vision and to the work
of making it come true. The originators of NIE did not have this
commitment, but they did get the funds: The result has been an
undistinguished organization. Herman Hollerith had no funds
but did have the commitment, and IBM has become one of the
great organizations of the 20th century.

The reason why this faith—this spiritual investment—on the
part of the originator(s) is so important is that the more significant the innovation, the more it requires that someone go beyond what he or she would have imagined possible to sell it to
clients or constituents. The more innovative the product, service, or policy, the less calculable is its risk in established terms.
Under these circumstances, people "buy" in at the **Investments**
stage on faith, and no one else is likely to exhibit faith if the
originators do not; hence, the primacy of spiritual investment at
this stage.

Also, the more innovative the product, service, or policy, the
less useful are any of the established procedures and channels
for making it come true. Indeed, they are increasingly likely to
block rather than to facilitate the innovation, whether intentionally or unintentionally. Thus, a significant innovation requires
more work than is initially imaginable. The originators and their
early colleagues must work over their heads and through de-
spair. Many entrepreneurs say afterwards that if they had known
what they would have to go through during the first several years

of their new business, they would never have started it. Albert Hirshman has spoken of "the principle of the hiding hand" in the economics of international development, claiming that few development projects would ever have been commenced if the true costs had been known at the outset.[2] Indeed, anyone who has ever lived through something as mundane as having a kitchen redone understands this principle all too well.

In large organizations, the need for commitment by an initial proponent of an innovation, if it is to succeed, is now widely recognized and well formulated in the concept of the "Product Champion."[3] The product champion is someone willing to put his career on the line in the struggle to secure institutional commitments for a prospective new product and to wrestle the product into marketable shape. The same need for a champion holds for the introduction of significant changes in service, in policy, in strategy, and in organizational culture, though somehow the phrases "Service Champion," "Policy Champion," "Strategy Champion," and "Culture Champion" do not have quite the all-American, Wheaties ring to them that "Product Champion" does. Rosabeth Kanter has developed the generic name "Change Masters," along with cogent descriptions of their modes of operation, for the persons and corporations that have the knack for managing innovation.[4]

The second most important investment necessary during this stage of organizing is the investment by a peer network in the nascent organization. When Angelo Roncalli was elected Pope John XXIII, he made his first political move before he went to sleep the first night of his papacy. He invited Msgr. Tardini—who had been the most influential member of the Secretariat under John's predecessor, Pope Pius XII—to become his secretary of state.[5] Tardini was perceived as a traditionalist and an opponent of John. Shocked at the request, Tardini remonstrated, reminding John that they had frequently disagreed in the past. "It made no difference," Tardini later reported, "The pope listened to me with kindness and interest, but to every point he replied: 'I understand, but I want you to be my secretary of state.' Finally I knelt down and offered him my obedience."

John's initial move within the byzantine peer network of the curia was, thus, consistent with his entire ecumenical, reconciling ministry, wedding the old with the new, tradition with radical innovation. Rather than banishing his enemies and fighting against them, he brought them as close as possible and worked with them for a more general transformation. This move dramatized the depth and reality of his commitment to his ecumenical vision for those very insiders most disposed to be cynical about any vision because they are in a position to see all the warts. It began the process of developing the spiritual and institutional investments necessary throughout the immediate peer network to eventually carry through the foundation-shaking, ecumenical Vatican II Council, peacefully transforming the largest single organization in the world. Not since the Council of Trent had the Catholic Church experienced renewal on such a scale. And the Council of Trent was occasioned by centuries of unattended corruption, the Protestant schisms, and a generation of religious war, rather than by an internally generated, ecumenical, peaceful wish for transformation.

On a scale more familiar to most of us, one entrepreneur launched his new business by writing to 200 former colleagues or clients, asking them for advice, money, or other resources, if they thought the proposal viable and worthy. Four warned against moving forward. In so doing, they alerted the entrepreneur to dangers and difficulties he might otherwise have underestimated until it was too late. Another 76 provided a wide range of more positive support, advice, access to resources at cost, free space for the start-up period, and some $10,000 of financing in the form of gifts.

Even when it is clear you require venture financing on a much larger scale, the most likely channel towards venture capital is through a peer network that can vouch for you. One entrepreneur developed an easily marketable piece of financial software but required $8 million to get going once he had demonstrated the prototype. This entrepreneur called a former business friend in New York, explained his problem, and was told to appear for a game of squash and lunch next week. He was to describe his concept to the person his friend would bring along, but say absolutely nothing about the financing. "Leave that part to me," said the friend. Eight days after the squash and lunch date, the entrepreneur had his $8 million. Two and a half years later, he sold his business and personally cleared over $13 million.

So important is the existence of a peer network willing to

invest time, energy, and intelligence, that a new organization is much more likely to succeed if the originators have a prior career and an established peer network before they try to create their own organization.

The third most important investment necessary during this stage of organizing is the investment made by "parent" institutions. Venture capitalists who take an equity stake in a new business are one obvious example of a parent institution. But typically there is in fact a complex network of institutional stakeholders in a new venture. Take a drug company that is considering marketing a new, brand-name pain killer in a market now characterized by cheaper generic products as well as the brand-name products that doctors have typically recommended. We can list at least nine major stakeholders in this situation whose willingness to invest in the new drug will determine whether it is a viable product. These stakeholders include the customers (patients), physicians, pharmacists, suppliers, government regulators, the company's sales force, the company's management, perhaps a holding company, stockholders, and so on.[6] Of course, not all of these stakeholders are usually thought of as parent institutions who need to make an up-front investment before the product is marketed. *But most of them can usefully be conceived that way.*

For example, many companies in widely varying industries have found that, despite their desire to avoid any unnecessary government regulation, the best way to do so is to take the initiative to negotiate regulatory guidelines and attitudes ahead of time, rather than "getting away with as much as they can for as long as they can" and then passively enduring (or reactively fighting) regulation when it cannot be avoided. The principle behind this finding is simply that of inviting parent institutions—in this case government regulatory agencies—to add to the organization's momentum early on, rather than resisting it later on.

IBM AT THE INVESTMENTS STAGE

If we return to IBM, the history of which we began to examine in the first chapter, we can gain an illustration of what the **Investments** stage of an organization can look like when viewed over a very long period. We can also gain insight into two of the (many) "secrets" of IBM's extraordinary record of entering and dominating four different industries over the past century (tabulating, mainframes, minicomputers, and micro or personal computers).

The first "secret" emerges from the **Investments** stage of Hollerith's original company, beginning with the first patent in 1884 and ending with the winning of the 1890 census contract. At this time, Hollerith fatefully decided to organize his business around leasing rather than selling his machines. This decision meant that the company had an active, long-term relationship to each of its clients and a commitment to servicing its machines, which in turn increased the company's stake in providing high-quality equipment to begin with. Moreover, the company could not measure its success simply in terms of its short-term revenues, but rather had to take other, more sophisticated financial ratios into account as well.

Hollerith's decision was undoubtedly more a matter of chance than of business genius, but through it he inadvertently created the basis for IBM's enduring commitments to quality and service. Or, to put this in the language of this chapter, IBM in effect invested in its clients up front, and so, over time, induced those clients to invest in IBM up front. Today, many of IBM's clients function like a peer network, buying into new products even before they are introduced. In the minicomputer market that Digital Equipment Corporation (DEC) dominated as recently as five years ago, for example, most of its major clients now have corporate data systems policies that dictate patronizing IBM, unless a competitor like DEC can be proved on a case-by-case basis to provide better value. Naturally, pressured executives will rarely make the investment necessary to document such a case, so this now gives IBM a tremendous competitive advantage in the minicomputer market and puts DEC at a comparable disadvantage. IBM has gained this degree of credibility by half a century's unwavering commitment to quality and service, the economic basis of which has been the lessor-lessee relationship. It will be interesting to observe whether IBM's increasing emphasis on selling rather than leasing (a change initially mandated by the government to break IBM's hold on the after market) will erode what has become a cultural value within the company.

If we step back, as we did in the previous chapter, and treat the entire period of Hollerith's firm until he sold it in 1910 as the **Conception** stage for IBM, then the period from 1910—when Charles Flint bought out Hollerith and created CTR—until 1915—when Thomas Watson, Sr., became CTR's president—displays the charateristics of the **Investments** stage. Two related aspects of this period stand out and confirm the analysis of this stage already offered earlier in this chapter. First, despite Flint's financial backing, the new firm did no more than tread water until Watson appeared on the scene. Indeed, other executives of the small conglomerate were planning to manipulate the price of the stock, and Flint himself might merely have resold the company, as he had many others. Thus, although Flint's financial resources were necessary for the **Investments** stage of the organization's development, they were neither the primary, nor the sufficient, condition for the firm's long-term success.

Watson was the critical ingredient, the "Organizational Champion," who actually restructured the organization in substantive terms. He created a small research laboratory under E. A. Ford, thus displacing Hollerith as the bottleneck of technological innovation within the company. He successfully opposed the stock manipulation, threatening to reveal it to the newspapers. And he won Flint's support to stop dividend payouts for 1914 and 1915 and to reinvest the capital into the company's development. In short, he had faith in the long-term productivity and profitability of the company, fought for this corporate dream, and generated faith in others (notably Flint). His moves turned CTR into a viable, focused, growing company (sales doubled and earnings tripled during the next five years).

Second only to the importance of Watson's overall personal investment in the organization, the decision to retain and reinvest the company's earnings was key. This is the second "secret" of IBM's success alluded to before. For the next 40 years, IBM rarely relied on capital markets for financing. Instead, it invested in itself. It may be that this level of investment in itself by an organization is analogous to the high level of investment entrepreneurs must initially be willing to make if a new organization is to succeed over the long term. In any event, no other economic organization has been as consistently successful by as many diverse measures as IBM during this century.

This chapter has focused throughout on the characteristics of the initial structuring of an organization at the **Investments** stage which augur well for long-term success in making the corporate dream come true. The emphasis throughout has been on the primacy of spiritual investments by the originators, on the secondary but still essential role of structural investments by peer networks, parent institutions, and other stakeholders, and on the tertiary role of financial investments. Spiritual and structural investments are always necessary. Financial investments are not always necessary at this stage. Spiritual and structural investments lead directly and reliably (but by no means inevitably) to financial investments. Financial investments do not lead directly to spiritual and structural investments. Indeed, to say that an organization achieves only financial investments at this stage, as in the case of NIE, and as in the case of CTR prior to Watson's advent, is to say that the corporate dream has already vanished before the body of the organization has been born.

In short, financial investment at this stage is not the primary determinant of an organization's future success. Interestingly, fewer and fewer venture capital firms have been investing in entrepreneurial start-ups in the 1980s. In general, they have not received reliable paybacks on their investments. Today, venture capitalists prefer to bet on organizations at later stages of development, organizations with a strong track record that are planning significant growth. Since adequate financing is not the primary determinant of future success for an organization at the **Investments** stage, it should hardly be surprising that venture capitalists were not experiencing reliable returns from new organizations.

At the same time, it is not surprising that Arthur Rock of San Francisco should be widely acknowledged as having the best track record in the venture capital business and yet be one of the few who still chooses to invest in those unreliable start-ups.[7] Why this paradox? Because Rock does not merely invest in new organizations financially. He speaks of himself as investing in people, not ideas or products. He discusses the prospective founders' dreams and their lives, not just technology and markets. Moreover, once he invests (both Intel and Apple were among his choices), he serves as a mentor on the appropriate timing for organizational restructurings. Typically, he advises the nascent company not to rush to get its product to market and not to rush into sumptuous corporate offices. In other words, he advises against rushing through the **Investments** stage and into the **Incorporation** stage prematurely.

In a business world dominated by the languages of technology, economics, and finance, Rock's intuitions about the requisites for long-term organizational success are unusual, counterintuitive, and spectacularly accurate. He is a venture capitalist with a profound appreciation for all that is at stake in the **Investments** stage and with a gift for investing simultaneously at the spiritual, structural, and financial levels.

Characteristics of the Investments Stage of Organizing

---

1. Originators or "champions" definitely commit to creating an organization, to "making the dream come true."
2. Early relationship-building among potential leaders, members, clients, and other stakeholders.
3. Peer networks and parent institutions make spiritual, structural, and financial commitments to nurture the organization.
4. Critical issues: authenticity, power, and reliability of the various commitments; financial investment appropriately subordinated to structural and spiritual investments.

NOTES

1. M. McCormack, *What They Don't Teach You at Harvard Business School* (Toronto: Bantam, 1984), p. 246.

2. A. Hirshman, *A Bias for Hope: Essays for Development in Latin America* (New Haven: Yale University Press, 1971).

3. T. Peters, and R. Waterman, *In Search of Excellence* (New York: Harper & Row, 1982).

4. R. Kanter, *The Change Masters* (New York: Simon & Schuster, 1985).

5. P. Hebblethwaite, *Pope John XXIII* (Garden City, N.Y.: Doubleday, 1985), p. 288 ff.

6. I. Mitroff, *Stakeholders of the Organizational Mind* (San Francisco: Jossey-Bass, 1983). The drug company example is drawn from Chapter 2, in which Mitroff treats this example much more extensively and for different purposes.

7. This judgment and the rest of the information on Rock presented here is drawn from M. W. Miller, "How One Man Helps High Tech Prospects Get to the Big Leagues," *The Wall Street Journal*, December 31, 1985, p. 1.

The Opportunist

The notion of opportunism and opportunists has both positive and negative connotations in American mythology.

In some ways, we like to think of ourselves as a nation of opportunists—flexible, pragmatic entrepreneurs, unconstrained by dogmas. We like to think of ourselves as action oriented, ready to search out and seize opportunities to build "a better mouse trap" or otherwise better our lives. We are impatient with those whom we suspect of using philosophy, religion, or political ideology as an elaborate mode of evading action.

In other ways, we regard the label "opportunist" as a criticism or even an insult. To call someone an opportunist can imply that he or she will sacrifice principle, friendship and organizational loyalty for short-term, narrowly self-interested, material gains.

The **Opportunistic** style of management to be described in this chapter includes all these connotations, but positive and negative. On the positive side, this style of management frequently is responsible for starting new organizations and bringing new products to market. One way of appreciating the genius of capitalistic economic systems is that they create incentives that draw **Opportunists** into the productive economic sphere where they generate goods for others as they pursue their self-interest.

These incentives are simultaneously drawing these same **Opportunists** *away from* the military, political, or religious spheres, where narrowly self-interested activity is more likely to be directly manipulative and exploitative of others.

On the negative side, however, the **Opportunistic** style of management counts only short-term, visible costs and benefits. It appreciates only the financial aspect of the **Investments** stage of organizing, not the structural and spiritual aspects. It does not help managers or organizations transform to later stages of development.

Managers at a later stage of development can choose to act opportunistically on particular occasions, reaping the benefits of opportunism. What is here called the **Opportunistic** managerial style is the style that results when a person experiences the opportunistic calculus as the *only* lens through which to view the world. The **Opportunist,** as here defined, *has* to act opportunistically on every occasion and thus suffers the limitations and negative consequences of opportunism. Hence, the portrait of the **Opportunist** presented in this chapter accentuates the limits of being opportunistic rather than the benefits of making and taking opportunities.

As indicated in the overview of developmental stages in Chapter 2, the **Opportunistic** style is appropriate for children who are in the full flush of mastering their own impulses, perceptions, and relations to the outside world—"the bike-riding, money-managing, card-trading, wristwatch-wearing, pack-running, code-cracking, coin-collecting, self-waking, puzzle-solving 9- or 10-year-old known to us all," as Robert Kegan has so evocatively described him.[1] If the child continues into adulthood without transforming beyond this evolutionary balance, however, the balance rigidifies.

The **Opportunistic** manager experiences things and people as essentially external, to be manipulated insofar as feasible, to be defended against as necessary. Capital and power are thus naturally seen as external phenomena (plant and equipment, military or financial resources), and human interaction is seen as a contest to get more.

For the **Opportunistic** manager, it is axiomatic that one must "play one's cards close to the vest," since others are doing the same. The Hobbesian equation, "Might makes right," holds. Similarly, the Golden Rule is in fact correctly represented by the phrasing of the current joke about it (The Golden Rule: He Who Has the Gold Rules).

The **Opportunist's** temporal horizon is short (the moment-to-moment turbulence of the commodities market feels fine; a quarter is an age). He or she lives in the narrow present, unconstrained by loyalty to past patterns or to future plans. Intimacy is attained through sex, team play, or some other shared physical adventure.

Corporate raiders seem to match this general description of the **Opportunist.**

ARE CORPORATE RAIDERS OPPORTUNISTS?

Let us examine one corporate raider, Irwin Jacobs. Jacobs is a man who could not manage a business (Grain Belt Breweries) profitably, but who has made millions buying and selling real property and waging takeover battles with Pabst, ITT, and others. He refuses to keep an appointment calendar and claims to have no managerial style whatsoever: "You can't predict what I'm going to do next because there is no track, no character to it. Our big asset is our flexibility, being able to move on a moment's notice."[2]

It all fits—the hatred of being "tracked"; the feeling that social norms are external constraints on one's freedom; not wanting to play by the rules; the restless activity with the short time horizon, searching out the main chance; the jungle fighter; the **Opportunistic** manager.[3]

Or, consider Chicago's Sam Zell, whose net worth in late 1985 was about half a billion dollars.[4] Years ago, Zell nicknamed himself the Gravedancer to celebrate his ability to rehabilitate bankrupt companies and thus profit from others' mistakes. Under the umbrella of his holding company, Equity Financial & Management, Zell is one of the nation's biggest landlords, among many other businesses. A motorcycle rider who is as likely to wear leather and swear at business meetings as he is to wear pinstripes, Zell will stomp cigars into white rugs at board meetings while forcing the resignation of the CEO. At Itel, seven of the eight top officers left in the year following Zell's takeover in 1984. Indicted in a federal tax shelter investigation in 1976, Zell make a deal with the government to testify if the charges against him were dropped.

Here, again, we see someone who delights in flouting social norms, a wheeler-dealer whose version of what is logical appears to be what he can get away with. Again, it all fits. Corporate raiders appear to operate in the **Opportunistic** managerial style.

But it does *not* all fit this easily. So far, this sketch of the **Opportunistic** manager shares a major trait of the **Opportunistic** managerial style itself: stereotyping. Stereotyping involves making black and white generalizations about a person's innermost essence based on a few external characteristics seen from a distance. In offering portraits of organizational stages and managerial styles, this book courts the dangers of stereotyping. The *intent* of the book is to help managers come closer to appreciating their own worldviews and those of their colleagues, superiors, subordinates *from the inside,* in order to better promote individual and organizational development toward an increasing capacity for making dreams come true. But the *effect* can all too easily be to create a faddish new set of stereotypes for managers to throw at each other *from the outside.* If these portraits are superimposed on persons stereotypically, their effect will be to obscure what dreams are shared, to impede restructuring, and to substitute short-term measures of success for long-term measures.

Managers may immediately wish to know how to measure these developmental styles in order to use test scores to select, place, reward, or promote others. This again would be an outside-in, **Opportunistic** use of the theory, rather than an inside-out use. The effect would be to label managers rather than to help them develop. (Fortunately, the methods so far devised to measure these styles are complex, expensive, and well guarded.)[5] In an effort to combat misuses of the theory, each chapter will address some of the typical ways that managers holding the perspective described in that chapter may misinterpret or act inappropriately on the theory as a whole.

To return to corporate raiders, they do not, of course, necessarily operate from an **Opportunistic** perspective. As much as the brief sketches of Irwin Jacobs and Sam Zell suggest this mode of vision, an equally brief sketch of T. Boone Pickens, whose pre-tax gains from corporate takeover attempts since 1982 exceed $100 million, can suggest the rare, late stage **Magician** style (described in the Postscript) that, through deep study, masters the social alchemy of transforming organizations, or, in Pickens' case, a whole industry. Pickens has a wonderful sense for both dialectic and story in conversation, and a lifestyle at once disciplined and relaxed rather than tense and hectic. He has lived the oil industry from the bottom up his whole adult life and feels passionately about it. He is pursuing a definite strategy to restructure ownership within the industry that he says is intended to benefit a wide constituency of small stockholders (and it has in fact done so in terms of increasing the value of their shares at the time of his takeover efforts). His emphasis on increased manager and worker ownership of companies as a key to better performance puts him near the forefront of a historical movement toward an economy that generates and rewards the human forms of capital.

The point is that it is very difficult to determine from the outside who is an **Opportunist.** This difficulty is increased by two factors. First, managers at later stages may choose to act opportunistically on particular occasions as part of a wider strategy serving wider goals. Momentarily and from the outside, such a manager appears to be an **Opportunist.** But the true **Opportunist,** according to this theory, is one who has *no choice* but to act opportunistically.

But here we encounter the second difficulty in determining who is a true **Opportunist.** Another of the primary characteristics of the **Opportunist** is lack of introspection, along with a wary, distant, distrustful, and manipulative attitude toward others. Hence, the **Opportunist** is the least able and the least willing of all the managerial types to offer "inside" information about himself to others (this is why Pickens' conversational openness is one clue that he is not at this stage of development).

Arnold Mitchell's research on consumer values, based on a developmental theory closely related to the theory proposed here, indicated that in the late 1970s about 16 percent of the population in the United States were "need-driven" consumers, his category that most closely parallels the **Opportunistic** style of management.[6] He describes such consumers as predominantly unplanning, distrustful, compulsive, and poor, whose buying behavior focuses on price, on basics, and on occasional impulse purchases.

The studies of managers shown in the table in Chapter 2 suggest that a smaller proportion of managers than of the general population function at the **Opportunistic** stage of development. Only one study showed any managers at this stage, and that study showed only 5 percent of a sample of relatively junior managers holding this perspective. **Opportunists** do not fare well in the educational system (which offers little in the way of immediate gratification), so it is not surprising that they rarely make it into the management of large companies. One study of a whole company showed no one measured as **Opportunistic** above the lowest ranks, with a strong correlation between later stage managerial style and promotion up the corporate ladder.[7] By contrast, **Opportunists** are disproportionately represented in the prison population.[8]

PORTRAIT OF AN OPPORTUNIST

The following description of a businessman was made by his daughter, an MBA candidate. Having made a serious study both of her father and of this theory, she believes he qualifies as an **Opportunist.** "The **Opportunist,**" she writes, "doesn't have the luxury of choosing whether to act or when or how, but is compelled to go forward. Failing to go forward could have dire consequences. This is the appropriate response to tough environments. My father came out of a tough environment."

> Born in 1916 on the west coast of immigrant parents, M was a teenager during the Depression, working summers on a communal farm, selling newspapers, peddling dope. His father would not let him leave college, so he worked his way through, booking bands.
>
> During World War II, he wrote correspondence for an officer who couldn't spell, smuggled liquor and slot machines into the

training camp, and booked entertainment. After the war, preferring cash businesses, M showed X-rated films, and dealt in coin-operated magic fingers, coin-operated radios, and coin-operated televisions.

This last, M parlayed into a hospital leasing business, avoiding service in Korea by a large donation to an army hospital, sometimes buying competing service businesses, expanding to avoid crashing. In one five-year period, M bought 60 companies. In one 10-year period, M sold the company as a whole, bought it back again, went public on the over-the-counter market, became the largest shareholder, and sold all the stock, in turn.

Always the style of management was the same, M on several phones at once, with files spread all about his office, wheedling, cajoling, selling, shouting, dealing. He enjoyed having his children play in the office; it unbalanced the "sharks" who came to make deals. His middle-class wife, who had married him under the impression he was a secure businessman, created home life, evening life, and vacation life that fit upper-class norms. This was her territory of order and good form that M would visit briefly from work, until their divorce.

After last selling the company, M was over 65. Divorced, his children now adults, wealthy by ordinary standards, M could obviously have retired. But the concept did not seem to occur to him. Instead, he continued looking for deals: discos, jewelry, auto repair franchises, bottled water, art, magazine ventures, real estate development, dress designers, safety deposit boxes, and backing rock and roll bands all got serious consideration: some got action. Today, after several years of losses, he has learned yet another business and is becoming a respected name within it.

Recently, M surprised his children by announcing that he was participating in a "personal growth" seminar. The children were less surprised when they learned the focus of the experience: firewalking.

Of all the evidence in the foregoing story that M is **Opportunistic,** perhaps the most impressive is his continuation in the same pattern after 65, long after he had survived the tough environments from which he came and the tough times of his early years. As his daughter suggests, M *still* "doesn't have the luxury of choosing." Other elements from the following list of characteristics are also evident in the portrait of M.

Elements of the Opportunistic Managerial Style

Short time horizon	Flouts power, sexuality
Focus on concrete things	Rejects feedback
Fragile self-control	Stereotypes
Hostile humor	Rules = loss of freedom
Deceptive	Punishment = eye for eye
Manipulative	Legal = what can get away with
Views luck as central	Right = even trade
Externalizes blame	Distrustful

One frequently hears speculation about whether famous personages, such as Albert Speer, Hitler's minister for production, or Henry Kissinger, Nixon's secretary of state, are **Opportunists.** As should be clear by now, it is extremely unlikely that they are, in the sense used here. The very fact that Speer and Kissinger could manage an aura of success amidst the most complex institutions argues against this; that they could articulate and enact long-term strategies, and later write extensively about them, strongly reinforces this argument.

The reader will reencounter Kissinger in Chapter 12, for his insights are used to illustrate the **Strategist** style of management. Some **Strategists** sound very much like **Opportunists.** Strategists become capable of seeing the different worlds that different people generate, as well as all the incongruent fragments of their own world. But they do not yet sense how to integrate them. All is confusion. All is relative. Under these conditions, a *chosen* opportunism can offer relative security. An *ideology* of opportunism can offer relief from relativistic confusion. This chosen opportunism has the advantage of comprehending a variety of managerial styles. Hence, Strategic Opportunism offers the flexibility to manipulate others in more subtle ways than someone limited to the **Opportunistic** perspective. Whenever we hear the **Opportunistic** voice articulated as clearly as in the next illustration, we are almost certainly hearing from a manager at the later, **Strategist** stage. A true **Opportunist** would not be able to articulate his premises as clearly as the following self-portrait does.

> By "dealing effectively," I mean the ability to get the job at hand accomplished or to get what you want from others. It is the simple

task of understanding their frame of mind, and then either working through that frame or possibly attacking it viciously, without mercy. Both methods work, but the important factor is to determine which approach will work best in any given situation. Although this theory works well on a one-to-one basis, it must be somewhat adapted for group use since further difficulties arise then. In that case, one must use the old military strategy of divide and conquer. If you can play the devil's advocate in such a manner that the others will jointly discredit each other's opinions, it is then possible to seem the voice of reason and the great compromiser, thereby insinuating the germ of your own idea into the group. Thereupon, by assiduous but understated and restrained means, you can eventually attain your goal.

I call this theory "Business as War," I assume that it will be frowned upon in more enlightened circles, but nevertheless it works and is, at times, necessary, apart from the amusement its application provides.

Let us examine the theory at work during some events in the trust department of "The Bank." The Bank is one of the largest fiduciaries in its region, and among the cognoscenti it is well known that it is notoriously mismanaged. At one point the turnover was phenomenal, many individuals staying for only a month or two. Recently, the tight job market has slowed the turnover somewhat. One sterling young lad stayed for only two weeks, during which time he still held his former position. We wondered where he would disappear to so frequently. At the end of the two weeks, he went back to his other job entirely without even informing The Bank.

I had been there for approximately two years when the events described took place. My work had been quite satisfactory, and I was making my rise through the several echelons. I had been called into a certain unit to straighten it out since it was suffering the effects of a lengthy line of incompetent administrators hired under various programs encouraged by Supreme Court rulings. Nicholas, the trust officer I worked under, is in the Social Register and spent most of his time preparing for the next America's Cup. The head of the backshop was the granddaughter of a rather large trust donor. She spent the day planning the home show for the Junior League.

After about a year, the unit was in shape and running smoothly. At that time, I had a review with the fellow who will play a major role in this narrative. He had many names among the staff, including Nicky No-mind and Wishy of the famed team Wishy and Washy. I am informed by knowledgeable sources that he drove with one foot on the gas pedal and the other on the brake. Rumor had it that he suffered a nervous collapse upon discovering that he was being promoted to trust officer. His grasp of tax matters was non-existent.

During an earlier review with Nicholas, I had received a raise and was told that six months hence, on the next review date, I would receive a promotion and a raise in recognition of and reward for my services to the social butterfly unit. Not being of the landed gentry, I, of course, raised the subject of filthy lucre. An increase of 15 percent was quoted. During the next review with Nicholas I received the promotion and the raise, but it was only about 8 percent. In my best Oliver Twistian fashion, I indicated that it wasn't enough, that I would like some more, that I had been led to believe that it would not be quite so niggardly and parsimonious. Nicholas was adamant (for once in his life). I must have misunderstood (the last bastion of the cornered). We parted.

An hour or two later, Nicholas asked if he might speak with me. Since he wanted to use one of the conference rooms, I knew that something "big" was up. He didn't want his secretary eavesdropping as usual, or perhaps he didn't want the *others* to see me dissolve into a quivering mass, thus disgracing myself and assuring a blackball for The Club for want of the old, stiff upper lip. We entered the conference room and sat facing each other: cold, impassionate Yankee and spirited yet calculating Italian.

(My thoughts at the time)

Nicholas: Some time, not today, I would like to have a chat with you concerning your career goals.

(Aha. Something's up. I wonder what it could be?)

Mercury: Well, we're both here. Why don't we have our little chat now?

(Let's see if I can draw him out.)

N: No. there's no hurry. I don't want us to feel rushed.

(The sleaze doesn't want to talk, does he? Let me try a little harder.)

M: I won't feel rushed. I don't have anything planned after work, and you don't usually leave until six.

(The last thing I want to waste time on is talking to this bonze, but it's better to get it over.)

N: No. No. There's no rush. I'd like to give you a little time to think about it.

(I'm thinking now, and what I'm thinking is that you are trying to pull a fast one. I'll get you to open up yet.)

M: It seems to me you have some ulterior motive in mentioning these "goals."

(There. That should get a response.)

N: How dare you, sir, impinge upon my integrity. Ulterior motive! I've never been spoken to like this.

(My god. I've created a Frankenstein. I hope he doesn't have a stroke. I'd be tempted to leave him here to croak.)

M: My dear Nicholas, you misinterpret what I say. I meant no disrespect. I merely used "ulterior" in its Latin sense. I have tremendous regard for you.

(I'd better try to calm him down a little. Flattery always works on these goosecaps. Gag.)

N: I'm sorry I blew up. I thought you were questioning my integrity.

(I should hope that you would apologize, you uncouth and unlettered lout.)

M: It's all right. No harm done.

N: Well, it's getting late. We better be going. I'm glad we got that straightened out.

(Double gag. I'd like to strangle the bastard. Too bad he didn't have a stroke. Just like a broad, blowing up like that.)

M: Good night.

This amusing interchange illustrates how a bad situation can be turned to one's advantage. Nicholas had thought he would put me in my place, but a frontal assault totally demoralized him. By lapsing into irrationality, I disoriented him and he had to retreat. Of course, any possibility of a future chat was out of the question for fear his disgrace might recur. A clever use of psychology to manipulate Nicholas was successful.

I received the balance of my raise during my next review and received regular raises and promotions thereafter. There was, of course, no mention of the incident, but Nicholas seemed to be of the opinion that we had gone through adversity together and were more tightly united. This was exactly what I wanted, and in order to further the illusion I even asked him to write a recommendation for The Club, which he gladly did. At times, when you ask someone for a favor, it puts him under an obligation.

This story presents us in technicolor with the inner life and perceptions of the **Strategist** who adopts the **Opportunistic** style as a chosen strategy. From the writer's perspective, the other players in his scenario are all contemptible chumps. Mercury's sharp-eyedness catches much that is wanting in The Bank. But his hostile, superior, demeaning attitude is the reverse of what is necessary to generate higher shared standards of performance, as well as the reverse of what is necessary to challenge and support others in their movement along the developmental continuum. Mercury's approach is also, clearly, poison to the possibility of trust within a group.

The bank that Mercury is describing is one that has recently been found in violation of the law for not reporting large cash transactions. One gains a new appreciation of the "systems failures" that banks have recently been discovering, as they investigate why they have violated the law. Mercury's portrait of The Bank shows us the environment that breeds such "systems failures" from the inside.

In dealing with **Opportunistic** managers, an organization must develop clear, well-defined, relatively just systems both for doing the work in the first place and for evaluating managers' performance. If the organizational systems are not in fact clear or defensible, the **Opportunist** will be the first to notice. Managers of **Opportunists** must not blanch at the possibility of open conflict, or else the **Opportunist** will easily manipulate them, as Mercury does Nicky No-Mind in the foregoing scenario. This means, in particular, that the **Diplomat** (to be described in Chapter 6), who prefers to smooth over conflicts (as Nicky does), will be at the mercy of the **Opportunist** (for whom mercy is not an operative concept).

The **Opportunist** is less likely than managers at any of the later stages to develop beyond this style because it has become more rigidified than the others by adulthood. It is part of the tragedy of human life that the Christian parable—"To him who has, more shall be given; and to him who has not, even that which he has shall be taken away from him"—appears to apply in a very precise way to development. People who reach adulthood without developing beyond the earliest stages appear to have the least chance of developing further then, whereas people who have evolved toward later styles of management by adulthood seem to have the best chance of continuing to evolve.

TRANSITION

In the previous two chapters, we have examined what "capitalizing on opportunities" means for an organization at the **Investments** stage of development and for a manager who, although chronologically an adult, has not evolved beyond the analogous, early-stage **Opportunistic** style of management.

The next two chapters examine the third stage of development for organizations and for individuals. At this stage, not external resources but patterns of behavior become the predominant reality. Performing in a timely fashion becomes a central concern. The criterion of timeliness is some existing authority, whether that be a market, an organizational hierarchy, or individuals who are perceived as holding high status. The organization must get products or services out the door and receive revenues and allegiance in return, or it will fail to achieve **Incorporation.** The individual manager at this stage is attuned to meeting organizational norms and avoiding or smoothing over conflict—to performing as a **Diplomat.**

NOTES

1. R. Kegan, *The Evolving Self* (Cambridge, Mass.: Harvard University Press, 1982), p. 139.

2. "Three Who Watch, Wait, and Strike," *Time*, March 4, 1985, p. 67.

3. Michael Macoby identifies "the jungle fighter" as one of four managerial types in *The Gamesman* (New York: Bantam, 1978).

4. P. Gray, "Breezy and Irreverent, Raider Sam Zell Runs a $2.5 Billion Empire," *The Wall Street Journal*, November 7, 1985, p. 1.

5. The measure used in the three studies on managers reported in Chapter 2 is Jane Loevinger's ego development sentence completion test which requires specially trained scorers (J. Loevinger and R. Wessler, *Measuring Ego Development*, vols. 1 and 2 [San Francisco: Jossey-Bass, 1978]).

6. Arnold Mitchell's research with associates is part of the SRI International, Values and Lifestyles Program (Palo Alto, California), as presented by James Ogilvy, the program's research director, at the Boston College School of Management, 1982.

7. H. Lasker, *Ego Development and Motivation: A Cross-Cultural Cognitive-Developmental Analysis of Achievement* (doctoral dissertation, Department of Sociology, University of Chicago, 1978).

8. L. Kohlberg, *Collected Papers on Moral Development and Moral Education* (Cambridge, Mass.: Center for Moral Education, 1976).

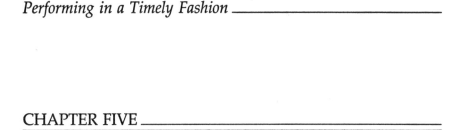

CHAPTER FIVE ——————————————————————————

The Incorporation Stage of Organizing

The **Incorporation** stage of organizing does not necessarily refer to legal incorporation but rather to physical, observable incorporation—to the time in an organization's development when it develops actual workspaces, selects members, and defines tasks for which more than one person shares responsibility. Such incorporation will not last more than a few months, however, unless the organization gets products or services out its doors in return for revenues—unless it performs in a timely fashion, as defined by the market it is addressing.

This stage can include the legal formation of the organization, but for-profit incorporation is, of course, only one of many possible legal, tax-related forms. The organization may start out as a sole proprietorship, a partnership, a worker-owned cooperative, or may seek not-for-profit status.

Obviously, it helps to develop the requisite capital (**Investments** stage) prior to purchasing one's equipment (**Incorporation** stage). But that does not mean it always happens that way. When these two stages get tangled up together, as they frequently do because the entrepreneur wants to get going, the resulting knots can become awesome. Fred Smith got Federal Express "off the ground" in January 1973 by buying and leasing his own fleet of Falcon 20s on the basis of short-term loans, pending venture financing that he expected any day. But the delays in the venture package continued until November of that year, and the company was broke as of February, the month after the Falcon deal. How did the company survive between February and November 1973? Smith rescued the company at the last moment by negotiating another bank loan. How did he secure this additional loan? Two years later, it was determined that Smith created a fictitious resolution on behalf of the Frederick Smith Enterprise Company. He also forged the signature of the company's board secretary. At his trial in December 1975, Smith admitted these actions forthrightly, but he defended them on the grounds that he had acted on behalf of the company before. He was acquitted.[1]

In the meantime, Federal Express continued to operate at a loss through 1973, 1974 and the first half of 1975. Its liabilities at one point exceeded $45 million before it had ever generated any net earnings. It rapidly became apparent that the November 1973 venture package would have to be supplemented by a second round of financing. Just as the second agreement was about to be signed in March 1974, Smith's forgery was discovered. Naturally, the investors were concerned about Smith's ability to attend to the company with a trial pending, so a new CEO was hired, with Smith demoted to president. The second round of financing was signed. And yet a third round of financing was negotiated in September 1974.

In January 1975, Smith was formally indicted for his forgery. The same night, after he was indicted, he hit and killed a pedestrian who was jaywalking, and then did not remain on the scene. The new CEO and several other members of the board of directors argued at the next board meeting that at this point Smith should be fired. But the other top officers of the company threatened to resign en masse and close the company down if Smith were removed. So the meeting ended instead with the CEO's resignation and with Smith as chairman of the board.

Such are the sparks when two stages of development become intermixed, but a very determined man refuses to let the mix-up defeat him and the organization.

In 1983, Federal Express, with Fred Smith still very much at the helm, became the first company in history to achieve $1 billion in revenues within the decade of its founding.

This story (of which only the barest outline is sketched here) may initially strike the reader as an unrepresentative soap opera.

But John Z. DeLorean's cocaine adventures on behalf of his be-leaguered automobile company start-up have a similar flavor. And when Thomas Watson was hired at CTR in 1913, he arrived as a convicted criminal (for violation of antitrust laws while em-ployed at National Cash Register) who had been fired from his previous position and faced a one-year prison term. (On appeal, a retrial was ordered but never held.[2])

Soap opera, yes. Unrepresentative, no. The actual birthing of an organization, like that of a child, is a moment of maximum risk, a moment that by its very nature involves extraordinary pressures, demands moment-to-moment life-or-death judg-ments, and requires virtually superhuman efforts. The jury that exonerated Fred Smith seems to have operated on the principle that all is fair in love and war and starting a business.

The particular problems that each organization and each leader faces at this stage are, of course, idiosyncratic. And the severity of the problems can certainly be compounded by an inversion and intermixing of two stages such as occurred in the develop-ment of Federal Express. But the need for persistence and unity in the face of an immediate threat to survival at the very outset of an organization's life is common.

Two additional start-up situations, very different from one another but both less personal in nature than the ones above, will illustrate how and why decisive action above and beyond the call of duty is a common requirement at the **Incorporation** stage. The building of a chemical or oil processing refinery is archetypically representative of **Incorporation** stage pressures. Because the eventual work involves flows and processes rather than parts assembled into units, the plant cannot be built piece-meal with production starting at once. Rather the plant must be complete before any processing can begin. For example, one par-ticular plan called for an 80-day construction period at a cost of $1 million per day. The capitalization plan required revenue-gen-erating production on the 81st day. Every day's delay beyond the initial 80 would cost the company an unbudgeted $1 million in expenses and still more in forgone revenues. As is inevitable, there were unforeseen snafus during the actual construction pro-cess. As the deadline approached, the crews worked night and day.

By contrast, a major new program for an existing not-for-profit bureaucracy like a university may appear to have no time deadlines whatsoever. Academics love to table proposals that they cannot agree on and bring them up again next year—if anyone remembers them by that time. But this is just the point: even in the academy, the timing of a project is not "academic." If—after a period of discussion during which faculty have a chance to argue about, modify, and decide whether to invest in some new concept—a decision about whether to do it is *not* reached, then the initiative is very likely dead for all time. Those who had invested most in creating and advocating the proposal are likely to feel betrayed rather than merely defeated and may choose not to reopen the question. At times like this, it is an illusion to believe that there is a freedom not to choose: "freedom not to choose" masks the choice not to do.

IBM AT THE INCORPORATION STAGE

As we have already seen in the previous chapter, Thomas Watson made no effort not to choose when he took over the leadership of CTR (IBM). One might have thought his position as a newcomer, along with the court sentence hanging over his head at that time, would have made Watson a mite tentative. Not so. Watson's early, strong decisions (already reviewed in the previous chapter) doubled revenues and tripled net earnings during World War I, by contrast to the previous three years (1912–14) when net earnings declined. This pattern of high net earnings relative to total revenues became characteristic for IBM. In 1939, IBM's total revenues were only slightly higher than the *average* of its four closest competitors (Burroughs, National Cash Register, Remington Rand, and Underwood Elliott Fisher), but its net earnings were almost equivalent to the *combined* net earnings of all the other four. In 1965, in a new industry (mainframe computers), measured against its seven closest competitors (Burroughs, Control Data, GE, Honeywell, NCR, RCA, and Sperry Rand), IBM's total revenues were *21 percent* as large as the total for the other seven, but its net earnings were *58 percent* as large as the combined net earnings of the other seven.[3] Needless to say, a pattern of high net earnings relative to revenue is a particularly advantageous pattern to set at a for-profit corporation.

Whatever specific characteristic patterns different organizations establish during the **Incorporation** stage, there is one pattern that they all set at this stage, though it is rarely recognized at the time. This pattern concerns whether the organization's actual functioning is consistent or inconsistent with its purported mission. Is its **Incorporation** consistent or inconsistent with its **Conception?** Does it practice what it preaches? Is it keeping its original promise? Is it making its dream come true?

Because an unimaginable number of contingencies arise between the initial fantasies and the eventual concrete establishment of the organization, and because these contingencies demand constant improvisation and compromise, it is virtually inevitable that there be some inconsistency between the ideal and the actuality. Of course, this inconsistency could hypothetically represent an improvement, for the initial fantasy may have been seriously incomplete or warped. But it is much more likely that the inconsistency will represent a diminishment of the original ideal. For, as Gregory Bateson explained to his daughter when she wondered why her room was always in a mess, there are an infinite number of ways for a room to be in a mess, and any random movement tends to mess things up. But there are only a relatively few ways for things to be in order, and they must intentionally be put that way.[4]

Here, the fact that business relies as heavily as it does upon the conceptual framework and language of economics can be extremely pernicious. As pressures mount and the entrepreneur finds himself sacrificing cherished elements of his or her original dream, what remains standing as the central element in the now-pared-down purpose? Probably, profit. Profit, we have learned, is the true ultimate purpose of a business.

Not so. Profit is a *condition* for continuing to do business. Profit is one among many measures of the relative success of a business. But profit is emphatically *not* the purpose of any business. The need to make a profit does not distinguish one business from any other. It tells us nothing about the distinctive order, the distinctive dream, of this particular business.

If we sacrifice the other elements of our dream to making a profit, we have in fact sacrificed *all* elements of our dream. Then, even if our business does not make a profit, we are in a mess. This mess is the more entangling and destructive in that we may continue to believe that everything must be in order because the business is making a profit. Being in a mess that one cannot even describe to oneself as a mess is to be crazy.

Rarely, though, is the issue so extreme. And it is certainly true, as well, that one's original fantasies are more likely than not to contain elements of self-indulgence. The market disciplines that strip us of these self-indulgences can be appreciated as spiritually liberating, enlightening, and sharpening. But the trick is to navigate the pressure of **Incorporation** in such a way as to slough off self-indulgence and, simultaneously, to realize the true kernel of the original dream.

To illustrate these abstractions, let us recall the new architectural firm, cited in the introduction, which was founded with the particular dream/mission of *building flexible, easily adaptable, creativity-enhancing spaces for fast-growing companies.* As it happens, most of the early commissions the firm receives are for residential housing. In order to get the business rolling and keep bread on the family table, the architect-entrepreneur accepts these commissions. His early drawings and models are received so enthusiastically that his reputation quickly mushrooms and he is submerged with requests to do residential housing. He is rapidly hiring staff—to help design *residential housing.* These people are not necessarily committed to the original dream. They are joining a firm that does residential housing.

Within six months, the architect/entrepreneur's original dream is in danger of being altogether lost amidst his "success." He is riding an emotional roller coaster, alternating among many feelings: exhiliration at "making" it, exhaustion from the constant act of "juggling in a whirlwind" and the concomitant fear of "losing it," and moments of soul-wrenching anguish when he fears that he has already irretrievably lost it—the original dream.

Paradoxically, this very anguish is the most hopeful element of his situation. If he did not feel this, he would almost certainly be lost in his success and his superficial (but nonetheless powerful) fear of dropping a ball on a day-to-day basis.

As it is, he jumps at a chance to move his office into a huge, old, abandoned plant. He leaves the shabby shell of the building untouched initially and builds attractive workspace islands and walkways throughout it, with movie set lighting. Displayed within these island studios are models of different buildings of the future.

Next, he stops designing buildings for two weeks, despite the pressures to stay on schedule, and designs a marketing brochure instead. He mandates counterhabitual "special effects" for every staff meeting, to embody the value of creative playfulness: Groucho Marx noses, mustaches, and glasses for all appear at one meeting, roving spotlighting for speakers and exhibits at the next.

Within two months, he has two major institutional contracts. By the end of the year, the business has decisively shifted toward corporate planning and design.

Now the firm's physical space is consistent with its mission. It *is* a flexible, easily adaptable, creativity-enhancing space for a fast-growing company. A member of the firm or a visitor to it sees, at a glance, the dynamic intertwining of the past (the plant shell), the present (the work islands), and the future (the model buildings—and also the plant shell which, transformed, represents the future of this adaptable space).

The firm's social atmosphere is also now consistent with its mission. Instead of being driven by external forces and fears, it *is* the internally driven, creative atmosphere that it claims it can help other businesses to attain.

IMPLICATIONS FOR CORPORATE PLANNING AND SOCIAL POLICY

What are the implications, if any, of the traumatic experiences of the **Incorporation** stage for corporate planning and social policy?

Over the past century, we have developed an elaborate health care system that mediates at the birthing of a child, providing a protective environment and significantly reducing infant mortality. Recently, a series of decentralized initiatives—such as Small Business Development Centers associated with certain universities, and large companies that godfather new ventures by taking a significant but not controlling equity position in them—represent tentative steps toward providing a protective environment for new businesses.

Japan is far ahead of the United States in this regard, having understood more than a generation ago that there is a specific period at the outset of a new venture, a new industry, and even in the development of a national economy when the developing social system needs special support and protection *in order to prepare it for rigorous competition thereafter.* The Japanese system of advisory (not compulsory) planning coordinated by the government Ministry of Trade (MITI), along with a financial structure that encourages banks to take continuing equity positions and board membership in companies, has proven remarkably effective at blending protection with competition at appropriate times within the Japanese economy.

Today, we are observing whether Japan will exercise similar discipline with regard to its external trade relations. After a generation of protecting its internal markets from foreign competition, Japan's enormous balance of trade surplus now invites it to take courageous initiatives to open its markets to foreign competition.

Despite our elaborate medical establishment today and what is superficially an apolitical problem of birthing children, the proper care for birthing mothers and newborn babies remains a subject of controversy, precisely because this particular developmental transformation is so dangerous and so supernaturally demanding. We can expect that the analogous political-economic issue of how to support the birthing of new businesses and industries will continue to be a subject of even greater controversy. And so it should be, for the proper response is almost certainly neither simple nor constant across countries and across historical periods.

For this controversy to be productive, however, debate in the United States must move beyond the false dichotomy of free enterprise market competition versus state-controlled socialism. History has by now decisively rendered this argument obsolete.

On the one hand, think of all the major economies in the world that have committed themselves substantially or totally to state-controlled socialism—the USSR, China, India, Yugoslavia, and Britain. All are now experimenting—with varying degrees of stiffness, stumbling, and ideological pain—with market mechanisms for price setting and productivity enhancement.

On the other hand, think of every major success of predominantly capitalistic economies since the Great Depression of the 1930s—the recovery of the U.S. economy at the outset of World War II, the European Common Market of the 1950s, and the Japanese miracle of the late 1960s and 1970s (from being classified as underdeveloped in 1965 to being the world's largest automobile producer in 1980). Without exception, each of these capitalistic successes has initially been fueled by unprecedented government intervention. The recovery of the American economy at the outset of World War II was prompted by a government deficit six times as large as any that Roosevelt generated in any year during the 1930s. The European Common Market in the 1950s grew from the Marshall Plan aid offered by the United States. And the Japanese "miracle" during the late 1960s and 1970s owes much not only to government guidance but also to the defense shield that the United States provided throughout this period.

To debate "capitalism versus socialism" is beside the point today. The interesting problem and the critical experiments today—both within companies and within countries—concern the *timing* and the *blending* of competition and cooperation.

The issue of *timing* can be stated as the issue of how to recognize and how to midwife major developmental transformations of the company or country, as these oscillate back and forth between a primary emphasis on individuation/competition/ centralization and a primary emphasis on interdependence/cooperation/decentralization.[5] In the developmental theory proposed in this book, the emphasis is on individuation and centralization in the first, third, and fifth organizational stages (**Conception, Incorporation, Systematic Productivity**). The emphasis is on interdependence and decentralization in the second, fourth, and sixth stages (**Investments, Experiments, Collaborative Inquiry**).

The issue of *blending* can be stated as the issue of how to create cooperative frameworks within which invigorating competition can take place. An example of a new way of blending competition and cooperation is the system of worker-owner enterprises that has developed in the Mondragon region of Spain. Every member of each business is a citizen with voting rights and a potential candidate for the firm's board of directors, as well as an owner whose share of each year's dividends is credited to his or her account. The individual worker-owned businesses are linked through a "second-order" system of institutions that are controlled in part by their own workers and in part by the other companies. These second-order institutions include a research institute, an insurance company, and a bank among others. The bank not only finances the existing worker-owned businesses but also maintains real-time financial information systems on each company, so that financial difficulties can be spotted early. The bank also has an entrepreneurial division that supports entrepreneurs who wish to found new worker-owned companies. After a predetermined period, the new companies must make it on their own. All the companies are in competition with the rest of the Spanish economy (and now the rest of the Common Market). The awesome record of this system of *cooperative* frameworks for building *competitive* enterprises is that over its first quarter of a century it supported the start-up of some hundred industrial enterprises *without a single business failure.*[6]

Characteristics of the Incorporation Stage of Organizing

1. Specific organizational goals and operating staff determined.
2. Recognizable physical setting, common tasks, roles, and initial legal form delineated.
3. Products or services produced in timely fashion that generates revenues.
4. Critical issues: (*a*) display of persistence, unity in the face of difficult choice or threat; (*b*) maintaining or recreating consistency between essential aspects of original dream and actual organizational arrangements.

NOTES

1. All the information presented here on Federal Express is derived from R. Sigafoos, *Absolutely Positively Overnight!* (Memphis, Tenn.: St. Luke's Press, 1983).

2. R. Sobel, *IBM: Colossus in Transition* (Toronto: Bantam, 1983), p. 40 ff.

3. The 1939 and 1965 IBM figures are computed from tables in ibid., pp. 83 and 161.

4. G. Bateson, "Metalogue: Why Do things Get in a Muddle," in *Steps to an Ecology of Mind* (New York: Ballantine Books, 1972).

5. A theory of business development through alternating phases of centralization and decentralization is presented by L. Greiner, "Evolution and Revolution as Organizations Grow," *Harvard Business Review* 50, no. 4 (1972), pp. 37–46.

6. D. Ellerman, *The Mondragon Cooperative Movement* (Boston: Harvard Business School Case Services, Case #1-384-270, 1984); and *The Socialization of Entrepreneurship: The Empresarial Division of the Caja Laboral Popular* (Somerville, Mass.: Industrial Cooperative Association, 1982).

CHAPTER SIX _____

The Diplomatic Manager

Like the opportunistic logic of the previous style of managerial development, diplomacy is one of the key elements that makes the social world work. And, just as calling someone "an opportunist" can be meant as a compliment or an insult, so too calling someone "a diplomat" can be positive or negative.

Sometimes calling someone a diplomat implies that he or she possesses just that exquisite sense of tact that permits both honesty and agreement about the most difficult issues, enhancing the self-esteem and dignity of all parties in the process. In this same positive vein, the diplomatic manager can provide loyalty and good will that functions as organizational glue.

At other times, the implication is that the "diplomat" avoids and smooths over all potential conflict, masking both true feelings and objective data in an effort to maintain a spurious public harmony at all costs.

As in the previous chapter on the **Opportunist**, this chapter on the **Diplomatic** managerial style focuses on managers for whom diplomacy is an end, not a means to some higher end. Consequently, it highlights the negative side of diplomacy—its limitations and ultimate costs.

For the **Diplomat**, the sentiments of family, work or play group, organization, or nation about appropriate patterns of behavior are the primary elements in the chemistry of social reality. Loyalty to the group and adherence to its definition of appropriate behavior are the ultimate tests of membership. The 1960s slogan "America: love it or leave it" was one expression of diplomatic logic.

At this stage of development, behavioral skills—the right moves or words at the right times—are seen as critical for gaining membership, working or playing to standard, observing the correct protocol, and developing value. For a person at this stage, value is defined not by oneself, but by others. Some thing or some action has value if it sells, if it influences others, or if high-status persons treat it as valuable.

The **Diplomat** is essentially past oriented, valuing continuity and stability. Conformity to group norms and leadership in exemplifying these norms are seen as the road to approval and happiness (and the Patty Hearst story, among many others, taught us long ago that conformity is just as likely in a "nonconformist" group as in any other).

For the **Diplomat,** behaving appropriately is the essence of civility, and civility is the essence of morality. Public error results in loss of face, but in no sense *merely* a loss of face, for loss of face is felt as loss of soul. Maintaining face and saving others' face are experienced not just as aesthetically preferable but as moral imperatives. The sum total of the sentiments of significant others about a certain issue becomes the **Diplomat's** sentiments about that issue. If the **Diplomat's** significant others are in conflict about the issue, the **Diplomat** feels that conflict as a conflict within himself or herself. Consequently, it is no wonder that public conflict is poison for him.

In his "consumer values" study, Mitchell estimated that 32 percent of the population were "Belongers," his category that most closely parallels the **Diplomatic** managerial style. He describes these consumers as conforming, traditional, and blue collar, whose buying behavior focuses on mass market items for family and home and on fads.

The three studies of managers cited in Chapter 2 found that less than 5 percent of the senior managers, 9 percent of the junior managers, and 24 percent of the first-line supervisors held the developmental perspective corresponding to the **Diplomatic** managerial style. These limited data suggest that the **Diplomatic** style limits one's chances for promotion.

Henry Ford II skipped the usual rigors of promotion. He is said never to fire a subordinate directly, but indirectly through third parties (and through the years he has fired many a number-two man in this way). Before he finally fired Lee Iacocca (leaking the information to a newsman who then unwittingly broke the news to Iacocca by calling him for verification), Ford paid McKinsey consultants $2 million for a study recommending Iacocca's demotion.[1] The **Diplomat**'s conflict-avoiding, indirect style can be expensive.

In 1981, Kathleen Kenefick, a young lender for Continental Illinois Bank, wrote a memo to her superiors saying. "The status of the Oklahoma accounts (particularly Penn Square) is a cause for concern, and corrective action should be instigated quickly."[2] In fact, corrective action was never instigated. Kenefick's message was explained away in the upper echelons as a personality conflict with her boss, and Kenefick left the company. A year later, Penn Square was closed by regulators, and Continental was left holding $1 billion in bad loans. In subsequent efforts not to scare depositors away by showing a big quarterly loss, Continental repeatedly manipulated its books to show profits, until its mammoth failure and federally supported reorganization in the spring and summer of 1984. The **Diplomat**'s smoothing-over, conflict-avoiding style can be expensive, indeed!

Elements of the Diplomatic Managerial Style

Observes protocol	Speaks in cliches, platitudes
Avoids inner and outer conflict	Feels shame if violates norms
Works to standard	Right = nice, cooperative, follow the
Suppresses own desires	rules
Sin = hurting others	Loyalty to in-group
Punishment = disapproval	Seeks membership, status
Conforms	Saving face essential

The phrase "organizational politics" leaves a bad taste in most people's mouths because it is so strongly associated with either the jungle-fighting **Opportunist** or the face-saving **Diplomat**. Harold Geneen spoke in language clear enough to discourage both of these types of managerial styles at ITT when he announced that anyone who tried to line up other managers to back his pet project in return for his later vote, or anyone who tried to force a more junior manager to give anything other than his honest opinion, did so in peril of losing his job. "Truth (goes) to the very heart of good management," writes Geneen.[3] "Decisions (have) to be based upon an honest examination of the facts and not be swayed by one man leaning on another through rank, threat, reciprocity, friendship, or whatever."

The trouble is that unless you create managerial systems that actually challenge managers to develop beyond the **Diplomatic** style, all you achieve by banning one sort of behavior or another is to create a slightly different sort of threat, reciprocity, and conformity.

Most programs aimed at generating greater managerial motivation, autonomy, responsibility, and creativity founder on the **Diplomat**'s loyalty to existing ways of doing things, along with his or her fear of public error and loss of face if a new behavior or a new product does not work. Take the various schemes to make managers more "participative." To the **Diplomat**, being participative means that you can avoid the controversy of advocating a new vision or strategy by asking everyone else for their ideas about what to do. In general, others don't respond well to such wide open requests. It is not their primary responsibility. They have not given it much thought. And they are a bit afraid that if they come up with a good suggestion they will be asked to implement it.

So, our **Diplomatic** participative manager begins to feel let down by his colleagues and a bit resentful when they do not participate, though he would never show such negative feelings in public. As nothing happens and senior management begins to insinuate that our **Diplomat** is not getting the job done, his frustration increases until he finally decides there is nothing for it but to take the initiative himself. When he does so, belatedly, he is astounded to discover that now people are madder than ever at him. They attack him for acting too slowly *and* for not consulting them about his final decision after promising to do so! He decides forevermore to excise the word "participative" from his working vocabulary (but continues behaving in basically the same noninitiating conflict-avoiding way).

A CLOWN BECOMING MORE THAN A CLOWN

Although the **Diplomat** may appear bland or unrelievedly positive or clownish on the outside, his or her concern with what other people think can lead to a cacophony of voices inside, especially in conditions of ambiguity or public conflict. The following passage from one manager's journal lets us hear some of these voices. This manager—a tall, rangy, athletic fellow with an open, competent expression—was well liked by colleagues. He was keeping this journal and trying a variety of exercises in conjunction with a management development process within his company. One of the exercises involved lying down at night after a difficult day at work, shaking and stretching the muscles and breathing deeply to begin to relax. Next, the exercise called for moving inward toward the real feelings evoked by the day's tensions while simultaneously allowing the mind to float back over one's lifetime, towards the earliest memory of an occasion that had generated similar feelings.

This manager's journal entry first describes his inner experience as he sat through a monthly management meeting without ever speaking. This was normal behavior for him on these occasions, though he frequently eased tensions before meetings officially began or at breaks by playing the clown. The management development training had made him aware that this pattern of "official" silence and "unofficial" clowning might be keeping him invisible when it really counted, thereby reducing his chances for advancement. So, the first part of this entry is an attempt to document what is keeping him silent. The last part of this journal entry describes his insight from trying the relaxing/memory exercise at night.

> People look at me and look away, I glance quickly at someone else and they glance away, retreat somewhere. Where? I look at the group leader. He looks mean as hell, the snarling, baleful glance of authority.
>
> I'd better say something fast. Hurry, say something, it only gets worse waiting! But it better be good. Something unique in a cool detached universal vein. Something that will impress them, but in what way? I don't want to say some stupid thing and sound like an idiot. I haven't said a serious thing yet at these management

meetings. I'm locked into the joke. I can't tell a joke now. Brother, you better produce. They're all waiting for you.

You're an adult. Say something adult. You are acting like a kid. I feel so isolated and alone. I am defeated, beaten, K.O.'d without ever landing a blow. Maybe if I started a fight I'd feel better. How childish can you get?

You are bad! Remember? You don't take nothing from nobody! Remember? Get mad, get tough, look tough, take it on a physical level, you can deal with that. So why don't you say something then? What should I say?

Why do I feel and act this way? It is as though there is someone else inside of me who never gets out. He thinks things, feels things, and yet, more often than not, cannot express his serious thoughts. I make light of situations, prefer to play the fool. My words and gestures say, "Relax everyone. See, I'm an idiot. Laugh at me and feel better, be my friend, like me." I have no fear of being a fool in public, but I have an absolute trauma about making a mistake when I am intending to be serious. As a reaction to this fear, I hold back from making serious comments in meetings. I only really talk to friends with whom I feel safe.

I remember when I was a very little person of about three, my father had a glass door leaning against a wall next to the house. I thought I'd be helpful and move it into the garage while he was at work, but due to a slight miscalculation as to the scope of the task, the door ended up in a million pieces on the ground. No one witnessed the deed so I reasoned that if I hid for long enough, I could avoid association with the crime ("What door?"). I went up to my room in the attic and hid under the bed for the rest of the day, falling to sleep in the process. I was so little that my parents never suspected foul play, and my father thought that the wind had blown it over. It just so happened that my sister had drunk some kerosene and that further served to camouflage my crime. My father had left the kerosene in an orange juice container in the garage, so he was more upset with himself than with the broken door.

This was the humble beginning of a rather illustrious career of retreat. If I look at the situation closely, I was a very serious little person trying to do an important and serious job and I blew it completely. In my subtle, adult way, I have refined the mechanics in that now I flee before I commit the crime, and manifest serious intention has become the crime. When I thought seriously of speaking at the management meeting, I experienced the same turmoil and desire to flee that characterized this early trauma. I felt that I had blown it when in fact I hadn't even attempted anything.

At the next meeting, the manager broke his pattern of silence. Previously, whatever learning he had done about becoming a more effective manager occurred within the limitations imposed by his role as a clown on public occasions. To the degree that his managerial ineffectiveness derived from this very limit, however, he could not, previously, become more effective. If anything, he had probably reinforced his own ineffectiveness by treating his clowning as his strength and as his "natural" style.

How had he finally come to see the very blinders that had previously been imprisoning his vision? At the meeting described in his journal and during the exercise he later tried at home, he had maintained the activity of self-observation, even though it generated great tension. Rather than being, and fleeing from, his inner conflict, as was his (**Diplomatic**) habit, he detached himself from the conflict within himself, continued to observe it, and later searched out its roots. He thereby earned an insight so powerful that it actually influenced him to act in a fundamentally new way.

The transformation in managerial style that this manager embarked upon as a result of his insight is a very unusual one for **Diplomatic** managers. Next to **Opportunist** managers, **Diplomatic** managers are the least likely to evolve beyond their current developmental stage and corresponding managerial style. A management development program that merely concentrated on introducing managers to new concepts, or to practicing new behaviors, would not have influenced this manager in any fundamental way. Like any clown, he could have mimicked the new practices perfectly in the training setting (probably drawing laughs from his colleagues by mimicking the trainers' tendentious tone of voice as well). And he could then have parodied them in management meetings as a tension reliever. But it is unlikely he would "really" change. If he were confronted on his clownishness by a superior, he would probably manage to make a joke of it, or else become terminally self-conscious about the matter, as he was in the meeting he reports above.

The point is that **Diplomatic** managers do not seek out negative feedback about themselves. Quite the contrary, they attempt to deflect it. They equate negative feedback with loss of face and loss of status. To tell them that it is constructive because it can help them achieve a goal they have does not make sense to them. No particular goal is as compelling to them as the implicit rule against losing face. In this context, the following finding is not surprising. A certain organization offers its members feedback, if they request it individually, on instruments used to measure their stage of development and managerial style. In four years, not one person measured as holding the **Opportunistic** or the **Diplomatic** styles asked for feedback. By contrast, about 10 percent of those measured at the **Technician** and **Achiever** styles (the next two developmental stages) asked for feedback; and *a majority* of those measured at still later developmental positions asked for feedback. These data indicate just how unusual it was for the clown in the foregoing story to begin to change his costume, mask, and public demeanor.

ORGANIZATIONAL CONDITIONS THAT SUPPORT DEVELOPMENT

Organizations interested in creating environments that challenge **Diplomats** to continue developing would do well to structure management development activities around real-time projects. **Diplomats** feel more at home in small work groups than in formal management meetings. They will reveal more of themselves and make friendships through which they can later be influenced. For such project groups to foster development, individuals must have clear leadership responsibilities (every member can hold a leadership role). Regular evaluation and feedback within the group must be mandated. And group members must have a mentor relationship to someone who does not have formal authority over them. Although these may at first sound like difficult conditions to create, they are useful not only for promoting managerial development but also for generating reliable high performance in semiautonomous project groups. Thus, the investment in creating these conditions has multiple payoffs.

It is through the inevitable tensions that arise between self-interest, group solidarity, quality production, and honest evaluation of the past and the future that development to later managerial styles can be fostered. Each of the early managerial styles focuses on one layer of social reality as truly real. **Opportunistic** group members will see issues through the lens of narrow *self-interest*. **Diplomatic** group members will be primarily concerned with establishing and maintaining *group solidarity* with minimal public conflict. **Achievers** will regard any time not spent on *quality production*—on making the best possible products and on achieving the best possible outcomes—as wasted time. So there will be conflict within almost any group, not only about whatever particulars are at stake, but also about what the stakes themselves are. The **Diplomat**'s skills in redirecting and avoiding conflict are sure to be exceeded, if not by the tangible, physical specifics, then certainly by the conflicting worldviews of **Opportunists** or **Achievers, Technicians** or **Strategists.**

It is important that conflicts not be artificially generated by the organization's leadership in the effort to promote development. Such artificially generated conflicts will naturally lead the victims to distrust those who fomented the conflict rather than to develop beyond their previous limits. The conflicts must be real—in the old-fashioned, pragmatic sense of real—occasioned by the real demands of organizational work and the real, but mutually incongruent, responses of the group members. Each **Diplomatic** manager—indeed, each manager holding any of the developmental styles—will risk further development only as he or she confirms that his or her current style is fundamentally incapable of resolving significant issues. Only such real and inescapable conflicts provide the material for creative solutions and for personal development when they gradually (or sometimes suddenly) emerge. It is particularly important for the **Diplomatic** manager to perceive high-status members of the organization as supportive of experimentation and personal change at such a point.

TRANSITION

In the past two chapters, we have been examining how organizations and managers reach the initial point of performing in a timely fashion. In the case of organizations at the **Incorporation** stage, a critical issue that determines whether they will continue to evolve is whether they are not only successful in external terms at this stage but also successful in the sense of remaining true to their original dream. In the case of managers who remain at the **Diplomatic** stage in adulthood rather than transforming beyond it during later teenage years, we have seen that the challenge of further development consists precisely in the fact that their view of themselves is virtually entirely mediated through others' views of them.

In the next section, we encounter the stages of development at which one finds most large organizations and rising managers. At the next stage of development, organizations break the mold that brought them success at the **Incorporation** stage with a series of **Experiments.** Managers break the mold of other-sanctioned behavior, give primary allegiance to some internally consistent logic, and begin to follow where it leads—thereby developing a **Technician** style of management.

NOTES

1. Lee Iacocca (with W. Novak), *Iacocca: An Autobiography* (New York: Bantam, 1984), p. 126.

2. This information and quotation comes from *The Wall Street Journal*, July 30, 1984.

3. Harold Geneen (with A. Moscow), *Managing* (Garden City, N.Y.: Doubleday, 1984), p. 134.

Restructuring to Make the Dream Come True

CHAPTER SEVEN _____

Experiments

In the period just after an organizing process coagulates into **Incorporation,** it immediately fluidifies again into a period of **Experiments.** At the **Incorporation** stage, the foremost challenge is to set limits, meet deadlines, and cut out activities that are inconsistent with the original dream—in short, to create a mold. At the **Experiments** stage, the foremost challenge is to try new ways of doing business, new ways to make the dream come true as the organization grows larger and the environment changes—in short, to break the mold. This is true whether we are looking at the 6-month history of a particular team project or the 100-year history of IBM.

During the **Experiments** stage, different ways of conceptualizing and carrying out the activity are tried out in relatively rapid succession in a search for a strategy and structure that works best for a particular team, with particular resources, in a particular environment, at a particular time.

Even in a largely prefabricated organization such as McDonald's, for which virtually every decision about colors, uniforms, products, packaging, and pricing is predetermined by the franchise agreement at the **Incorporation** stage, the early days of the new franchise tend to be vibrant. Virtually all organization members can feel directly and daily the challenge of meeting various environmental tests for which even all of McDonald's prepackaged logistics provide no automatic response. Later, this period is likely to be canonized in myths about "the good old days."

In 1985, a new McDonald's franchise opened every 17 hours somewhere around the world. Back in 1980, June Torris was one of the first women to make the jump from store manager to store owner at McDonald's when she acquired an ailing franchise in Dallas. She had already proved herself as a manager by taking one store from red to black and quadrupling the profits at another, so McDonald's offered her a Business Facilities Lease. The very fact that she was a woman and that something different clearly had to be tried in this store gave the **Experiments** stage a special flavor. Moving about the store and the community like a friendly whirlwind, Torris worked the grill, developed a new commitment to "fast, friendly service" among her crew, and visited local merchants to find out what she had to do to reclaim them as customers. Each move was a miniexperiment. Business as usual is a phrase that simply does not apply to June. In less than three years, she earned enough to be able to buy the franchise outright.[1]

At each stage of organizational development, the more original and uncharted the new organizing process is, the more pronounced this stage will be. At the other extreme from a McDonald's franchise, virtually every facet of what the Peace Corps was attempting to do when it was founded in the early 1960s involved exploring previously unknown social terrain. At the most mundane level, job titles, responsibilities, and reporting lines in the Washington central offices changed on a monthly basis, sometimes even weekly.

Selection and training procedures were in constant turmoil. How do you select for hundreds of different types of jobs in a hundred different cultures? How can you tell who will survive, thrive, and contribute to settings halfway around the world? How can you train people to deal with unanticipated dilemmas? Since there were no obvious, authoritative answers to these questions based on prior experience, different Peace Corps training camps were explicitly based on different educational philosophies and methods. Hence, each training design was explicitly experimental.

Because the political stakes were so high, even more disturbing questions arose once a Peace Corps contingent arrived in its assigned country. How was the contingent to relate to the U.S. ambassador there and to the host organization and host government? Take a Peace Corps volunteer assigned to Nicaragua in 1969 as a rural development specialist, in association with the central bank's mandate to fund decentralized, peasant, agricultural development. Was this volunteer a member of the bank like other employees whom the bank could fire? Did the volunteer owe allegiance to the Nicaraguan government's policies? Was the volunteer subordinate to the U.S. ambassador and to the U.S. government objectives in Nicaragua?

All these questions were severely tested in short order. Many members of the first Peace Corps contingent to Nicaragua came to believe on the basis of their early experiences and research, that the bank was not really funding decentralized development, as mandated by the Alliance for Progress funding source, but rather was systematically diverting these funds to the Somozas and other large landowners who exercised oligarchic control over the government itself. These volunteers did not wish to participate in a charade of development, but their appeals to the government fell on deaf ears.

The U.S. ambassador himself counseled patience, noninterference, and respect for the self-determination of the Nicaraguan people. To the volunteers, this sounded like a smokescreen and like a betrayal of the "little" people and the ideals of the Alliance for Progress. In protest, they developed a strategy of phased resignation. If this strategy did not elicit a constructive response, it would leave Nicaragua without a Peace Corps contingent, to the embarrassment of officialdom in both countries, the volunteers hoped. The strategy was to be implemented *unless* the Peace Corps contract between the United States and Nicaragua was revised and clarified to more nearly assure the implementation of the stated intentions of the rural development program.

Put in terms of this developmental theory, the **Incorporation** stage had become radically inconsistent with the Peace Corps dream at the **Conception** stage, at least from the volunteers' perspective. The strategy outlined above was an **Experiments** stage effort intended to destroy the results of the **Incorporation** stage and reincorporate. Obviously a traumatic process, whether it succeeded or failed.

One third of the Peace Corps contingent reluctantly resigned and returned to the United States before the restructuring occurred.

Episodes like this around the world led to repeated restructurings of the Peace Corps itself, as well as to restructurings within the countries. This ferment may well have been necessary to the accomplishment of the Peace Corps' mission. Certainly, though it still exists, the Peace Corps has moved off the stage of history as its functions have been increasingly routinized. The Peace Corps is no longer presented as a leading element of U.S. foreign policy and is no longer in the headlines and the TV news.

THE EXPERIMENTS STAGE AT IBM

In between the extremes of a "prefabricated" McDonald's and an "unprecedented" Peace Corps, the continuing story of IBM's development offers an illustration of the **Experiments** stage painted in intermediate hues. The reader will recall that we delineated the **Conception** stage of IBM as the period between 1879 and 1910 when Herman Hollerith invented and commercialized his tabulator. We identified the **Investments** stage of IBM as the short period between 1910 and 1913 when Charles Flint bought the company, merged it with two others, and then brought Thomas Watson, Sr., on board. We described the period between 1913 and 1918 as the **Incorporation** stage because Watson became president and made a series of critical decisions that established the company as a worthy and profitable independent entity.

The period between 1918 and 1924 can be considered the **Experiments** stage in IBM's century-long history. Watson unified the sales force for all three divisions of what was then still CTR. He instituted what he called the Hundred Per Cent Club, giving bonuses and privileges to those salesmen who fulfilled their sales quotas each year. The motivational and organizational twist to this system consisted in setting quotas at levels that fully 80 percent of the sales force could meet. Each year that a salesman topped 100 percent and received a bonus, his quota was raised.

This merit system, unlike those that reward only a small minority and generate envy, succeeded in raising the morale of a large majority of the sales force, in annually raising productivity standards, and in weeding out those least inclined toward this activity. Although this was an experiment in the CTR context, it was an almost exact copy of a system that Watson had previously worked with at NCR. In any event, it worked in the new setting; from then until now, "sales" has been the privileged route to the top at IBM. Tom Watson, Jr., started in sales when he joined the company after World War II, en route to succeeding his father, and so did IBM's current chairman and CEO, John F. Akers.

In other experiments between 1918 and 1924, Watson, Sr., invested in new construction and unveiled the first new product from A.E. Ford's research group, a state-of-the-art printer-lister that presented the information gathered by the Hollerith tabulators and sorters. Watson increased inventories, betting heavily on the new product and on continued prosperity. To finance these moves, he took short-term loans from Guarantee Trust, a practice so common to business that no one would have considered it an experiment.

But Watson had taken the loans just before the recession of 1920–21. Suddenly the company was in jeopardy, finishing 1921 with a net deficit for the only time in its history. Everyone's wages were slashed by 10 percent and, in the effort to reduce inventory, Watson discontinued production of the new printer-lister, even though demand continued strong.

Betting heavily on a state-of-the-art product is certainly an experiment, but if it fails one can conclude that the product or the timing was off and try again. Watson, however, concluded that the very notion of borrowing to bet heavily on a state-of-the-art product was the mistake. Thereafter, he maintained high cash reserves and a policy of "technological followership" rather than leadership, depending on the company's sales force and reputation to gain market share. So, as in most cases of organizations during the **Experiments** stage, not all the particular experiments at CTR worked, and the conclusion drawn from the failures deeply influenced the future character of the organization.

The final experiment of this era, and the frame setter for the next, was the company's adoption of a new name in 1924, leaving behind its jerry-built identity as Computing-Tabulation-Recording and becoming International Business Machines. Actually, in keeping with the theme of experiments, Watson tried out this name twice before applying it to the company as a whole—first giving it to the Canadian subsidiary of CTR in 1917, later to the Latin American operation.

THE CRITICAL ELEMENT IN TRUE EXPERIMENTS

Whether the actual experiments tried out at this stage are as minimal as in a McDonald's franchise, whether they are intermediate as in the case of CTR/IBM, or whether they are as unprecedented as in the Peace Corps, the critical element in true experiments is one that is, in principle, difficult to articulate. The true experiment is a disciplined stab in the dark that goes beyond the intellectual alternatives that one could have formulated prior to the creative movement. This point emphasizes how difficult it is to use any conceptual scheme such as developmental theory and simultaneously experiment in a given setting. For, at its best, an experiment probes toward what is unique and previously unformulated about the present situation. Yet, as adults, none of us approach new situations concept free. How can we use preexisting conceptual schemes without being trapped by them? How can we use preformulated concepts to see and enter unformulated territory?

A graphic image of the disciplined stab-in-the-dark principle is conveyed in comparing adults and kids experimenting with a Rubik's cube. Adults approach the cube thoughtfully, turn it around, develop a plan of attack, pursue it a little while till they see it is not going to work, study the cube again more respectfully, try another approach slightly less energetically, get frustrated, try a third time hopelessly, and give up. Kids attack the cube and begin to manipulate it apparently at random, watching the swirl of changing patterns for clues about next directions, and wind up coordinating the colors in astonishingly short times. This child's play is the archetype of the **Experiments** stage—not the adult scientist's laboratory experiment that is, at best, totally preplanned and controlled.[2]

In organizations, the very fact that the different members approach problems from fundamentally different developmental perspectives could be an enormous advantage at the **Experiments** stage, if people were not unconsciously imperialistic about their own worldview. A solution that integrates two or more perspectives is more likely to represent a true experiment than a solution, however catchy and plausible, based on only one perspective. The technician who invents a brilliant new software package for business people wants to name it Quark-Count based on an elegant feature of the internal design. The salesman laughs him off and suggests Easy-Count instead, as one component of a series of packages, each to start with "Easy." The technician is insulted and regards the proposal as virtually unethical. The salesman's suggestion trivializes his invention and renders it an anonymous member of a series of technically unrelated packages.

Depending on the strength of the two personalities, their hierarchical relationship, and the culture of the company, one or the other suggestion will win out. But Quark-Count, however elegant and interesting it may seem to some, is the less experimental of the two solutions because it remains within one language universe. As much a cliche as it may seem at one level, Easy-Count is the more sophisticated, dialectical solution, marrying technical-mathematical complexity with consumere(a)se. (Also, with the advantage of hindsight, it is possible to report that this company's "Easy" series is now its principal money-maker.)

Characteristics of the Experiments Stage of Organizing

1. Alternative legal governing, administrative, physical, production, selection, training, or reward structures practiced, tested in operation, and reformed.
2. Alternative financial, marketing, and political strategies practiced, tested in operation, and reformed.
3. Critical issues: (a) Truly experimenting—taking disciplined stabs in the dark—rather than merely trying out a limited number of preconceived alternatives; (b) Finding a viable combination of strategy and structure that can be systematized for the next generation or the next stage of organizing.

THE ILLUSION OF THE ETERNALLY YOUTHFUL ORGANIZATION

Because the **Experiments** stage is so vibrant, and because the entrepreneurial types who start organizations usually assume that stable systems necessarily stifle creativity, it is not uncommon for businesses to resist the transformation to the next stage of **Systematic Productivity** or else, later, to try to return to the **Experiments** stage in order to reinvigorate the business. But it does not work to try to hold back or turn back the developmental clock. The recent history of Digital Equipment Company illustrates the eventual costs of holding back the clock, and the recent history of Dana Corporation illustrates the mixed outcomes of trying to turn back the clock. Let us look briefly at each of these companies.

Digital Equipment Corporation (DEC) is the second largest company in the computer industry, but a distant second to IBM. DEC's founder, Ken Olsen, is still its CEO today. A scientist-entrepreneur who virtually created the minicomputer industry, Olsen generated a lively, entrepreneurial company that grew by leaps and bounds throughout its first 20 years, without losing its challenging, decentralized atmosphere. *In Search of Excellence* celebrated its ability to grow big without becoming overly bureaucratized.

But even before *In Search of Excellence* appeared, during the late 1970s, many employees of the company felt a balance had tipped from invigorating diversity to the random chaos of nearly 40 independent business units, with no organizational integration among engineering, manufacturing, marketing, and service except Olsen himself. Not until 1983, when DEC's revenues were plunging by over 30 percent from the previous year, did Olsen move to simplify the structure to fewer than 10 divisions. The thrust from diversity to unity was strongly symbolized in November of 1984 when Olsen publicly announced the Venus superminicomputer (two years late) standing under a banner reading "One Company, One Structure, One Message."

By this time, however, IBM was twice as big and growing three times as fast as DEC in DEC's own minicomputer segment of the market. Perhaps even more important, a third of DEC's vice presidents had quit in the previous two years. They could feel their entrepreneurial independence becoming increasingly limited. But they lacked a shared vision of entrepreneurial *inter-*dependence—a shared vision of organizational development that painted the transformation to **Systematic Productivity** as itself the truly entrepreneurial challenge for DEC at this time, as itself the true organizational experiment for DEC at that time. Confirming the lack of shared vision, an informal poll of 50 company managers, taken a week after Olsen's "One Message" press conference, found that none of them had any idea what the company's purported "One Message" was. Thus, the transformation from decentralized, entrepreneurial company to disciplined, coordinated company was at once belated and rushed, at once traumatic and inconclusive, and more polarizing than unifying in its initial effects.

Olsen remains the key player at the company, maintaining a technician-oriented rather than consumer-oriented culture, at a time when the company desperately needs symbols of new direction. It is conceivable that a debacle of the scale that traumatized Polaroid in the early 1980s and forced out its scientist-founder, Edwin Land, may eventually occur at DEC.

A recent study argues that needed organizational transformations are regularly blocked by current top management, and that collapse of the company or replacement of the top management team en masse are frequent, not rare, outcomes.[3] Conversely, among the most successful entrepreneurs—such as Bill Poduska of Apollo Computer, whom we met in Chapter 2—are those who know themselves and their organizations well enough to sell the enterprise just before they and it turn sour together by trying to stay forever young.

But perhaps Olsen is himself capable of transforming to a later stage of managerial development and capable of taking seriously criteria for organizational success other than technical leadership. Or else, perhaps Olsen is already at the **Strategist** stage of development and his apparent **Technician** style is more chosen than compelled. In this case, a change to an **Achiever** style is not so difficult as a full-scale developmental change.

In 1986, there is evidence that Olsen is focusing on the whole organization as a system, as an **Achiever** would, more than he is on the technical process of new-product development. He is evidently supporting his new chief financial officer in establishing centralized financial controls, and the company has launched a focused advertising campaign. Moreover, one technical requirement that Olsen insisted upon even during the many years of relative decentralization happens to fit the **Systematic Productivity** stage very well and is now emerging as a significant competitive advantage for DEC. Olsen has always required that DEC's different systems be mutually compatible. As integrated networks become the industry's leading edge, systems compatability gives DEC an advantage that no other major company can claim.

Dana Corporation was another of the 43 companies celebrated as excellent in *In Search of Excellence*. Rene McPherson, Dana's CEO in the 1970s, tried aggressively to debureaucratize the company. He threw out the thick policy manuals, halved the layers of authority, cut corporate staff by four fifths, and thereby tripled sales per employee. He appeared to be rejuvenating the company by moving it back from the **Systematic Productivity** stage to the **Experiments** stage, and by one significant (but short-term) criterion—sales per employee—he was succeeding.

But Dana was a big, mature company and did some of the things big, mature companies do, such as acquiring new companies. These acquisitions failed in both strategic and implementation terms. Although the strategy had been intended to diversify Dana, the acquisitions actually tied it tighter than ever to the light truck market. Moreover, three of the aquired companies suffered severe drops in profit within a year of purchase.

In the meantime, McPherson graduated from Dana to the deanship of the Stanford Business School, and he tried out the same informal **Experiments** stage approach there that he had at Dana. But the faculty members did not respond well to the language that appealed to blue collar workers at Dana, so this second attempt to turn back the clock did not work by any measures, and McPherson left after two short years.[4]

The sorts of organizational systems necessary to strategize and implement acquisitions successfully, or to manage independent professionals such as the academics at Stanford, are not **Experiments** stage phenomena at all, but rather late-stage organizing phenomena that we will explore in Chapter 11 on the **Collaborative Inquiry** stage. The solution to the problem of how to maintain an entrepreneurial climate in a mature organization is not for it to revert to adolescence, but rather for it to develop systems that reward rather than inhibit calculated risk taking. Also necessary is an understanding of entrepreneurship that does not refer just to cowboy independence and to marketing concrete products. Managers must understand how generating transformation within the organization itself demands entrepreneurship. Managers must understand that at a certain point, leaving the decentralized **Experiments** stage and entering the more centralized **Systematic Productivity** stage represents precisely the experiment—the disciplined stab in the dark—required by their mandate of managing the corporate dream.

NOTES

1. "McDonald's Franchises; The Making of an American Tradition," *Asset Based Finance Journal* 6, No. 3 (Winter 1986), pp. 7–13.

2. For a paean to, and more stories about, the experimenting entrepreneur, see G. Gilder, *The Spirit of Enterprise* (New York: Simon & Schuster, 1984).

3. P. Nystrom and W. Starbuck, "To Avoid Organizational Crisis, Unlearn," *Organizational Dynamics*, Spring 1984.

4. McPherson suffered severe injuries in an automobile accident during his deanship at Stanford, and this was the immediate and public cause of his departure.

The Technician

Just as an organization moves from the particular form or mold of its **Incorporation** to a period of fluid **Experiments,** so a manager moves from conformity to what historically has been good form at the **Diplomatic** stage of development, to a more fluid willingness to experiment and break the conventional mold at the **Technician** stage.

When (and if) managers move beyond the **Diplomatic** stage of development, they turn other people's preferences into variables in a wider situation rather than determinants of their own actions. As it does at each period of transformation from stage to stage, the question arises, at least implicitly: What determines the validity of actions? How can I know reliably what to do? Rebelling against the emotional other-directedness of the **Diplomatic** stage, nascent **Technicians** take an introspective and intellectually coherent objectivity as the source and aim of activity.

Technicians no longer identify with what makes them the same as the others in the group. They identify more with what makes them stand out from the group, with the unique skills that they can contribute. They depend less on others' judgments of quality, more on their own judgment and ability. In fact, because they are actively differentiating themselves from the group, they are frequently defiantly and dogmatically counterdependent, the late adolescent defying all forms of authority other than the authority of their chosen craft and "craft heroes."

In their new passion with understanding for themselves what causes what and with exercising the power of their skill, **Technicians** focus almost exclusively on the *internal* logic and integrity of their arena of expertise, often setting perfectionistic standards. They can be obsessed with efficiency but are frequently indifferent about effectiveness. They are not yet focused—as they will become when they reach the next equilibrium at the **Achiever** stage of development—on the overall performance of any system (including themselves) in a wider environment. Instead, they tend to overlook the wider and messier dilemmas of integrating their arena with others.

David Stockman's story of his years as the Reagan administration's budget director vividly illustrates the strengths and limits of the **Technician** style of management.[1] Stockman's ability to learn a department's budget inside out in several days' time was awesome to his co-workers at the Office of Management and Budget. His ability to rework budget figures based on new assumptions, again and again, discovering new ways of achieving goals, was equally startling. His ability to experiment also extended to imaginative ways of presenting information—such as the time he developed a multiple choice quiz for the president, allowing Reagan to make his own choices about what budget cuts to make and then testing whether his cuts added up to what was needed to balance the budget (as we all know, they never did). Note that these strengths are predominantly analytic and technical in nature, dealing with the internal logic of the budget.

Stockman's limitations are the shadow of his strengths. The very title of his book—*The Triumph of Politics: Why the Reagan Revolution Failed*—suggests that he views politics not as a creative process for integrating different arenas and resolving conflicts of perspective, but rather as a process of undignified compromises that contaminate the internal logic of a pure objective standard— *his* ideology. "To make a revolution," he tells us, "required defining fairness in terms of exacting abstract principles—not human hard-luck stories." The president turned out not to be Stockman's kind of revolutionary—"he sees the plight of real people before anything else."[2]

A politician more to Stockman's liking was Jack Kemp: "His head, like mine, was stuffed full of sweeping theories, historical knowledge, and insights about the patterns of things. . . . As I had been, he was searching for his own Grand Doctrine." Kemp's "intellectuality of approach . . . made him stand out like a lighthouse in a sea of fog."[3] In these comments, we see the value the **Technician** places on internal intellectual coherence and on standing out from the group.

The **Technician's** focus on internal efficiency at the expense of external effectiveness is evident in the way Stockman briefed the president about budget cuts:

> Instead of giving him a bird's-eye view of the budget, I gave him a worm's-eye view. We sat there happily hacking away at CETA (job training) and foodstamps, $300 million here, $100 million there. That's all they saw. . . . We had browbeaten the cabinet one by one into accepting the cuts. . . . In my haste to expedite the revolution, I had inadvertently convinced the chief executive that budget cutting was an antiseptic process, a matter of compiling innocuous-sounding "half-pagers" in a neatly tabbed black book.[4]

House Majority Leader Jim Wright's comment that Stockman knew the cost of everything and the value of nothing sharply summarizes the result of focusing on efficiency at the expense of effectiveness.

Technicians typically work closely but impersonally with subordinates, checking up on all details, taking over in a very direct way in emergencies. Bradford and Cohen offer the following illustration of what they call the "Manager-as-Technician":

> One of our clients was head of computer services for a large government agency. As brilliant as he was irascible, Warner had no tolerance for governmental rules and regulations. He and his staff did whatever was necessary to get the job done. Although his department was highly effective in solving technical problems, his style left a trail of strained relationships with other department heads. His ability to cut through red tape won him great admiration and allegiance from his subordinates, who thought of him as a wizard. On the other hand, other departments were reluctant to use his department's services, which left his group more isolated than was desirable from the agency's point of view.[5]

Managers at the **Technician** stage are extremely ambivalent about receiving feedback about their performance or themselves. Still influenced by their passage through the **Diplomatic** stage, they reject the implication that *they* read into all feedback, that they should be influenced by it simply because another feels that way. They no longer believe that group norms are necessarily right and necessarily the criteria that should guide behavior. At the same time, they have not yet fully assimilated the perspective of the **Achiever,** according to which feedback can help achieve goals. **Technicians** are identified with the means—the skill, the technique—not yet with the goal. Hence, the notion that other or additional means may more effectively achieve a goal is felt as a personal criticism of their skill, i.e., of them.

Because **Technicians'** identities are so interwoven with their particular skills—because they *are* the technical skill rather than *having* it—they virtually cease to exist when the skill is not being exercised. Blue collar workers nearing retirement frequently tell stories of others who died within a year of retiring.[6] High-technology engineers and project managers frequently tell stories about terminal depression in between projects.[7]

Unlike **Opportunists** and **Diplomats,** who together probably represent something less than 15 percent of the managerial population today, **Technicians** almost certainly represent the most prevalent style of managing. The three studies of managers cited in Chapter 2 found 47 percent of the senior managers, 43 percent of the junior managers, and 68 percent of the first-line supervisors at the **Technician** stage of development. Because this style of managing is apparently so prevalent, we will take a more detailed look at it in the following pages than we have at any of the other developmental styles so far.

In the previous chapter, we saw that the "disciplined stabs in the dark" an organization must take at the **Experiments** stage are, at best, more like the experimenting children do with a Rubik's cube than the experimenting that adults do as laboratory scientists. This comparison helps us to understand the limitations of the **Technician** as a leader. The **Technician** functions more like a laboratory scientist than like a child with a Rubik's cube. The independence from the status quo and group pressures that the **Technician** gains in developing beyond the **Dip-**

lomatic stage is a narrow independence, constrained by a tightly structured logic.

In *The Soul of a New Machine*, the biography of the embryonic development of a new computer at Data General, Tracy Kidder describes the tensions between Tom West, product champion of the Eagle computer, and the whiz kid engineering "perfection-ists"—nicknamed the Hardy Boys and the Microkids—who work for him. The following excerpt illustrates these tensions between an **Achiever** (West) and **Technicians** (the whiz kids).

> On the Magic Marker board in his office, West wrote the follow-ing:
>
> *Not Everything Worth Doing Is Worth Doing Well*
>
> West reviewed all of the designs. Sometimes he slashed out fea-tures that the designers felt were useful and nice. He seemed con-sistently to underestimate the subtlety of what they were trying to do. All that a junior designer was likely to hear from him was "It's right." "It's wrong," or "No, there isn't time."
>
> To some the design reviews seemed harsh and arbitrary and often technically shortsighted. Later on, though, one Hardy Boy would concede that the managers had probably known something he hadn't yet learned: that there's no such thing as a perfect design. Most experienced computer engineers I talked to agreed that absorbing this simple lesson constitutes the first step in learning how to get machines out the door. Often, they said, it is the most talented engineers who have the hardest time learning when to stop striv-ing for perfection. West was the voice from the cave supplying that information: "Okay. It's right. Ship it."[8]

TECHNICIANS' RESPONSES TO AN IN-BASKET TEST

The difference in administrative style between the **Technician** and a later stage managerial style, such as that of the **Strategist,** is strikingly illustrated in a study that examined how managers holding different developmental styles handled an in-basket exer-cise. This exercise asks the manager to spend two and a half hours dealing with 34 items in the in-basket of the general man-ager of the Bradford Consolidated Fund, a position that he or she has just assumed in midcampaign because of an accident to the predecessor.[9] The Bradford Fund has a 35-member board of trustees, a half dozen paid staff members, and a large volunteer organization. The 34 items concern a wide variety of issues, including a report that shows a historic decline in community contributions to the fund, a confidential letter from one staff member complaining that another staff member has unilaterally and inappropriately fired a secretary, and a memo from the business manager suggesting that the fund switch its printing contract to a company that has been a major contributor. The new general manager has the former incumbent's calendar and must handle the 34 items as he or she sees fit on this Sunday afternoon, before having met the staff and before leaving to take care of a final commitment for his or her former job on Monday and Tuesday. Participants in this exercise not only write whatever memos and letters they wish, make appointments, and outline meeting agendas, but also fill in a form at the end describing their reasons for acting as they did.

The general findings of this study were that **Technicians** and **Achievers** were more likely to solve problems *as these were initially defined for them.*[10] They also delegated responsibility for implementing decisions to others *in a unilateral fashion.* By contrast, managers scored at the later, **Strategist** stage of development were more likely to *redefine the presented problems in ways that interrelated them*, were more likely to take actions that would *generate additional information as well as get something done*, were more likely to *use specific issues as opportunities to test the vision, strategy, and style of the other players*, and were more likely to *seek feedback from those to whom they proposed delegating a task* about how they would recommend proceeding.

The **Technicians** put a high premium on speed and completeness in measuring their own success in the exercise. As one put it, "I assumed I had to complete everything in some manner, deal with everything, so I read through the whole thing very quickly. I put the items that seemed less important aside, and my feeling was that I had to deal with the important issues very quickly. . . ."[11] Another said, "Once I get into the job and see what I am doing . . . personally I don't like to leave stuff on my desk. I (want to) at least get some sort of action or make suggestions and then let them do my job for me while I am gone."

The **Technician's** style and the questions that it does not address emerge vividly if we look at a couple of the specific actions of one such person enacting the role of general manager of the Bradford Consolidated Fund:

> When the representative of the local Nursing Association complained that, at the last panel meeting, the association was given insufficient time to present their allocation needs, with the result that an inadequate allocation was made,"Jack" responded by asking his secretary to reschedule 30 more minutes at the next meeting. His reasoning was "unhappy people hurt contributions."
>
> "Jack's"quick rescheduling suggests responsiveness to the Nursing Association's isolated concern, but ignores the question of why the association was given "insufficient" time in the first place. What in "Jack's" response is to prevent the fund from making the same mistake (if indeed it is a mistake) in the future? Also, "Jack" either mistakes the Nurses' Association (which is a receiver of funds) with a contributor, or else draws a direct correlation between receivers and contributors, which seems questionable.
>
> In responding to a letter from the editor of a local newspaper indicating that the paper has yet to receive the information on the fund requested earlier for a feature article, "Jack" wrote a memo to his director of public relations, saying simply: "Handle—*Monday.*" His reasoning was that the director needed a "kick in the ass," it was "his fault" for not responding earlier.
>
> While it seems highly plausible that his response will get the job done, it ignores the question of why such an important and reasonably simple job was not done in the first place. Hence, similar errors of public relations may well recur.[12]

THE DIFFICULTY IN OFFERING FEEDBACK TO A TECHNICIAN

How ambivalent the **Technician** tends to be about receiving and digesting feedback is illustrated by the following story. The setting is the corporate office of a large retail chain. A senior manager participated in a study of her developmental stage and managerial style, and one of her subordinates asked to participate as well. The study offered participants feedback on the results if they wished it. The senior manager felt that she had benefited from this experience.

The subordinate also was eager to receive the feedback and invited the senior manager to participate with the researcher in the feedback session (as well as in a follow-up session the researcher required in order to assess the effects of the feedback). Gene, the subordinate, was measured as in transition between the **Diplomat** and the **Achiever** stages of development, at the **Technician** stage.

Upon receiving this feedback (along with some explanation about what these terms mean), Gene verified that from his point of view he was indeed in the midst of a major transition. He said that upon joining the company he had felt enthusiastic about working in teams and helping others, but that he was increasingly realizing that the managers who got ahead were the ones who were basically out for themselves. Gene interpreted the difference between the **Diplomatic** position and the **Achiever** position as the difference between *concern for others* and *selfish goal maximization*. The researcher twice suggested that persons holding each worldview can be both "concerned for others" and "selfish," but will mean different things by these terms.

In an effort to offer a concrete illustration of this abstract notion, the senior manager mentioned a project that she and Gene were working on. Gene had not produced a certain product by an agreed-upon date and had not spoken about the matter. The senior manager had heard through a third party that Gene felt incapable of doing the task but did not want to disappoint her. The senior manager wondered out loud whether Gene's "paralysis" in this case might by symbolic of a transition, with the **Diplomatic** mode of not losing face or disappointing others in conflict with the task orientation of the **Achiever**. The senior manager pointed out that Gene's decision not to discuss the problem could be interpreted as selfish (to avoid losing face) and as not concerned with the other (the senior manager's need to complete the project).

Gene was initially embarrassed by the use of the "real-life" example, but it seemed to make the point clear. Probably more important to Gene, he and the senior manager together redesigned the project, and the senior manager asserted that she did not regard this one "failure" as characteristic.

Two weeks later, however, during the follow-up conversa-

tion, Gene was openly hurt, angry, and resentful. In his recon-
struction of the feedback session, the other two had attacked
him and his value system throughout the session, advocating
selfishness rather than concern for others, and blowing up a very
minor issue of timing into an attack on his very being. He further said that he had decided to approach the company more
"cynically" hereafter and just treat it "as a job to be done" rather
than caring for the other people.

Now the senior manager felt hurt and angry. What she had
said out of concern for Gene, Gene was attacking and devaluing.
Although the senior manager by now understood enough about
developmental theory to appreciate the underlying difficulty that
Gene had in digesting feedback, the senior manager spoke about
her feelings in an effort to bridge the distance between them.
This cathartic opening led to a long conversation reviewing numerous recent incidents in which Gene's wish to please others
and wish to perform well had generated painful knots for him.

After this session, both Gene and the senior manager adopted
a slightly greater reserve with one another, and Gene's performance improved markedly. Seven months later, Gene was measured as having completed the transition to the **Achieving** stage.
Two years later, speaking long distance from another company,
at which he had accepted a new position. Gene thanked the senior manager both for her interventions and for her later reserve. Gene acknowledged that he had felt overexposed at the
time and had appreciated the senior manager's willingness to
step back. But now Gene saw the entire episode in a positive
light, feeling that a new kind of clarity and confidence had been
conceived within him during the turmoil and the subsequent
calm.

As the foregoing story shows, just below his self-motivated,
critical perfectionist exterior, the **Technician** experiences much
painful confusion. He does not wish to expose his painful confusion, not because he will lose face as the **Diplomat** might feel,
but because his developmental movement is toward internaliz-
ing the source of his actions within himself. He wants to be able
to understand and fix himself, thank you very much, just as he
wishes to be able to understand and fix a marketing problem or
a machine.

Elements of the Technician's Managerial Style

Interested in problem solving	Wants to stand out, be unique
Perfectionism	Critical of others and self
Longer time horizon	Torn between loyalty to self and
Seeks causes, motives	group
Sees contingencies, exceptions	Chooses efficiency over effectiveness
Values decisions based on merit	Ambivalent about receiving feedback
Sense of obligation to wider moral	Dogmatic
order	
(not just current in-group norms)	

If the developmental categories presented in this book are thrust upon **Technicians,** they will feel "labeled" by them. They may very well respond with scorn and contempt at the very idea of allowing oneself to be defined by someone else's theory. And, how strongly they feel this! In the study of developmental stage and managerial effectiveness cited earlier, the reader will recall that no managers who were measured as **Opportunists** or **Diplomats** asked for feedback and that under 10 percent of those scored as **Technicians** asked for feedback. Another finding from that study is particularly relevant here: of the **Technicians** who asked for feedback, nearly half expressed explosive emotional reactions during the feedback session, somewhat as Gene did in his second session in the story above. No one else except those **Technicians,** among over a hundred persons who sought feedback in the study, ever responded explosively.[13]

Let us suppose, though, that someone inhabiting the **Technician** style of management becomes fascinated with the sheer elegance and internal coherence of developmental theory upon reading this book. What might this person conceive to be an effective way for an organization to encourage the development of its members? We can return to Tracy Kidder's story about the building of the Eagle computer at Data General for a clue:

> Alsing created the Microteam. He chose its members and he gave them their first training, with some help from Rosemarie Searle. Nowadays it takes a computer to build a computer, especially when it comes to building microcode for one. Alsing figured that before the Microkids did anything else, they must learn how to manipu-

late Trixie. He didn't want simply to give them a stack of manuals and say, "Figure it out." So he made up a game. As the Microkids arrived, in ones and twos, during the summer of 1978, he told each of them to figure out how to write a certain kind of program in Trixie's assembly language. This program must fetch and print out the contents of a certain file stored inside the computer. "So they learned the way around the system and they were very pleased," said Alsing. "But when they came to the file finally, they found that access to it was denied them."

The file in question lay open only to people endowed with what were called "superuser privileges." Alsing had expected the recruits to learn how to find this file and, in the process, to master the system. He was equally interested in seeing what they would do when they found they couldn't get the file.

One after the other, they came to him and said, "I almost have it."

"Okay," said Alsing, "but you don't have it."

In the end, most Microkids went to Rosemarie. Alsing had conferred with her beforehand. She was to help the Microkids find the file, if they asked. They learned something, Alsing felt. "If a person knows how to get the right secretary, he can get everything. It was a resourceful solution—one of the solutions I hoped they'd find."[14]

Borrowing this training method, the **Technician** might very well encrypt developmental games within the company's computer and leak the word that something pretty special is hidden there, perhaps even offer prizes or bonuses for those who "win." One important advantage that such a method for provoking development offers is that any explosive emotional reactions are easily sublimated into computer warfare rather than more direct, personal attacks. For example, Alsing's first game with the Microkids generated a response:

> Not long after . . . the "Tube Wars" began. As a rule, it was the kids against Alsing. In one commonly used gambit, a Microkid would sit down at a terminal and order Trixie to open up Alsing's files. The Microkid would then move the files to a new location. Returning from coffee or lunch, Alsing would find his files gone. He'd hear tittering from the cubicles nearby. And he would know he'd been "tube-warred."
>
> "What did you do to me?" he'd cry.
>
> "Find out, stupid," a voice would answer.

A related story describes the trick that scientists in a research and development group played on one of their colleagues. The trick got out of control and stopped being funny very quickly. As a way of not having to listen to his family problems, which appeared to be depressing him and lowering his productivity, the scientists let their colleague know that they had a computer hookup to MIT's well-known Eliza program. Eliza simulates a Rogerian therapist who essentially just listens to the client and occasionally plays back the most recent comment in slightly different words, in order to encourage the client to continue talking.

The depressed man was unexpectedly eager to learn more about Eliza, so his colleagues sat him down at a terminal downstairs while one of them rushed upstairs to listen in and offer occasional Eliza-like responses. The depressed scientist thanked them, closed the door, and wasted no time pouring out his troubles to the machine. Taken aback, his upstairs colleague tried to think of some way to end this unanticipated invasion of the other's privacy. Finally, he had Eliza say, in a very un-Eliza-like way, "You are using this talking to avoid facing up to what you can do. I would advise you to buy a dog for companionship and work harder than you have for a long while, and you will find that time takes care of all the other problems." The scientist typed in a "Thank you for your advice," signed off, and thenceforward went out to his car at breaks to give his new dog a walk.

His productivity rose as well, but only slightly. His colleagues began asking themselves what Eliza might have said instead, to influence the quantity and quality of his work more dramatically. But then, six months later, the scientist again approached his colleagues for access to Eliza. The joking ceased. They claimed the program could no longer be accessed (and, in fact, access has been limited to Eliza because so many people seemed to be developing a dependency on "talking" with her).

Hopefully, all organizational **Technicians** will properly decode the moral of the Alsing and Eliza stories and will avoid playing games with the development of others. Managing the corporate dream is no mere technical process but rather a profound aesthetic and ethical challenge.

The moral for managers at later stages of development, who hope to help younger colleagues develop beyond experiencing the pains and limitations of the **Technician** stage, is less clear.

Offering **Technicians** unsolicited negative feedback ("Your style just doesn't work!") is clearly dangerous and unlikely to be effective. Even offering solicited feedback is unlikely to help, as the study cited earlier found. Since **Technicians** pride themselves on their own capacity to think things through, asking them to diagnose and propose remedies for situations where their approach appears questionable may offer the best chance of influencing them. Refrain from offering advice. Instead, patiently confirm all the ways in which their approach is problematic until they seem motivated to solve this problem.

What if a colleague or subordinate whom you believe may be at the **Technician** stage seeks to dismiss the problem? The most influential type of response is likely to be one that does not insist the **Technician** face the problem yet simultaneously makes clear that you cannot yourself dismiss the problem because to do so would betray your commitment to the objective, real-world facts. Since the **Technician** also holds the ideal of objectivity, he or she is likely to gnaw on this bone of contention in private. Raising the issue again later, in a reflective, inquiring manner, may show that the **Technician** did not altogether dismiss the matter and is now ready to treat it as a problem to be solved.

At this point, the **Technician** may be willing to join in a coauthored scientific experiment in which he or she experiments with different managerial approaches in search of more effective results. The more tightly defined these experiments are at the outset, and the more objective and countable are the results, the more comfortable will the **Technician** be, even if the ultimate outcome that the mentor envisions is a relaxation away from an overly controlled, overly focused, spuriously objective style of management.

TRANSITION

In the previous two chapters, we have been examining how organizations and managers break the mold and go beyond the initial pattern of socially acceptable behavior that they adopt at the **Incorporation** stage, in the case of organizations, and the **Diplomat** stage, in the case of individuals. We have seen how exhilarating and how tricky it is for organizations to engage in true **Experiments**—disciplined stabs in the dark. And we have seen how individual managers begin their search for an internally coherent system of action by adopting a rigorous and limited **Technician's** logic.

In the next two chapters, we examine how organizations and managers develop a "logic of success," how they develop a system for interacting with the environment that is not merely internally coherent but also externally effective. The primary challenge to organizations as they move from the relative decentralization of the **Experiments** stage to the relative centralization of **Systematic Productivity** is how to avoid overemphasizing a narrow **Technician's** logic. The primary challenge to individual managers as they move to the **Achiever** stage is how to digest negative feedback in a way that improves their effectiveness.

NOTES

1. D. Stockman, *The Triumph of Politics: Why the Reagan Revolution Failed* (New York: Harper & Row, 1986).

2. Article on, and excerpts from, Stockman book (ibid.) in *Newsweek*, April 21, 1986, p. 41.

3. Ibid., p. 43

4. Ibid., p. 55.

5. D. Bradford and A. Cohen, *Managing for Excellence: The Guide to Developing High Performance In Contemporary Organizations* (New York: Wiley, 1984), p. 34. Although Bradford and Cohen do not discuss developmental theory, their three managerial types—the Technician, the Conductor, and the Developer correspond very closely to the developmental portraits offered in this book of the **Technician,** the **Achiever,** and the later stages outlined in the Postscript.

6. W. Torbert and M. Rogers, *Being for the Most Part Puppets: Interactions among Men's Labor, Leisure, and Politics* (Cambridge, Mass.: Schenkman, 1972).

7. T. Kidder, *The Soul of a New Machine* (New York: Avon, 1981).

8. Ibid., p. 119.

9. "Consolidated Fund In-Basket Test" (Princeton, N.J.: Educational Testing Services).

10. D. Fisher, K. Merron, and W. Torbert, "Meaning Making and Management Effectiveness (presented at Academy of Management, Chicago, August 1986).

11. K. Merron, "Strategies for Managing Ambiguity" (paper developed for Action Effectiveness Research Project, Boston College School of Management, 1983).

12. Ibid., p. 41.

13. Fisher, Merron, and Torbert, "Meaning Making." Also, K. Merron and W. Torbert, "Offering Managers Feedback on Loevinger's Ego Development Measure: Exploring the relation between developmental stage and managerial behavior" (working paper, Boston College Graduate School of Management, 1983).

14. Kidder, "The Soul," pp. 105–106.

CHAPTER NINE _____

Systematic Productivity

Systematic Productivity—the whole point of organizing, most people would say. At this stage, the organization is finally doing at full throttle what it set out to do. Attention is tightly focused on consistent implementation of systematic procedures for accomplishing the predefined task. Objective, quantitative measurements of the marketability or political viability of the product or service become the overriding criteria of success. Standards, structures, and roles are usually formalized and presented in deductive, Aristotelian terms insofar as possible—in short, as a pyramidal organization chart.

IBM, between 1924 and 1946 when Thomas Watson, Jr., joined the company, represents a classic case of **Systematic Productivity.** Watson, Sr., remained CEO throughout that entire period. Both revenues and retained earnings more than quadrupled even before World War II began. The competitive advantage that IBM gained over its foremost competitors has already been described in Chapter 3, but it is important to emphasize here that this outcome was in no sense foreordained. To industry observers in the mid-1920s, it appeared that NCR and Burroughs both had firmer customer bases than IBM, while both Remington Rand and Underwood had wider product bases and more financial resources.

The strategy of Watson and IBM throughout these years was a severely classic "stick to the knitting" strategy. The company made no major acquisitions and no unrelated acquisitions what-soever. It continued and expanded its leasing strategy, with its clear premium on quality and service over the long term, rather than quarterly profit peaks. It invested steadily in research and development from its own retained earnings rather than through borrowing in the financial markets.

As simple as this strategy may sound in brief summary, we have seen how it evolved through 30 years' experience. This strategy is not a consultant's recommendation. The *organization as a whole*—not merely a single person or a small group—learned to *implement* this strategy—not merely to espouse it—and then *stuck to it* under all the various pressures and temptations to change it over a 20-year period.

Moreover, as simple as the strategy sounds, it is not merely internally consistent, and is not merely restricted to the financial language of dollars and cents, but rather relates three qualitatively different realms to one another. IBM's strategy:

1. Keeps the company's *mission* well focused.
2. Puts a premium on actual *operations* through the focus on quality.
3. Keeps the company closer to the *market* by the emphasis on service.

Thus, IBM's strategy before, during, and after the 1930s was complex in the sense that it interwove the four realms all organizations must interweave to be successful—intuitive mission, rational strategy, actual operations, and market outcomes.

IBM's success during those years was aided by Watson's rare ability not to falsely dichotomize reality. This ability is evidenced first and foremost in the balance that he and the company achieved among the four realms just mentioned. To treat only the bottom line (current market outcomes) as a truly significant measure of success is one way of falsely dichotomizing reality.

This ability not to falsely dichotomize reality was also evident in Watson's understanding of relations between business and government and between business and universities. While most leading businessmen railed against Franklin Delano Roosevelt and the New Deal during the 1930s, Watson was proclaiming the New Deal "a research laboratory, with President Roosevelt the greatest research engineer the world has ever known."[1] Willing to pitch in to help, IBM landed the biggest single contract of the 1930s, the new Social Security Administration contract in 1936.

Watson was also the first businessman in his industry to appreciate the value, as a long-range sales strategy, of training scientists and the next generation on his machine. He abundantly supplied the Columbia University Statistics Bureau as well as the research facilities of other universities.

The strategy of Watson and IBM in fact represented a form of reasoning that is rare among organizations of all kinds today. Although it accomplished phenomenal results in quantifiable measures of market outcomes, IBM was not driven by the deductive mode of reasoning that usually reigns supreme at the **Systematic Productivity** stage of organizing. Instead, the strategy itself was a reflection of a set of historically evolved commitments to a particular mission, to operational excellence, and to customer service. The ultimate test of the value of actions within the company was not simply whether they followed deductively from a strategy statement, but rather whether in microcosm they represented all that the company stood for in terms of mission, operations, and service. Analogical reasoning, not deductive reasoning, can make this kind of comparison and judgment. Let us explore the differences between these two forms of reasoning—these two forms of systematizing productivity—since they are so central to this stage of organizing.

ANALOGIC AND DEDUCTIVE LOGIC—INTEGRATING THE TWO

Two fundamentally different types of reasoning systems vie for the soul of the organization during the **Systematic Productivity** stage. The first and more common type of system can be called "digital," "deductive," or "Aristotelian." This type of system attempts to organize the relevant reality in terms of a single, internally consistent set of symbols that are deduced from certain minimal assumptions or axioms. The logic is binary and dichotomous (on/off, 0/1, A/not−A), following Aristotle's "law of the excluded middle" (something is either A or not−A; it cannot be both A and not−A, nor halfway between A and not−A). For well-formulated problems within the same symbol system, this type of reasoning can be done with enormous speed and precision, especially when aided by digital computing machines such as IBM today builds. This is the type of reasoning system that Western sciences, such as physics or economics, represent and that bureaucratic organizational charts, with their clearly delineated spheres of authority, spans of control, and chains of command, also represent. This is the type of organizing logic with which we are most familiar in today's large organizations.

This type of instrumental, logistical reasoning is very powerful when and if its assumptions are correct. Indeed, IBM has long represented an ideal of well-articulated bureaucratic systems in such areas as hiring, training, and performance evaluation. But this type of reasoning is not sufficient for business success. It must be properly subordinated to analogical reasoning.

The trouble with deductive logic for action purposes is that—unlike IBM's strategy in the 1920s and 1930s—it is fundamentally insulated within itself and its assumptions. If its categories and assumptions happen not to fit intuitive, operational, and market realities well, this system can only make incremental internal changes or else eventually be overwhelmed by the external reality. All corporate, military, educational, or national strategies run the risk of being predominantly this type of system—of being or becoming insulated within themselves—of losing contact with intuitive dreams that can inspire cooperation, with operational excellence that creates tangible values, and with the markets and other constituencies that the organization is supposedly serving.

A second difficulty with deductive reasoning for action purposes is its dichotomous quality. Dichotomous reasoning hides transformation. For example, dichotomous reasoning can categorize companies as either young or mature and describe the characteristics associated with each state, but it cannot describe the process by which companies successfully transform from young to mature. Yet the task of organizational leadership is precisely to help the organization evolve successfully through the several transformations required to mature. Indeed, all productive human action involves the transformation of materials and attitudes from raw to cooked, from natural to artifactual, from alien to familiar, from intangible dream to tangible product. Hence, dichotomous reasoning misses the very life of business.

Dichotomous "either-or" reasoning also generates unintended "win-lose" dynamics (e.g., business versus government, business versus education, business versus labor). Such reasoning can generate unproductive tension and conflict where it is unnecessary and can miss opportunities for collaboration and "win-win" solutions to dilemmas.[2]

What is remarkable about the IBM strategy of the later 1920s, 1930s, and early 1940s is that it framed all of its deductive systematizing of strategies, structures, and roles within a wider type of reasoning system. This wider type of reasoning was not self-insulated; it connected vision to market and did not dichotomize the company from other institutions (government, universities).

It is important for the future of business, science, and education to begin articulating the outlines of this wider logic. In the absence of such an outline, science and education retain Aristotelian, deductive logic as their highest ideal and arrogantly denounce as hopelessly subjective the seat-of-the pants, intuitive "gut feel" that business people often describe as guiding their decision making. Also, in the absence of such an outline and guiding ideal, business decision making can actually become hopelessly subjective or else an inharmonious and counterproductive mixture of the deductive and gut-feel approaches.

This wider logic that a strategy can reflect and help to institutionalize during the **Systematic Productivity** stage of organizing can be called an "analogical," "constitutive," or "Anaxagorean" system.[3] This type of system is intellectually much less familiar to us. The very fact that everyone recognizes at least Aristotle's name, whereas few know of Anaxagoras, suggests how long ago we began to forget about this type.[4] This type of reasoning system is also unfamiliar to us precisely because it is not merely intellectual. Analogical reasoning does not proceed linearly within one dimension from beginning to end inferring one part from another. Rather, it compares wholes from different dimensions of reality to one another.

For example, if I say to you, "Make up your own mind how to act—don't take anyone else's advice!" there is nothing internally inconsistent within the statement. "Don't take anyone else's advice" is a logically deducible corollary of the proposition, "Make up your own mind how to act." But there is a significant inconsistency between the content of what I am saying (the strategy I advocate) when I make that whole statement and the process of what I am doing (the behavior I enact). I am, after all, asking you to take my advice "not to take anyone's advice." To see this inconsistency as it occurs in action, you must be simultaneously alert to two wholes and their relationship to one another—to the cognitive dimension and the action dimension of speech. No amount of sophistication in the realm of deductive logic alone serves to spot this inconsistency.

Granted, no internally inconsistent business strategy is likely to be much good. The argument here is not in favor of analogical reasoning *instead of* deductive reasoning. That would be "either-or" dichotomous thinking. The argument here is for deductive reasoning appropriately nested within analogical reasoning. For a deductive, internally consistent strategy can be just as useless as an inconsistent strategy if it does not succeed in knitting together the dimensions of intuitive dream, cognitive planning, operational action, and market or historical outcomes. One of the principle differences between deductive and analogical reasoning is that analogical reasoning is constantly at work comparing and knitting together whole units from these different dimensions. Each event in one dimension raises the question of consistency among dimensions.

Another example: if your company's strategy is to acquire another company, the immediate analogical question is how this can be accomplished in each dimension: how the two can become one—not just in conceptual terms (i.e., legally and financially)—but in intuitive terms (sharing a vision and sense of identity) and in operational terms (cutting costs by sharing activities and managerial know-how).

During the 1970s, American companies were not likely to be asking analogical questions when considering mergers or acquisitions. Instead, they were taking their cues from deductive modes of analysis like the Boston Consulting Group's (BCG) famous matrix for making strategic investment decisions in companies. This matrix divides companies into four types—the young and questionable "Wildcat," the fast-growing "Star," the large market share "Cash Cow," and the "Dog" whose growth rate and market share are dwindling. The logic of the matrix is predominantly deductive. It represents a single, conceptual system of symbols in that both variables used to create the matrix—the company's growth rate and its relative market share within the industry—focus on the marketability of the product in financial terms.[5] This matrix is self-insulated in two major ways. First, it refers only to the strategic level of decision making, not to the intuitive and operational levels. Second, at least two of its three transitions (Star to Cash Cow and Cash Cow to Dog) represent developments within relatively large companies at the **Systematic Productivity** stage. Thus, although the BCG matrix claims to tell us about the full life cycle of products and companies, it in fact hides the major transformational challenges of development highlighted in this book. And, although it claims to determine what sort of companies should buy (Cash Cows), what sort of companies should be bought (Stars), and what sort of companies should be sold (Dogs), we should not be surprised that in practice, acquiring firms during the 1970s rarely succeeded in integrating and developing synergies with acquired firms.[6]

Moreover, since the very notion of raising analogical questions relating strategy to practice is unfamiliar, it is not surprising that the conclusion many businesspeople drew from the lack of synergies accompanying acquisitions in the 1970s was not that there was something about the art of choosing and actually implementing acquisitions yet to be learned, but rather that one should continue as before but not even try to integrate the acquired firm and not expect any synergies.[7] They concluded that one should simply allow the acquired firm to continue to manage itself in a decentralized fashion. But this strategy is virtually impossible to implement. For even the reporting requirements to the parent company feel like an erosion of the acquired company's independence that can anger, frustrate, and depress its members.

Robert Townsend, president of Avis, quit shortly after ITT acquired Avis and wrote in *Up the Organization: How to Stop the Corporation from Stifling People and Strangling Profits*, "two and two may seem to make five when a conglomerate is making its pitch, but from what I've seen they are just playing a numbers game and couldn't care less if they make zombies out of your people."[8]

Townsend's passionate language illustrates another difference between deductive reasoning and analogical reasoning. Feeling has no place in deductive reasoning. By contrast, feeling is the basis for choosing which analogies between dimensions to examine at a particular moment in analogical reasoning.[9] Townsend captures this in his analogical equation in the foregoing quote; he locates a fundamental inconsistency in the approach of conglomerates to the head and the heart: in head terms they add value and generate synergy (two plus two add up to five), but in heart terms they subtract value (turn people into zombies). In settings where deductive reasoning alone is applied, the suppression of feeling results in alienation between dominating logic and rebelling feeling. The formal, proclaimed organization comes to be opposed by the informal actual organization, and productivity falls. The colorless, "purely rational" financial manipulations of conglomerates come to be opposed by a colorful and emotional assortment of "greenmailers," "white knights," "golden parachutes," and "poison pills."

An organization that defines itself during the **Systematic Productivity** stage in terms of deductive reasoning alone generates its own opposition and thereby squanders enormous amounts of potentially productive energy. As in the case of IBM, only deductive systems lodged within a wider analogical system that has been implicitly discovered during the organization's earlier stages of development will institutionalize the organization in a way that is likely to endure and to generate increasing growth and energy.[10]

The Analogic of a Smokejumping Season

The functioning of a smokejumper forest-fire-fighting unit provides a vivid example of a more balanced relationship between deductive, "scientific" reasoning and analogical, "intuitive" reasoning in determining an organization's strategy and actual practice at the **Systematic Productivity** stage. Precisely because a balance between deductive and analogical reasoning is unusual in contemporary organizations, the following description of smokejumpers may seem unbalanced, unusual, and extreme, rather than balanced. But note how the well-established rituals associated with each fire season highlight and aid organizational transformation through the different stages of development. Note also how the deductive science of fire fighting is appropriately integrated with and subordinated to the analogical art of fire fighting.

Each and every fire-fighting season begins with a two-week-long "refresher" session during which the jumpers must satisfactorily perform a number of activities before they requalify for this season. The first activity is a multifaceted endurance test which includes running, pull-ups, sit-ups, push-ups, and carrying a 110-pound pack. There is also classroom work on first aid, radio communications, logistical information, rule changes, equipment and procedural updates, etc. One also prepares for three practice parachute jumps by doing hours of parachute landing rolls, climbing trees, rappelling, and exiting from a mock aircraft.

Informal conversations are rampant at the beginning of each season. Veterans and rookies (known as "neds") swap stories at a rate that would satisfy the most prodigious storyteller. The coming season is inevitably envisioned in mythic proportions: the forests will burn with a fury unseen in written history. [*These mythic stories can be seen as part of the* **Conception** *stage of the season.*]

The commitment of smokejumpers at the beginning of each fire season is usually very high if for no other reason than because of the danger and excitement of the work and the pure enjoyment that is anticipated. This commitment is solemnized in the first refresher jumps, for parachuting is the single most dangerous act in the whole process. The danger raises the question why one continues to pursue this career. At the same time, there is much competition among the jumpers as to who works hardest and longest. This friendly rivalry elicits a high degree of commitment in another way.

The aid of the parent organization in the art of smokejumping is recognized as a necessary evil. Most jumpers see the relationships between the local smokejumping unit and the rest of the Forest Service as somewhat feudal. Smokejumpers belong to one of the few subunits within the Forest Service that is largely independent, not reporting to the local Ranger Station and funded from a separate line in the federal budget. Nevertheless, the Forest Service's Fire Management Team is the unit that decides how many and which fires the jumpers get to attack. This relationship is considered evil by the jumpers because these decisions are based on many factors other than how fires may best be physically extinguished—political factors at the federal, regional, and local level.

In many organizations, it may take some imagination to discover participants' spiritual commitment to the chosen endeavor. Not so in the case of smokejumpers. Jumpers worship a fire god called Ernie who determines how many fires there will be, who gets them, and whether they will reach the ground safely in bizarre circumstances. If things are slow, or if a certain cluster of jumpers do not get to go on any fires, the rest of the jumpers will demand a greater spiritual commitment to Ernie—by partying until they drop! This form of hedonistic or pagan worship may seem quite foolish, and it may seem that jumpers undertake it in a lighthearted way. Yet most of them in fact believe in it, using such phrases as "honest partying clears your karma."

An example of the seriousness of this call to spiritual commitment can be seen in the concept of the "plug." When there have been no fires for a long time, the jumper who is scheduled to be the first one out the airplane's door in the event of a fire is known as the "plug." This jumper is viewed as plugging up the door so the rest of the jumpers cannot get out onto a fire. The plug becomes the focus of many party plans. The object is to propitiate Ernie, so the plans often show little regard for the plug's feelings. Those that resist may be tricked, abused, or intimidated. Thus, a plug's karma actually does determine the type of treatment he receives. [*The refresher jumps, the parties for Ernie, and pulling the "plug" are Investments stage rituals.*]

The development each season of the smokejumper unit into "a fine-tuned fire-fighting machine" requires at least one good "fire bust" (a period in which many fires break out, leaving no time for anything else). In a quiet season, this stage may never be reached, and the old salts will leave with the sense that "we never really tested our metal." [*The first "bust" represents the Incorporation stage.*]

The terrain, weather conditions, political conditions, time of day, amount of resources, intensity of the fire, and the particular makeup of a team combine to make every fire an experiment. However, many patterns for a given summer are set early in the season: whether a fast attack or letting the fire burn itself out is the best strategy; whether water will help; or how far away from the fire to construct a fire line (a cleared area) and how wide it should be. [*Experiments stage.*]

In the smokejumping game, the whole point is to be fighting and extinguishing fires (note that most jumpers do not view success as having no fires). The deductive logic and technology of modern science is applied to this end in the form of computerized lightning strike detectors, weather prediction, aerial observation, fuel content analysis, etc. But a much more intuitive type of reasoning remains the primary basis for strategizing on fires. A common smokejumper belief is that two factors determine events on any fire: the weather and luck. And since weather is a matter of luck . . . so much for scientific knowledge of fire behavior. Actually, however, smokejumpers treat fire science seriously under two conditions: when the fire is not too threatening and when the "book" approach confirms the jumpers' wishes. But if the fire is running wild, and Ernie is doing strange things such as making the fire jump ahead of itself, make "fire devils" (tornadolike whirls of fire), or burning downhill and into the wind, then one's strategizing must be as wild and canny as Ernie's and "seat of the pants" fire fighting is the rule. [*Subordination of deductive to analogical reasoning at the Systematic Productivity stage.*][11]

This story provides a review of all the early stages of development, partly because each fire-fighting season has a distinct beginning and end, and partly because the smokejumpers' analogical reasoning generates rituals that systematically highlight and aid organizational transformation.

Each fire season progresses through the organizational stages of **Conception** (informal conversations about the mythic fires ahead), **Investments** (the refresher jumps, parties for Ernie), **Incorporation** (the first "bust"), **Experiments** (determining the best strategies for this season), and **Systematic Productivity** (appropriately balancing deductive fire science with analogical fire-god-like alertness). Furthermore, because of the seasonal nature of fire fighting and because of the analogical rituals created to kindle wild fire by wild partying and wild risks, these different stages are quite plainly visible to the jumpers themselves. They recognize the importance of systematically transforming through the stages and of balancing deductive and analogical reasoning in order to achieve a successful fire season (even though they do not, of course, use the theoretical language of this book).

Obviously, the smokejumpers are unusual. Most organizations today overconcentrate on deductive systems as they mature. Four serious negative consequences result from the widespread overconcentration on deductive systems at the **Systematic Productivity** stage of development:

1. As we saw in Chapter 7 on the **Experiments** stage, some companies try to avoid entering the **Systematic Productivity** stage in order to avoid losing their liveliness. This strategy does not work.

2. Because deductive logic aims at *generally* valid conclusions, it falsely generalizes deductively systematic productivity

as the acme of all organizing. One result is that organizations are pushed at a forced pace toward the **Systematic Productivity** stage, without sufficient recognition of the qualitatively different dilemmas posed at each stage; hence, the high "infant mortality" rate for new ventures, as discussed in Chapter 5.

3. Treating deductive reasoning and **Systematic Productivity** as the acme of organizing also obscures the very possibility of still later stages of organizational development.[12] This results in the unnecessary demoralization of mature companies in mature markets. If mature organizations have only distasteful images like Cash Cow and Dog to look forward to, our economy is in serious trouble today.

4. Treating deductive systems as the acme of organizing leaves us in a fog about how to run and how to evaluate all those organizations that do not have clear predetermined objectives and outcome measures, that is, the entire not-for-profit and public sector. There is no simple measure of productivity for all those organizations that provide intangible services or experiences rather than tangible products, or whose purpose is to raise questions about what frameworks are appropriate for judging success and productivity in the first place. In a society that does not widely recognize the possibility of creating analogical measures of productivity that test whether interplay among an organization's mission, strategy, operations, and outcomes is harmonious, not-for-profit and public organizations are more likely simply to *avoid* applying *any* measure of productivity to themselves.

It is important to emphasize at the end of this chapter that the analogical systems at the core of IBM's success in the profit sector and of the smokejumpers' esprit de corps in the governmental sector are not described as such by the organizations themselves. These are not self-conscious organizations that have deliberately structured analogical systems for themselves. Likewise, the majority of organizations that are primarily deductively bureaucratic at this stage have not deliberately and explicitly chosen that structure with awareness of alternatives. Rather, the implicit historical development and cultural context of the given organization usually determine whether its primary allegiance at the **Systematic Productivity** stage is to deductive or analogical systems. It is only at the next stage of development, to be examined in Chapter 11, that an organization as a whole begins to become self-conscious about its culture and operating systems.

Because the deductive sciences have become the secular religions of modernity, the cultural context of organizations today strongly legitimizes the development of deductive systems and largely obscures and delegitimizes the development of analogical systems.

Characteristics of the Systematic Productivity Stage of Organizing

---

1. Attention is legitimately focused only on the systematic procedures for accomplishing the predefined task.
2. Marketability or political viability of the product or service, as measured in quantifiable terms, is the overriding criterion of success.
3. Standards, structures, and roles are taken for granted as given and formalized, usually in deductive, pyramidal terms.
4. Reality is usually and most easily conceived of in deductive terms as dichotomous and competitive: win-lose, rational-emotional, leader-follower, work-play, personal-professional, practical-theoretical.
5. Critical issue: whether earlier development has provided a strong and appropriate analogical system that frames, and is not distorted by, the deductive systems developed during this stage.

NOTES

1. R. Sobel, *IBM: Colossus in Transition* (Toronto: Bantam, 1983), p. 84.

2. R. Nielsen, "Toward a Method for Building Consensus during Strategic Planning," *Sloan Management Review* 22, no. 4 (1981), pp. 29–40, and "Cooperative Strategy," *Strategic Management Journal* (forthcoming 1987).

3. This distinction is described in detail in J. Ogilvie, *Many Dimensional Man: Decentralized Self, Society, and the Sacred* (New York: Oxford University Press, 1977). Karl Mannheim makes a closely related distinction between "instrumental" and "constitutive" rationality in *Ideology and Utopia* (New York: Harcourt Brace Jovanovich, 1936). Gareth Morgan makes an equally closely related distinction between "bureaucratic" and "holographic" reasoning and organizing in *Images of Organization* (Beverly Hills, Calif.: Sage, 1986), pp. 95 ff. Another related notion of fundamentally different types of logic, and how a recognition of these differences influences our approach to science, is presented in I. Mitroff and R. Kilman, *Methodological Approaches to Social Science* (San Francisco: Jossey-Bass, 1978).

4. Anaxagoras was a teacher of both Socrates and Pericles who held that man is analogous to the universe, that the microcosm is analogous to the macrocosm.

5. The only Anaxagorean element in the BCG matrix is that it compares

two different perspectives on marketability to one another. The company's growth rate compares its current state to its own history; its market share compares its current state to the industry as a whole. Thus, the company's current state is being compared to two "wholes"—itself (previously) and the industry.

6. M. Porter, *The Competitive Advantage* (New York: Free Press, 1985), pp. 318–19

7. Another move in the face of these difficulties was to analyze those cases where major strategic change seemed to be successful in operational terms. This has led to a model of dialectical movement back and forth between strategizing and implementing, as a corrective to the "deductive" model (J. Quinn, *Logical Incrementalism*). This model imports something of the "inductive" scientific method into strategizing and is a step in the direction of Anaxagorean logic.

8. R. Townsend, *Up the Organization: How to Stop a Corporation from Stifling People and Strangling Profits* (New York: Alfred A. Knopf, 1970), p. 95.

9. At any given moment, there are a large number of potential analogies to the issue at the focus of one's attention. One can think in terms of spatial scale, analogizing from a personal issue to the group situation to the organizational, to the national, to the global; or in terms of the temporal scale, analogizing from the immediate stakes to what is at stake within one's career, one's lifetime, the organization's lifetime, the civilization's lifetime, or human history as a whole; or in terms of the existential dimensions of each moment, namely, intuitive dream or purpose, cognitive strategy or plan, behavioral operation, and effects in the external world. The fact of multiple possible analogies faces each of us with a continual paradox that deductive science cannot formulate, much less resolve. On the one hand, no predetermined methodology can resolve ahead of time what analogies will be the most fruitful to explore at a given moment. On the other hand, there must be disciplines for testing the validity of one's feelings about what analogies to explore from moment to moment—that is, for distinguishing between feelings that are merely subjective and feelings that are attuned to wider social and deeper spiritual rhythms. If there are no disciplines for widening, deepening, and attuning awareness, then there is no analogical "logic." This book attempts in many different ways to illustrate analogical reasoning and disciplines leading to it, but the book can go no further than to persuade readers to seek out help in beginning or continuing to exercise such disciplines for themselves. As Ogilvie puts it (in his book, *Many Dimensional Man*, p. 239), "Anaxagorean logic . . . must be lived in a synthesis of wholes rather than looked at in an analysis of parts. By its own partiality, by its implicit invitation to quiet armchair reflection, the written word is not suited to an introduction to Anaxagorean logic. That logic needs the activity of a Pericles . . . to overcome the fixed framing that words alone invite."

10. Nobel economics prize winner Herbert Simon promulgated the notion that human rationality is necessarily bounded (capable of making instrumental choices between well-defined alternatives, but not of constituting order from chaos) and that it therefore operates best within the bounds of bureaucracies (*Reason in Human Affairs* [Stanford University Press, 1983]; with J. March, *Organizations* [New York: John Wiley & Sons, 1958]). In the terms used here, Simon claims rationality is limited to Aristotelian logic. Powerfully descriptive of contemporary reality, this theory becomes demonic as a prescriptive theory

about the limits of human and organizational nature (see W. Torbert, "Educating toward Shared Purpose, Self-Direction, and Quality Work: The Theory and Practice of Liberating Structure" *Journal of Higher Education* 49, no. 2 [1978], pp. 109–33).

11. This story is edited from a course paper by doctoral candidate Patrick Withen (Department of Sociology, Boston College, 1985). Withen is a longtime smokejumper. I am grateful for his permission to publish his description in this form.

12. Recently, increased academic attention has been given to the notion of historical stages of organizational development (e.g., K. Cameron, and D. Whetten, "Models of the Organizational Life Cycle," *Research in Higher Education*, 1983), but these models typically collapse all development beyond **Systematic Productivity** into one stage vaguely named "Elaboration of Structure," implying "more of the same" rather than transformation to something qualitatively different. Similarly, current strategic guru Michael E. Porter (see note 6) implies the possibility of a qualitatively different form of organizing beyond **Systematic Productivity** when he criticizes the recent focus in strategy on portfolio management of diverse decentralized companies and advocates focusing on what he calls "horizontal" strategy that exploits interrelationships among business units for earnings-enhancing synergies.

The Achiever

When MBA students begin their search for a position following graduation, they are typically encouraged to view their effort as a "job campaign." They are told to take initiative and follow through on job opportunities, and to demonstrate commitment through action to the point where they will stand out from other candidates. Legends about ingenuity and persistence paying off are retold. Harold Geneen's initiative in becoming executive vice president and chief operating officer of Raytheon in 1956 fits this mold.

Seeing an announcement of his predecessor's departure, Geneen called the office of Charlie Adams, Raytheon's CEO. Adams' secretary followed her instructions and asked the caller to send in his resume, but Geneen interrupted:

"I don't want to do that, I want to find out if there's a job open, and if there's a job open, the sort of job it is."

Lillian couldn't answer that, and he continued before she could cut him off. "I think it's unfair to expect anyone to send in a resume without even knowing if there's an opening. And if there's an opening, it's unfair to conceal it. That means it's not open to everyone qualified."

In the space of a couple of minutes he had turned her around, made her feel their procedure was incorrect. That upset her. She took his name and number, said she would try to find the answers and call him back. Then she walked in to Mr. Adams and described her experience. He listened with interest. He respected Lillian, knew she had considerable experience dealing with all sorts of callers. Anyone who could so swiftly penetrate her defenses must be extraordinary. He arranged to have (a vice president) talk to the man. Gratified, Lillian returned to her desk, made her promised call, and was very courteously thanked. She put the receiver down with a smile, stared at the man's name to fix it in her memory: Harold S. Geneen.[1]

Geneen later made his name as CEO of ITT, where between 1959 and 1977 he acquired over 300 companies, increasing sales to 25 times their size when he started, and increasing per share earnings by 10 to 15 percent each quarter compared to the previous year *for 58 consecutive quarters*. Geneen is at once the prototype for the **Achiever** style of management, and at the same time a major influence in legitimizing this style of management as a normative model for other managers during the 1960s and 1970s.

Two convictions about business guided all Geneen's work and helped him and others move beyond a **Technician**'s concern with the substance of particular products to an **Achiever**'s concern with the overall results of a business system. His first conviction was that the purpose of business was not the creation of any particular product (e.g., airplanes), nor even the performance of any more general function (e.g., transportation), but rather to make money for shareholders. His second conviction was that successful operation of a large business required continuous monitoring and analysis of current, detailed financial information.[2] These two convictions dovetail nicely, integrating means and ends, in that they both focus on business in the abstract terms of deductive, market economic theory. And ITT's actual bottom-line performance during the Geneen years certainly grants these convictions at least initial credibility.

How many managers are **Achievers**? Our figures represent approximations, of course. The three studies of managers originally cited in Chapter 2 found that **Achievers** represented 33 percent of the senior management sample and 40 percent of the junior management sample, while none of the first-line supervisory sample measured at this relatively late stage of development. The junior management finding is probably a high estimate for junior management generally, since the entire sample held MBAs. In his study of consumer values, also cited in earlier chapters, Mitchell estimated that 26 percent of the population were "Achievers." He described this market segment as a high-income group, as motivated by success, fame, or leadership, as materialistic, and as interested in both efficiency and comfort.

To gain a closer impression of one **Achiever's** day-to-day managerial style, we can return to Harold Geneen during his days at Raytheon, before his role as CEO and his growing legend at ITT hallowed his activities to the point where the organization as a whole was shaped to his style. At Raytheon, Geneen entered as an unknown quantity into a corporation with other strong leadership figures, but a corporation with a history of not having strong management controls.

> Geneen began by holding meetings and asking questions. In the beginning, these were financial: the controller's office was asked for books, accounts, records, proofs. The meetings and the questions would last for hours, well into the night. First the financial men and then the engineers learned to their amazement that he could read pages of statistics as other men read prose. Then he could, from memory, cite items and the pages upon which they appeared.
>
> (He) was fond of late meetings that extended from dinners at the Red Coach Grill in Wayland. There were regular attendees . . . . Other men came and went. . . . The conversation . . . revolved eternally about Raytheon business problems, systems, people, markets. . . . Finally the meetings expanded to the point where Geneen had his assistants bring charts . . . (filled) with the names of other companies. One of Geneen's points was that 80 or 90 percent of the business done in the United States was nongovernmental. He was, therefore, talking about fundamental changes in Raytheon. The word had not yet been coined, but he was thinking along conglomerate lines. . . . To Geneen, this was what strong drink, women, and music might be to other men.[3]

What comes across most vividly in this description is the sheer *passion for hard work*, not as an isolated individual but rather *as part of a group creating and monitoring some system*. Later, Geneen himself would write, "The best hope of achieving . . . a climate in which each fellow would want to carry his own share . . . was to jump in the boat, grab an oar, and start pulling along with the other men."[4] In his writing, Geneen distinguishes between management, which is objective ("You want to accomplish an objective, to get from here to there, and your performance can be measured"), and leadership, which is subjective ("The very heart and soul of business, . . . the ability to inspire other people, . . . difficult to define, . . . cannot be taught in school").[5] But what comes through in every description of Geneen is his passion for objectivity (goal achievement measured by "unshakable" facts), a passion so great that it displaced other ordinary avenues for expressing passion.

"I often told colleagues," Geneen tells us, "that business was as much fun as golf, tennis, sailing, dancing, or almost anything else you might want to name. The pleasures were different from those of eating an ice cream sundae. Business provided intellectual challenges that stimulated and fed one's mind. They were every bit as good in their own way as the momentary pleasures of gobbling down one's dessert, and they were more durable. The sweetness lasted longer."[6] So much for all other passions and pleasures!

Such was Geneen's passion for objectivity that he was very hard on many people's sense of subjectivity. The reader may recall his harsh policy, described in Chapter 6, with regard to any business activity that he interpreted as "office politics." At Raytheon, and again at ITT, he made wholesale changes in top management personnel in an effort to put the best people in each job. At Raytheon, he also brought in a psychologist who assessed every employee (except for the two other members of the office of the president, who refused) searching for future "stars," or, as he put it, "the upper one third of the upper one tenth."[7] Each of these moves may be constructive under certain circumstances, but Geneen was categorical about them, not circumstantial. At Raytheon,

> "He made people nervous," recalls Charlie Resnick. . . . "He struck me as brilliant, but hard. He gave men hell if they made a mistake—and kept silent when they did something well."
>
> Charlie Adams attended Geneen's meetings when he could, and sat quietly through most of them. He had chosen to give his executive vice president room to run and was not going to change that understanding. But on one occasion Geneen's treatment of one man was, Adams says, "so painful" that Adams was aroused.

In the midst of his remarks, therefore, Geneen was abruptly recalled when Adams turned to him and said, in an iron voice, *"Stop that."*

Geneen flushed and fell silent; it took the meeting several minutes to recover its balance. Later Geneen went to Adams' office. His manner was extremely courteous, and he wondered what had upset the president.

"In the navy," Adams (said), "we took note of men who misbehaved. Later, they were chewed out—in private. In the future, if you choose to rebuke a man, do it privately. Fire him, if need be. But don't publicly humiliate people. It hurts the team."[8]

What might be overlooked in this episode, and what is perhaps most characteristic of the **Achiever**'s managerial style, is the fact that Geneen took the initiative to seek out what he knew would be negative feedback about his behavior. The **Diplomatic** manager would avoid such feedback if possible. The **Technical** manager would feel very ambivalent about such feedback. By contrast, the **Achiever** is so clearly focused on, and identified with, his goal that if he is not achieving it he wants to know that so that he can do something differently in order to increase his chances of achieving it.

In other words, negative feedback has the positive value for the **Achiever** of making it more probable that he can achieve the goal. As rational and obvious as this point may seem, developmental theory shows what a long path we must come to reach this point and helps to explain why people in organizations so frequently act as though they do not understand this point.

Elements of the Achiever's Managerial Style

Long-term goals	Results-oriented
Strives for excellence	Welcomes behavioral feedback
Future is vivid, inspiring	Feels like initiator, not pawn
Chooses ethical system	Distinguishes ethics from manners
Appreciates complexity, systems	Works conscientiously
Respects individual differences	Seeks mutuality in relationships
Seeks generalizable reasons for action	Guilt if does not meet own standards
Blind to own shadow, to subjectivity behind objectivity	

But, what the last excerpt about Geneen also begins to reveal is the shadow side of the **Achiever**'s style.[9] Precisely because the **Achiever** is more systematic and more open to new information than any of the earlier styles, he or she is likely to be among the more effective and more confident managers in any situation. The **Achiever**'s passion for objectivity, for "unshakable facts"——whether it be Geneen's, or a lawyer's, or a doctor's, or a scientist's, or a journalist's—can easily lead to the belief that he or she *is* objective. The **Achiever** does not yet recognize that this objectivity is not absolute but rather is defined as objective by its own framework of (nonobjective) assumptions.

Like managers at earlier stages of development, the **Achiever** views the framework of assumptions that he or she "inhabits," not as a framework at all, but rather as "the way the world really is." Consequently, a manager like Geneen cannot imagine that a rebuke like Adams' has any real validity. Since Geneen's behavior is clearly goal oriented, any failure to reach the goal must be someone else's fault. That his own goal-oriented behavior could be responsible for destroying a team and making a goal unreachable does not make sense to him. More than likely, Geneen hears in Adams' rebuke only a displeased superior with too much of a **Diplomatic** perspective, and the threat that the corporation may start to make decisions based on subjective, ego-salving, political criteria rather than on objective, business-building, economic criteria. He imagines that his own position is apolitical, and he strives consciously to be as unegotistical as possible (Geneen excoriates egotism as the worst disease that can afflict an executive[10]).

Geneen's "hardness" will seem to him a duty he owes to the corporation and to other managers. To remain silent in the face of error will seem to him a betrayal of the corporation and of the other person, whom silence would condemn to continue blindly in his ineffectuality. And, of course, on any given occasion this may be perfectly true. But treated as always and necessarily true, these dicta become dictatorial.

Although Geneen's managerial style clearly rewarded other managers who were **Achievers**, it is not at all clear that it supported development by managers toward the **Achiever** style, let alone beyond it. Although Geneen's style in general clearly improved the **Systematic Productivity** of the firms he acquired, there is no evidence that he could nurture either early stage organizations or organizational development to later stages beyond **Systematic Productivity**.

Geneen was assiduous in seeking behavioral feedback that could improve his goal achievement, but he was blind to feedback that could throw the very framework within which he was operating into question. What other people view as his political interventions (e.g., intense Washington lobbying in support of ITT's acquisition of Hartford Insurance, volunteering funds to the CIA to prevent Allende's election in Chile, subsidizing the 1972 Republican convention in San Diego[11]), Geneen viewed simply as clearing the way for managers to manage. He even chooses not to mention these controversies in his autobiographical book, *Managing*. He also chooses not to mention that despite the spectacular overall growth in size of ITT during his tenure there, per share earnings increased less than for an average stock on the New York Stock Exchange.[12] Although Geneen hates addictions of all kinds—whether to alcohol, drugs, or ego—he is himself helplessly addicted to a limited conception of business and of life.

The previous chapter introduced the distinction between instrumental, deductive, Aristotelian rationality and constitutive, analogical, Anaxagorean rationality. The **Achiever** treats instrumental, Aristotelian rationality as all that rationality is. The axioms that frame instrumental rationality, constituting the system as a whole, are "given," or "taken for granted" from the outset, and remain unexamined. The possibility of a constitutive, Anaxagorean rationality remains unimagined, unattractive if suggested, and therefore unexplored. In offering the opportunity to obtain whatever goals one may desire, instrumental rationality appears to be all that is necessary for the good life. It even has the virtue of appearing at once morally neutral (supports any goal) and morally imperative (the basis of all desirable results). The assumptions provide the foundation for the myth—so attractive in our time—of the at-once-objective-and-socially-responsible professional—whether scientist, doctor, lawyer, accountant, therapist, or civil servant.

What kind of organizational systems can help the **Achiever** begin to develop awareness of, and take responsibility for, the limits and costs of his or her entire approach? Because of the

Achiever's relative competence and relative openness to feedback, organizational "inquiry systems" that bring anomalies to his attention are of use. Such inquiry systems are illustrated in the next chapter. However, the **Achiever** will unintentionally tend to translate feedback about the limits of his or her entire framework into behavioral feedback to be used to improve goal achievement. Consequently, the **Achiever** needs close supervision from a manager or consultant at a later stage of development if he or she is to transcend the addiction to work-related goals.

An openness to working with feedback, characteristic of the **Achiever** style, is evident in the following case. The reader is invited to examine this case with an eye to the ways in which, despite his own best efforts, the manager translates feedback he receives about his approach into a plan for action that still embodies the original approach.

> My firm recently completed a large design engineering project for an industrial client, with Jim serving as project team leader. A smaller design project spun off of the larger one, and this was also to be run by Jim. The first project was delayed, however, and he could not possibly handle both of them at the same time. Therefore, the second project was assigned to Barry to lead, with myself as principal engineer. Barry and Jim have the same job position and relative status in the company.
>
> It was assumed that Jim would "phase in" Barry as project head and then would bow out himself. The changeover period would allow Barry to establish client contact and learn the peculiarities and standards of the work to be done for this particular client. But the transition did not take place. What ensued was a power struggle. Barry did not appear technically skilled enough to handle the job. At the same time, Jim, having done the "dog work and wheel spinning" on the first project, wanted to fly through the second project on momentum, making a big profit and collecting the associated credit for doing so.
>
> Jim ended up with control of the project with Barry as his assistant. The project is now 90 percent complete, but we are going to go over budget by a long shot, as did Jim's first project. I did not work on the first project, but in my opinion both of them could have made the target budget.
>
> As I look back, Jim employed a mystery-mastery strategy (meet own objectives irrespective of group, control unilaterally, minimize

expression of negative feelings [13]) in attempting to control the project group. It was extremely frustrating to work for him. The project team had all kinds of target dates for individual contracts, but no clear definition, ever, of what exactly the contracts were to encompass. This should have been handled by Jim. I conceptualized the overall scope of the project in a design memorandum to the client in the first month of work. Jim would not allow deviations from this memorandum, which was approved for him, for fear of losing face. The kinds of changes I wished to make were improvements as a result of further details worked up by me and other project team members as the job progressed. He wouldn't hear of it.

Information was transmitted through Jim from the client and distributed to the project group. He withheld this information from the group until he could completely absorb it and feel on top of things, and one step ahead of Barry. Barry became extremely defensive and unwilling to make decisions without checking with Jim first. The entire project group became extremely mechanical in their work. They waited for explicit instructions, didn't comment on improvements they thought should be made, and became extremely distrustful of one another.

I went home one evening and decided as principal engineer to attempt to change things for the better by assuming some leadership responsibilities. I set up a meeting with Jim, Barry, and myself the next morning to explain to them that the other project team members and I felt incompetent and totally ineffective under the techniques of project management being used. I thought I had some good ideas about what should be done.

I opened the meeting:

"I hope you don't get mad, but . . . this project suffers from a lack of control. I know I've made some errors, but I feel that they stem from my frustration with the way things are going. There is no communication. Can we discuss the problem we have?"

I had been working under a boss who used a mystery-mastery leadership style. In attempting to assume some leadership responsibility, I now fell into the same mold. I attempted to minimize negative feelings by starting off with "I hope you don't get mad." I made a judgment that I did not test publicly in assuming the problem was "lack of control." I was self-protective in excusing my errors. All through the meeting, I suppressed my intense feelings of aggravation.

I came out of the meeting with more task-oriented schedules, directives that were now going to be given by me instead of Jim, feelings of increased competitiveness and distrust, and a "get the job done and over with" attitude. I find it hard to believe now, but I actually felt good about the meeting at the time!

The project will be completed next week in spite of itself. The meeting did absolutely nothing towards improving the effectiveness of the project team. I am slated to work for Jim again soon and have determined not to let this type of situation develop again. Jim and I are soon to discuss how performance can be improved. I have some ideas.

A climate of social inquiry has to be developed! I am going to suggest that the next project be discussed openly among the team members before we begin and at fixed intervals after we begin. The conceptual design memorandum which we will prepare before we begin detailed design should be understood by all as just that—a "conceptual" memorandum for purposes of explaining to the client what we are doing for them. It is to be an informative statement subject to change within budget limitations, pending ongoing project group recommendations as design proceeds. It is not to be a noose.

Tasks will be given to individuals along with all the necessary and available information for them to come up with what they think is a good plan. The pieces of the plan will be put together, discussed, and revised by the group as a whole. In my opinion, the project team is small enough and competent enough that this format will not be wasteful. There is going to be a shift in emphasis from what we are going to do (task) to how we are going to do it (process). Are we going to use models, sketches, parts of a previous design, site visits? The whole idea being to "cultivate the quality of attentiveness necessary to follow the interplay of purpose, process, and task."[14]

Perhaps my biggest problem will be in using self-disclosure, supportiveness, and confrontation in promoting an inquiring mode of interaction when I speak to Jim about my ideas. I will have to present them as just that—"ideas," subject to evaluation. I will have to be supportive if he has incongruous ideas but confront him with the possibility of going over budget for the third time.

This manager's self-study brilliantly illlustrates both the strengths and the limits of the **Achiever** style as it begins to reach beyond itself. The writing shows a clear understanding of complex systems of ideas (in this case about different interpersonal styles—a "mystery-mastery" style and an "inquiring" style).

Moreover, the self-study shows a dramatic willingness to apply the ideas to the manager's own experiences, virtually an eagerness to analyze his own mistakes in his original initiative. The manager sees that his opening comment at the meeting he called with Jim and Barry—a comment that might be interpreted as innocuous and inoffensive—in fact set a tone for the meeting. Even the question at the end of that comment is a challenge more than it is an opening to their point of view. A prior set of questions, which would have the effect of including the other two in the definition of the meeting rather than blaming them, would be, "Are you aware of how much these difficulties are lowering the group's productivity? Are you experiencing problems with the project too? How do you understand these difficulties?"

From his analysis, our **Achiever** develops what seems to him an entirely new blueprint for managing a project, a more participative team-oriented approach which he is determined to implement successfully. One can hear his enthusiasm. This is the way to make it work! But then, in his final paragraph, he sees the tip of an iceberg that may sink his vision. He sees that, to be internally consistent, he must treat his new blueprint just as he is proposing they treat a conceptual memorandum at the beginning of a relationship with a client—as "subject to change," not "a noose."

Whereas the tone of the two paragraphs proposing his new management process is euphoric—the social engineer laying out utopia—the tone of his final paragraph is momentarily tentative again, on the verge of an awareness that the "inquiring" style of management is not so much a solution to all managerial problems as a demand that the manager balance the tension between task and process, between his mode of vision and others, from moment to moment to moment. This awareness vanishes through the sieve of the **Achiever**'s goal-oriented logic again and again and again. The likely scenario when this manager meets with Jim is that Jim will experience the manager's plan as an attempt to exercise unilateral control, and he will resist it. Feeling Jim's resistance, this manager's commitment to his new vision will lead him to fight for it all the harder, thus further confirming Jim's view.

From an initial attempt to correct himself with negative feedback, our **Achiever** is likely to bounce quickly back into a positive feedback loop vis-à-vis Jim. That is, each one of the pair is likely to feel *reinforced* in his initial assumptions and behavior by the other's response, even as the two of them become increasingly polarized. The **Achiever** seeks to achieve in terms of his or her own framework and is neither inclined nor competent to question the validity of the framework itself and possibly reframe his or her approach in the midst of action.

TRANSITION

In the previous two chapters, we have been examining what organizations and individuals look like, feel like, and think like at the stage of development when they crystallize into a system that produces or achieves success in a reliable fashion—when they develop not just a socially acceptable pattern of behavior, and not just an internally coherent logic, but a logic of success— at once acceptable, coherent, and effective.

But what happens when the environment or the system itself changes radically? As we saw in the final paragraphs of this chapter as well as in the portrait of Harold Geneen, the logic of success promises continued success. If it is a predominantly deductive logic, the system does not even include the possibility, let alone the ability, to question its own assumptions—to reframe itself. Yet mature organizations and senior executives in the 1980s regularly face radical changes because of deregulation or global competition or acquisition or changing technology. What type of organizing and managing can question its own assumptions and appropriately reframe itself without ceasing to produce in the meantime? The next two chapters on generative organizing address this question.

NOTES

1. O. Scott, *The Creative Ordeal: The Story of Raytheon* (New York: Atheneum Publishers, 1974), pp. 263–64.

2. R. Schoenberg, *Geneen* (New York: W.W. Norton, 1984).

3. Scott, *The Creative Ordeal*, pp. 271, 285–86.

4. H. Geneen (with A. Moscow), *Managing* (Garden City, N.Y.: Doubleday, 1984), p. 130.

5. Ibid., pp. 127–28.

6. Ibid.

7. Scott, *The Creative Ordeal,* p. 287.

8. Ibid., p. 290.

9. For a description of Geneen's style that highlights its shadow side and negative consequences, see R. Pascale and A. Athos, *The Art of Japanese Management* (New York: Simon & Schuster, 1981).

10. Geneen, *Managing,* ch. 8.

11. For details, see R. Sobel, *ITT: The Management of Opportunity* (New York: Times Books, 1982), particularly chapters 15–17.

12. J. Lorie, "The Wizard of ITT," *The Wall Street Journal,* March 18, 1985.

13. The notion of two fundamentally different interpersonal styles of management, only the less common of which invites and digests "frame-changing" feedback, was initially developed by C. Argyris and D. Schon, *Theory in Practice: Increasing Professional Effectiveness* (San Francisco: Jossey-Bass, 1974). See also W. Torbert, "Interpersonal Competence," in A. Chickering, *The Modern American College* (San Francisco: Jossey-Bass, 1981).

14. W. Torbert, "Educating toward Shared Purpose, Self-Direction, and Quality Work," *Journal of Higher Education* 49, no. 2 (1978), pp. 109–35.

CHAPTER ELEVEN _____

Collaborative Inquiry

At the **Collaborative Inquiry** stage, organizations not only produce goods or services but do so in ways whereby members continually reexplore the authority and legitimacy of the organization's various structures, strategies, and systems, with a regular process for amending them. The organization *is* no longer any particular structure. It *has* structures. And it has inquiry systems for restructuring, and it is these with which it identifies more closely.

The organization at this stage of development deliberately fosters inquiry about its mission and about whether its structure, operations, and social outcomes are consistent with its mission and are beneficial. In other words, the question of whether the organization functions so as to make the corporate dream come true begins, for the first time, to become explicit and to be tested as part of the regular functioning of the organization. It is not just the board of directors and the CEO of the organization who address this question. A much wider spectrum of the organization's membership participates in this inquiry process, whether through participation in ownership of the firm (e.g., leveraged management buyout or Employee Stock Option Plan), or through managerial and shop floor participation in Quality of Working Life projects, or through systems of performance review and career development.

Norberto Odebrecht, CEO of Odebrecht S.A., holding company for one of Brazil's largest conglomerates in civil construction and related industries, has developed an explicit philosophy (and published it in book form) that guides his company in the turbulent Brazilian environment.[1] This philosophy treats every manager as a responsible partner in the firm. Odebrecht argues, on the basis of having rescued his father's company from bankruptcy after World War II, that every line manager should be treated as a "partner-entrepreneur" who participates in the creation of business goals, directives, and budgets for his or her area of responsibility each year and whose compensation directly reflects the productivity of that business unit. Spurred by Odebrecht, the senior management at the company persisted throughout the late 1970s in developing an annual planning process and legal structure that implement this philosophy.

So much energy was devoted to creating this planning process because Odebrecht understands entrepreneurship, not as an individual manipulating impersonal economic forces, but rather as *an educational process among persons*. He defines the entrepreneurial leader as one:

> who is able to establish, maintain, and broaden the confidence of the men he leads, through the creation of economic conditions for the survival, growth and perpetuity of the organization.

> who continuously reaches higher levels of maturity.

> who performs the non-delegable educational function of developing other leaders, including that one who will replace him

> who masters the spoken language which is his primary instrument of action.[2]

These words are not mere "commencement speech" rhetoric. Odebrecht goes on to emphasize the difficulties facing the entrepreneurial leader. The entrepreneur must identify others' potential and match it to the right opportunity at the right time, thereby developing a loyal relationship, resembling that of a father and son:

> But paternal love, in order to be true, cannot be mixed up with "paternalism." Examining, treating and performing the task of serving the client is a hard job, full of suffering. An authentic father does not prevent his son from suffering; he prepares his son

to face it and overcome it. Frequently, the dialogue between the leader and the man becomes hard and painful for both parts.[3]

These words, in turn, gain significance and power when one knows what Odebrecht has paid for them. No one within the company would read the father-son reference as a "mere" analogy. For Odebrecht and his own son engaged in a generation-long struggle within the company. Over a period of years the father, as president, was based, with his deputies, in Salvador, while the son, as executive vice president, was based, with his deputies, nearly 1,000 miles south in Rio de Janeiro. The two executive teams frequently strained against one another in terms of both substance and style. Yet they remained engaged, developing the planning process as an inquiry system which encouraged semi-annual review and restructuring of priorities between the two executive teams. They thereby generated a more vibrant, fast-growing company, with the unusual advantage of headquarters presence in both northern and southern Brazil.

As already stated and as illustrated by the Odebrecht S.A. example, when an organization moves from the **Systematic Productivity** stage to the **Collaborative Inquiry** stage, its identity becomes lodged less in its current structure than in its capacity for restructuring. It becomes capable of restructuring to meet unforeseeable market and political conditions, restructuring as subgroups within the organization develop, and restructuring to more consistently enact the corporate dream. In regard to acquisition, merger, and divestiture activities, the organization becomes capable of restructuring intentionally and appropriately rather than as a defensive reaction or as a victim of others' initiatives. The organization at this stage of development also tends to restructure its definition of success, moving away from a single outcome criterion of success to multiple criteria of success. The organization balances concerns for short-term efficiency, middle-term effectiveness, and long-term legitimacy so as to enhance all three over the long term.

Very few organizations fully achieve this stage of development, as desirable as it may sound in the abstract. One reason for this is that, as we have seen in the previous chapters on managerial stages of development, almost all managers operate at stages of development that do not accept the possibility, much less the practice, of using feedback to restructure themselves or their organizations. Hence, few managers can take effective leadership in guiding an organization to this stage, and most managers unawaredly act in ways that obstruct the development of **Collaborative Inquiry.** Despite the cliche about business as "a school of hard knocks," few managers in fact emulate Odebrecht in taking as their core responsibility the creation of an educational process within their immediate work group and for the organization as a whole.

A second reason that very few organizations evolve to this stage of development is that, as we saw in Chapter 9 on **Systematic Productivity,** we have not had attractive images of mature organizations (recall the BCG categories Cash Cow and Dog) to serve as guides. Hence, we have an incomplete vision of what **Collaborative Inquiry** should look like, why it would be desirable, and how much commitment, pain, and trial and error we should be prepared to expend in order to generate and maintain it. Certainly, no manager that views an organization's purposes as limited to **Systematic Productivity** would dedicate the energy Odebrecht has to its annual planning process.

The organization that probably comes closest to representing **Collaborative Inquiry** is the U.S. government, or rather its skeletal structure and circulatory system as set forth in the Constitution, the Bill of Rights, and the subsequent amendments. As we all know, the Constitution provides a well-defined process for self-amendment and fundamental inquiry. Each election of legislators and executives provides an opportunity to reexplore the authority and legitimacy of the current structure of law and the ongoing process of governance. Inquiry about the system's purpose and about the consistency or inconsistency of its actual operations is deliberately fostered by the freedoms of assembly, speech, and press guaranteed in the Bill of Rights, and by the independence of the judiciary as well. The Supreme Court, in particular, tests whether current laws or actions are consistent with the American corporate dream as articulated in the preamble to the Constitution and by our system's analogue to philosopher-kings (and queen), the justices.

Over 200 years, the effect of this carefully calibrated self-restructuring system has been to generate a degree of legitimacy for the U.S. government among its own citizens unparalleled in any other country. It is the longest surviving continuous government in the world. And this system has been able to survive, and mend the wounds of, severe civil war. Abraham Lincoln was able throughout the Civil War to appeal to the pacifying and reconciling dream of union (rather than focusing primarily on the divisive slavery issue) because the union for which he spoke was of this self-amending, self-inquiring kind.

Beginning with the **Collaborative Inquiry** stage, all of the later stage organizing systems are frameworks that permit participants to create a variety of specific structures within them. The sciences, professional associations, trade associations, labor federations, and sports leagues all share something of this character. All of these are procedural frameworks that surround specific organizations. The argument here is that a specific organization can also identify itself primarily as such a procedural framework within which divisions, projects, and issues compete for attention and other resources.

Two basic questions arise about such procedural frameworks. First, are they truly self-regulating—that is, self-regulating in the service of some wider common good than their own self-aggrandizement? Put differently, are they truly self-amending—that is, self-amending in the sense that they can debate and potentially reform not just peripheral elements of their structure but also their fundamental assumptions?

Second, can organizations that truly encourage inquiry also succeed in practical, "bottom-line" terms? Or does the energy devoted to inquiry necessarily reduce the energy devoted to productivity, perhaps even "paralyzing" the organization?

There is no simple, historically persuasive answer to these questions. In asking them, we arrive at the leading edge of social evolution, a leading edge arrived at as long ago as in the Athens of the fifth century B.C. but a leading edge still little explored.

In his magisterial work *Politics and Markets: The World's Political-Economic Systems*, Charles Lindblom shows that no existing social systems encourage, much less guarantee, full freedom of inquiry. In this regard, he asks, "Can we expect . . . any society to debate its own fundamentals? Has there ever been one that did?"[4]

The fact that the United States passed the 14th amendment after the Civil War can be cited as a rare example of an organized system amending a fundamental structural element. But the debate was hardly nonviolent. Moreover, some would argue that the long-term success of the American government is due to the good fortune that its 6 percent of the world's population controls 42 percent of the world's wealth. And many would argue that "government" and "inefficiency" are synonymous, so that however well the U.S. government exemplifies inquiry systems characteristic of the **Collaborative Inquiry** stage of organizing, it does not serve as a useful model for businesses facing practical day-to-day demands and competition.

Obviously, it is difficult to reconcile the fundamental inquiry that establishes legitimacy with the timely action necessary for efficiency and effectiveness. Just how difficult is emphasized when we recognize that contemporary science—our foremost model of inquiry—is itself fundamentally inadequate as a guide. For scientific inquiry as we know it today:

1. Is conducted outside of "real time" pressures insofar as possible.
2. Emphasizes deductive rather than analogical reasoning.
3. Generates conclusions intended to amend general theories applicable across times and places, not specific actions uniquely appropriate here and now.[5]

Hence, scientific inquiry as we know it today would very likely paralyze an organization were executives to await its results before acting. Moreover, recommended actions would very likely not be appropriate to the unique elements of the situation. The later chapters of this book offer an introduction to *action inquiry*—a kind of analogical inquiry in the midst of daily pressures that enhances the timeliness of actions (and thus their legitimacy, effectiveness, *and* efficiency). The rest of this chapter offers some glimpses of organizations developing inquiry systems.

The first point to make, having just highlighted the difficulties of institutionalizing inquiry, is the practical bottom-line importance for organizations, once they have reached the **Systematic Productivity** stage, of creating such self-critical, self-amending, self-legitimizing systems. Many organizations have no external watchdog to keep them honest and sustain their legitimacy. First and foremost among these are the external watchdogs themselves—the press. Next are the supposedly self-regulating professionals such as doctors and accounting firms. In recent years, resentment, lawsuits, and insurance premiums have grown astronomically in response to the perceived arrogance, self-protectiveness, and destructiveness of these erstwhile hallowed industries. Accounting firms, fearful that they may lose their legislated monopoly over auditing, have developed new forms of mutual self-regulation including audits of one another. More and more newspapers are developing an ombudsman role to do investigative reporting on the way other reporters manage the stories they cover. These represent beginning efforts at creating inquiry systems.

An organization may also wish to develop inquiry systems in order to change its environment. However productive the organization may be, the environment may be reducing the organization's effectiveness. At the **Collaborative Inquiry** stage, the organization does not take the existing environment as a fixed constraint, just as it does not take its own structure for granted.

The Philippines Advertising Counselors, Inc., can serve as a useful illustration of a company that reframed the industry and market of which it was a part. In the 1960s, the senior executives of the company recognized that corruption within the industry as a whole was keeping both the industry and company small, unprofessional, and incompetent, with most large Philippine advertising accounts going to U.S. firms. In response, the company's senior executives initiated an industrywide trade association in the Philippines, developed a code of ethics, defined enforcement procedures within their own company, and adopted the motto "Profit with Honor." Today, the company is the largest in the industry in the Philippines, and both it and its Philippine competitors have significantly increased their market share in the Philippines in comparison with the American firms.[6]

Two other occasions when it can become practically important for an organization to develop beyond the **Systematic Productivity** stage occur when it decentralizes, or when a longtime chief executive who has molded the company's success approaches retirement. When a firm decentralizes, the president of each division appropriately holds operating responsibility for the systematic productivity of that division, and the corporate chief executive appropriately generates an inquiry system among the divisions that improves the corporation's *overall* efficiency, effectiveness, and legitimacy. Otherwise, the corporate chief executive's initiatives override and undermine the division presidents' authority, creating confusion and distrust.[7]

A new chief executive will inevitably change the tenor of an organization. If the former chief executive is credited with making the organization a major success, as Thomas Watson, Sr., was after 40 years as president of CTR–IBM, then organization members are likely to fear and resent the change, and this very attitude can become a stumbling block for the successor. In such a situation, the successor is probably best off not merely trying to continue in the former image, nor merely changing priorities, but rather honoring the predecessor and introducing a qualitatively new agenda which the strength of the company now makes possible.

This is what Thomas Watson, Jr., did during the decade between 1946 and 1956. Starting at IBM as a salesman, he became president in 1952 and chief executive officer in 1956. Watson, Sr., gradually stepped back, making John Phillips an interim president in 1949, then working directly with his son from 1952 on. Whereas Watson, Sr.'s, focus was on sales, the customer, and the existing business machine market (i.e., **Systematic Productivity**), Watson, Jr.'s, focus was more on research and development, the nascent computer industry, and the future (i.e., on inquiry systems and restructuring, characteristic of **Collaborative Inquiry**). Watson, Jr., doubled IBM's long-term debt in 1951–52 in order to enter the computer industry (we have seen how averse Watson, Sr., was to debt). He also agreed to the divisionalization of the company, first into two parts—Domestic and World Trade, his brother Dick becoming president of the latter. Then in 1956, he met in Williamsburg, Virginia, with 110 IBM top executives and together they decentralized IBM Domestic into five divisions, each with profit responsibility.

In giving up direct control, Watson, Jr., was exercising a qualitatively new kind of leadership. With this relaxation of tight control, IBM bolted forward in terms of bottom-line growth. It had taken Watson, Sr., four decades to build the company to $333 million in gross revenues. Watson, Jr., added an additional $333 million in gross revenues in three years.

This very brief sketch of a decade of change at IBM illustrates a successful succession of chief executives and a successful divisionalization of a company, facilitated by Watson, Jr.'s, exercise of a qualitatively different kind of vision and power from that of his father.

IBM's move from mechanical tabulators to electronic computers during that decade illustrates yet another practical reason why companies can gain by transforming to the **Collaborative Inquiry** stage of development. In a rapidly changing environment, any number of company members may see or think of opportunities for innovation. An effective company will seek to maximize the entrepreneurial sense of initiative and the executive sense of ownership and responsibility that its managers and even its workers feel in order to increase the likelihood of turning perceived opportunities into productive results. All the management innovations that come and go—Theory Y, Theory Z, 9,9 leadership, Quality Circles, QWL programs, matrix organizations, leveraged management buyouts, Employee Stock Option Plans, and worker cooperatives—are attempts from different angles to create **Collaborative Inquiry,** where authority is not merely exercised from the top down but rather shared, tested, and reestablished more widely.

The management innovations just cited can be arrayed along a spectrum from informal, interpersonal changes in management style (Theory Y, Theory Z, 9,9 leadership), to more formal, parallel structures that offer some power to lower level employees (Quality Circles, QWL programs, matrix organizing), to actual changes in the ownership structure of the firm (leveraged management buyouts, ESOPS, and worker cooperatives).

Of all these innovations that a particular firm can try at a particular time in its history, only worker cooperatives, in which all employees of the firm are citizens of the firm with equal voting rights, spreads the **Collaborative Inquiry** mode of organizing throughout the firm. It is not surprising that this is also the rarest of the nine innovations listed here, for it requires the deepest commitment to, and the greatest skill in implementing, **Collaborative Inquiry.**

The trouble with all these managerial innovations—the reason why they tend so often to turn into fast-fading fads—is that they are rarely undertaken with sufficient respect for the fundamental commitment required to accomplish this developmental transformation. One or two elements of **Collaborative Inquiry** are emphasized, others are neglected, and the time scale necessary for a large organization to accomplish such a transformation is severely underestimated. The chief executive, or whoever is initially championing the managerial innovation, may attempt to control its adoption by a unilateral exercise of power, unaware that this only reinforces the existing, top-down, deductive approach to authority and power. Or else, the innovation's champion may altogether forfeit attention to existing power realities and production requirements in his or her enthusiasm for the ideal of **Collaborative Inquiry,** succeeding only in losing credibility day by day.

An organization that has fully evolved to the **Collaborative Inquiry** stage would have gradually interwoven all of the following characteristics:

Characteristics of Collaborative Inquiry

1. Explicit shared reflection about the corporate dream/mission and actuality/history in the wider social context (recapitulating **Conception**).
2. Open rather than masked interpersonal relations, with disclosure, support, and confrontation of apparent value differences (recapitulating **Investments**).
3. Systematic evaluation and feedback of corporate and individual performance on multiple indexes (recapitulating **Incorporation**).
4. Direct facing and creative resolution of paradoxes (which otherwise become polarized conflicts): inquiry-productivity, freedom-control, quantity-quality, and so forth (recapitulating **Experiments**).
5. Interactive development of, and commitment to, unique, self-amending strategies and structures appropriate to this particular organization at this particular historical moment (recapitulating **Systematic Productivity**).

As the foregoing chart shows, the process of transforming an organization from the **Systematic Productivity** stage to **Collaborative Inquiry** is a process of explicitly recapitulating, and thereby potentially correcting, the organization's earlier implicit developmental history. In other words, the organizational development of **Collaborative Inquiry** is in some ways analogous to an individual's development of self-reflective capacity through therapy or some other form of self-study.[8]

It is not by chance that the five characteristics of **Collaborative Inquiry** describe a process of transformation rather than a "steady state" logic arrived at after some transformation. In moving toward **Collaborative Inquiry** and still later stages, an organization is developing dynamic structures, strategies, and systems that recognize and support appropriate transformations rather than resisting them. Means and ends cease to be dichotomous qualities and become closely interrelated instead. Paradoxically, collaborative inquiry is the appropriate means for generating **Collaborative Inquiry.** The organization is becoming self-educating, self-restructuring.

One manager—the youngest corporate vice president at a *Fortune* 100 electronics firm—describes how he organizes business meetings according to a dynamic strategy that encourages transformations within each meeting. Here is an example of collaborative inquiry being used on a micro scale, as a means to attain the end of shared ownership in the decisions reached at the meeting. Moreover, this vice president's mandate over the next five years is to generate a general change in the culture of the company so that its information and performance evaluation systems cultivate, highlight, and reward innovation and excellence. Hence, his long-term, organizationwide mandate is also to lead the company from the **Systematic Productivity** stage of development to the **Collaborative Inquiry** stage.

The electronics firm vice president does not, of course, use the language of this book, but the stages he describes correspond remarkably to the developmental steps presented here. An undergraduate mathematics major, this manager regards the Pythagorean octave as organizing all activity. Of business meetings, he says:

> The first note "do" is the leader's vision for the whole meeting. It has to be both crisp and inspiring. It's got to surprise people just a little—jog them awake, make them reconsider what they came in prepared to do. [Conception]
>
> "Re" is the first response, the first chorus from the group. The leader has got to allow for this if he wants a creative, committed meeting. How he choreographs that first response determines how far the meeting can go. [Investments]
>
> "Mi" is the first concrete decision of the meeting. If it's taken early on and makes sense to everyone, there's a general loosening

up, and the rest of the meeting is likely to fly. **[Incorporation]**

A lot of meetings end there, but if you want to go further, you've got to realize there's a big interval between "mi" and "fa." The leader can best bridge this interval with a new structure for the meeting. "Fa" is primarily the group's note again, so the leader's structure should be something that brings out the chorus, something like breaking into subgroups on different issues. **[Experiments]** (*He goes on to discuss the rest of the "meeting octave."*)

But the actual meeting can also be viewed as the middle part of the octave between the two intervals. In this larger perspective, the premeeting preparation is the first part of the octave and the postmeeting follow-up is the final part.

At the macro end of social organizing, one suggestion for national industrial policy that emerges from attention to this whole developmental theory and to the **Collaborative Inquiry** stage in particular is to replace the antitrust division of the Justice Department and the antitrust law with legislation that mandates certain forms of self-regulation within each industry among the mature, large-market-share companies. The largest companies controlling 25 percent of the market might be subject to the most demanding self-regulating disciplines; the next largest companies comprising the next 25 percent of the market would be subject to a somewhat less demanding set of disciplines, and so forth. Smaller companies could voluntarily implement such systems if they saw it as in their interest to do so. Some such system would help to turn regulation from a nasty, negative, government function to a positive function of professional and trade associations.

CASE STUDY OF THE EFFECT OF INQUIRY SYSTEMS

The following case illustrates the five self-educating characteristics of the **Collaborative Inquiry** stage on the middle scale of an entire organization over a several-year period. The case describes a unique MBA program that embodies these five characteristics, teaches students how to enact them, and thereby aids their development toward later stage managerial styles.

Some readers may initially feel that creating a self-educating MBA program may be easier than creating a self-educating business or political agency. After all, education is a priority for a school but not necessarily for other settings. Such readers can look forward to Chapter 16, which offers an extended case about the "fits and starts" of a *Fortune* 100 manufacturing firm transforming toward self-educating **Collaborative Inquiry.**

Ironically, however, schools are no more likely to be self-educating and self-restructuring organizations than businesses, hospitals, or governmental agencies. Indeed, universities, with their system of tenure for professors, are in many ways structured to withstand change and to protect the individual's right not to be influenced by feedback. Let us look very briefly at where most universities stand in relation to the five characteristics of **Collaborative Inquiry** (shared reflection, open interaction, performance feedback on multiple indicators, creative paradox resolution, and unique, self-amending structures).

With regard to shared reflection, even though professors are paid to be reflective *within* their own disciplinary specialty, they are no more likely than other managers or professionals to engage in explicit, shared reflection *across* departmental lines about the corporate dream of their school or university as a whole. With regard to openness, perhaps because professors are supposed to *think* in theoretical and objective terms and be open to new data, when they come to *act* in their own institution the subjectivity, the petty particularism, and the behind-the-back qualities of their interpersonal relations are frequently more evident than openness. With regard to performance evaluation, end-of-the-semester student course evaluations are nowadays common, but it is frequently months before the professor sees the results, and the results rarely have any direct effects on salary increments or promotion, much less the professor's behavior when he or she next teaches the same course. With regard to creatively resolving paradoxes, the great paradox of university education is how eternal, dispassionate inquiry can inform the immediate, passionate action choices we each face in our daily lives. In individual courses and in the overall structure of university life, this paradox is rarely posed, more rarely faced, and still more rarely resolved.

All in all, a strong argument can be made that it is harder to create a self-educating school than a self-educating business. The argument is supported by the fact that the collaborative inquiry systems of the MBA program to be described are unique.

With these introductory reflections, we can turn to the case itself. After its first 15 years of existence, a certain graduate school of management had achieved national accreditation for its MBA program—one measure of reaching the **Systematic Productivity** stage of organizing. Over the following two years, faculty reexamined the school's mission and curriculum, ultimately agreeing on a whole package of major changes.[9] The changes included new required courses such as International Management and a mandate that students spend almost 50 percent more time in class than before. But the main effect of the changes was to make more explicit the faculty's commitment to teach students not just how to *think about management*, but how to *manage*—how to *act effectively* in multinational settings. Overall, then, these changes represented *characteristic 1* of the **Collaborative Inquiry** stage—shared reflection leading to a new and more focused statement of mission, truer to the original corporate dream.

This qualitatively new mission was to be accomplished through a series of inquiry systems interwoven into productive systems. For example, most management schools encourage informal student study groups to prepare daily assignments or term projects. This management school formalized the study group process by assigning a heterogeneous group of students to each group and assigning it two semester-long projects, making these groups a closer analogue to business settings with assigned colleagues and multiple, competing projects.

Several systems surrounded these project groups. A second-year student with special training was assigned as a consultant to each group to provide the members with an external perspective on their efficacy in working together. The presence of the student-consultant increased the likelihood that the groups would develop open interpersonal relations (*characteristic 2* of **Collaborative Inquiry**).

Also, each group member was required to take a leadership role. There were two project leaders, a meeting leader, an evaluation leader who helped the group evaluate itself systematically, and a process leader who helped redirect the group at any time in its meetings when it appeared unproductive. These roles helped to assure systematic evaluation and feedback of individual and group performance (*characteristic 3*). (Note that these methods of organizing project groups can be used, with minor variations, in virtually any large organization. They also match the kind of setting recommended earlier [Chapter 6] as helpful to the continuing development of managers at the **Diplomat** stage.)

In addition, several different course papers required students to study their own actions in their study groups, to evaluate their leadership effectiveness from different theoretical perspectives, and later to experiment with new actions that promised greater effectiveness. Thus, young managers were not merely thrown into difficult action situations to learn by sinking or swimming but rather were surrounded by organizational systems that encouraged inquiry, documentation, feedback, and experimentation. They were exposed not only to hard knocks but also to a school of hard knocks.

In their second semester, students were required to take still more responsibility for their actions. They selected their own consulting teams this time, developed their own internal leadership structure, developed their own research and consulting relationship with a local business or not-for-profit organization, and contracted for support from a faculty advisor and a second-year consultant. These teams were to be responsible not just for presenting their clients with a valid diagnosis of whatever problems they had originally contracted to study, but for doing so in ways that encouraged implementation and greater effectiveness on the part of the clients. Thus, students were being asked to face directly the paradox that most academic settings avoid— namely, how to wed reflection and action, inquiry and productivity, eternal validity and immediate effectiveness (*characteristic 4* of **Collaborative Inquiry**).

The tensions of this paradox were brought to a crescendo at the end of the semester, just before final exams. The projects ended, not only with the traditional academic paper but also with a public oral presentation competition, judged by visiting executives and scholars for both analytic credibility and presentational effectiveness, with both video and verbal feedback to the teams. Students received no academic credit for participating in this competition but sometimes won positions at graduation because companies viewed their performance in the oral competition as a more significant predictor of on-the-job success than course grades.

In a still more fundamental innovation, the program as a whole was treated as an ongoing inquiry process. Faculty who taught within the program participated in public midsemester course and program evaluations. The faculty team discussed the results of these midsemester evaluations together within one week after they were received and decided, in turn, how they could best be discussed with students. The formal and informal discussions of the data—along with the subsequent change or lack of change in both student and faculty attitudes and actions—would highlight the stakes, the difficulties, and the skills involved in acting effectively to generate organizational change. By holding up a mirror that reflected the organization in action, the ivory tower would be transforming itself into the real world. Just how much of a shock to the system this can be, we will examine more closely below.

On a still larger or longer term scale, this MBA program planned to avoid territoriality and to institutionalize inquiry by appointing a new faculty team every two years and asking it to review the program and amend its structures. Such frequent role turnover is, of course, not at all unusual in most institutions. More unusual, the program carried on longitudinal research to test how students responded to the new mission, structures, and activities; to test whether these in fact generated developmental changes in students toward later developmental perspectives; and to test whether such movement correlated, in turn, with greater managerial effectiveness once graduates reentered the work world. In all these ways, the program as a whole institutionalized a self-educating process that encouraged all participants to reflect in the midst of action, to do research and seek feedback on their performance, and to develop greater interpersonal effectiveness.

Longitudinal Research Findings on the MBA Program

In its first four years, the longitudinal research uncovered several facts of particular interest. Most concretely, they tell us something about how the program actually operated and how students and the wider environment responded to the changes. Standing back a little further, we can learn something about how an organization generates change in the developmental perspectives of its members. Standing back still further and looking at the organization as a whole, we can see how an institutional inquiry process can raise new questions about an organization's mission and strategy.

The research discovered that the first two classes to go through the restructured program registered much higher overall satisfaction at graduation than prior classes.

Second, it showed that students operating at the later developmental stages of managing performed managerial tasks more effectively than those operating at earlier stages. Also, project groups with more students at later stages of development received better grades on projects and better ratings from their consultants with regard to efficient use of time, effective decision making, and support for one another's learning.

Third, it showed that no student ever moved more than one developmental transformation during the two years of the program, and that on average the program generated no developmental change in its students. Furthermore, it showed that almost all of the (relatively few) students who moved toward later developmental perspectives during their two years in the program were ones who not only completed the first-year activities described above, but who also voluntarily took an intensive course in Developmental Theory and Consulting Practice during the summer between their two years and then, during their second year, served as consultants to first-year project groups.

Fourth, and finally, the institutional research showed a dramatic change in the developmental position of students choosing to *enter* the program, as the following table shows:

Developmental Position	Entering Class of:	
	1980	1983
Prior to **Achiever** Stage of Development	58%	25%
Achiever	40	50
Strategist	2	25

Taken together, these findings indicate that this restructured MBA program came to be perceived by applicants as very different from the former program, attracted a different group of students to the program, and was experienced as more satisfactory than the former program by the students who went through it.

The findings are also consistent with the notion that later

developmental perspectives generate greater managerial effectiveness, as well as the notion that organizational inquiry systems can support development toward those perspectives. At the same time, the findings seem to offer clues about how long and intense an individual's commitment to acquiring new action skills must be before a measurable change in developmental position is likely to occur. One year of occasional, more or less required participation in organizational inquiry systems of the sort described here is *not* enough. Two years of highly committed participation, chosen by the MBA candidates who became project group consultants during their second year, can be enough.

These research findings in some ways serve to confirm the appropriateness and efficacy of this organization's mission, strategies, and operations. The findings also show that the organization changed in a way that invited students at later developmental stages to attend, but not in a way that provoked developmental change in most of the students in attendance. These findings in turn raised new questions for the faculty and administration: did they wish to redefine the school's mission yet again to include within it promoting this kind of development? Did they wish to construct additional organizational inquiry systems in order to more broadly support students' development? In this way, an institutional research process can function over the long run as an organizational inquiry system that raises fundamental questions about organizational mission and strategy.

In the meantime, the unique mission, strategy, and operations of this management school brought it to the attention of other management school deans who changed their ranking of the school from below the top 100 to among the top 30. Hence, in this MBA program, the inquiry systems characteristic of the **Collaborative Inquiry** stage fostered dramatic improvement in the school's visibility and competitive position.

An Illustration within the Illustration

The very distant overview so far offered of the organizational inquiry systems built into this MBA program does not convey the liveliness, the subtlety, and the controversy that institutionalizing inquiry demands and creates. A closer look at one of these inquiry systems—the public midsemester evaluation process—can show more clearly what is at stake: how organizational inquiry systems surface not only *secondary* data about other times and places to be analyzed reflectively but also *primary* data about one's own effectiveness in, and about the very definition of, the ongoing situation in which one is currently participating. All of us implicitly and incompletely use such data to orient ourselves from moment to moment. But explicitly bringing such primary data to the surface and testing their validity is unusual in most organizations and offers both significant risks and significant potential returns.

Explicitly bringing primary data to the surface can agitate us because it will, from time to time, inevitably mean making conflict open. As implied in the chapters on the earlier managerial styles, few managers can resolve open conflict openly and effectively. Many managers assume that open conflict can only have a negative effect on individuals' self-esteem, on esteem for the organization, and on the eventual outcomes of the ongoing situation. At the same time, explicitly bringing primary data to the surface can correct undetected problems, generate restructuring, and increase effectiveness. An organization cannot operate at the **Collaborative Inquiry** stage unless its leadership is effective at managing open conflict and unless its personnel in general are becoming increasingly effective at doing so.

Let us examine the operation of the public midsemester evaluation system in this MBA program in order to form a clearer impression of the risks and opportunities.

After the first midsemester evaluation in the fall of 1980, both students and faculty changed their behavior in the one course that received a negative evaluation, and the learning environment in that course improved markedly during the second half of the semester. In the first eight semesters of its use, the midsemester evaluation served primarily to confirm the overwhelmingly positive response of students to the program as a whole, thus strengthening the faculty's confidence, while permitting numerous "fine-tuning" adjustments which further improved collective morale. In particular, 38 of 48 courses received predominantly positive evaluations. Of the other 10 courses, the general consensus was that the learning atmosphere of 5 improved significantly the same semester and of 3 more during the subsequent offering. Moreover, of the faculty members who stood for tenure in the first four years after the restructuring of the program, all those who were (or had been) members of the program's faculty team received tenure, while the only ones not to receive tenure had not been members of the program team.

These facts no doubt played a role in sustaining this organizational inquiry system, but they did not in any sense make it "safe" on every occasion. Consider the following series of events.

During one semester, the informal information network suggested there might be two generally problematic courses. Students were invited to fill out the midterm evaluations overnight, in response to a student request for more time to do the questionnaire justice. Less than half the class returned the questionnaires the next day. Later inquiries indicated that some felt they were unimportant because they had not been thoroughly discussed the previous semester (when no program elements had been identified as problematic by a majority). Others felt that the faculty was treating the questionnaires as unimportant by not allocating enough class time to fill them out. These details suggest how easy it is to throw organizational inquiry systems off track.

Of the questionnaires returned, 4 of the 39 responses could be interpreted as personally insulting to the faculty member with whom students experienced the most dissatisfaction, and all the responses were critical of this particular course. This faculty member, in turn, had the least experience with the program, had no previous experience with receiving and responding to data about ongoing activities, and had created a course with little predetermined structure.

This faculty member's inclination was to dismiss the data on the grounds that it was not complete and that students had misused the evaluation privilege. A two-hour faculty meeting devoted to the question of how to treat this data seemed to influence him not to dismiss the data out of hand. But when he actually discussed the matter with his two sections, he chided them for their juvenile approach to the freedom and responsibility demanded by his course structure and by the evaluation process. And he invited no discussion of the matter.

TOTAL MUTUAL ALIENATION!!! All student suspicions about the inauthenticity of this organizational inquiry system and about the unapproachability and incompetence of this faculty member were instantaneously confirmed. (Events like this one frequently lead to the breakdown of labor-management cooperation efforts, such as Quality Circles, in business settings.)

Three aspects of the action skills and systems interwoven throughout the program partially retrieved this situation. First, some students had developed enough trust in the program as a whole and enough action competence to be able to insist politely on continuing the discussion for just a moment, to apologize for the personal remarks, to verify that these represented only a small minority of the comments, to specify one or two concrete instances where they believed changes might enhance the achievement of the instructor's goals, and to ask whether he would like to explore these possibilities outside the class session. This action dramatically changed the tone of the immediate setting, reinforced the sense of competence and empowerment of those taking the action, and eventually resulted in some helpful small changes in the course.

Second, over the next two weeks, three other faculty members did use the feedback from the midterm evaluations, as well as other primary data as they occurred in classes, to explore more deeply into the roots of disharmonies and invent creative, nonpolarizing solutions. In the mood of heightened alertness on the part of students (and faculty) about whether the program was "for real," these faculty actions more than counterbalanced the earlier event.

Third, as these events were taking place, students were simultaneously at the point in their consulting projects with business clients where they were recognizing, in quicker or slower succession:

1. That there were serious differences in the ways they and their clients defined the business problems to be solved, despite earlier effort at consensual problem definition.
2. That clients tended to be unaware of how their own interactional patterns created and maintained the technical and strategic problems they knew they faced.
3. That the student consulting teams themselves by and large had yet to develop the alertness, courage, and skill to use both primary and secondary data to help their clients see and change the relationship among the technical, strategic, and interactional layers of their business problems.

In general, these insights served to increase students' humility about their own action effectiveness and to decrease their harshness in judging others' (similar) lack of effectiveness.

This case within a case illustrates many features of the organizational inquiry systems characteristic of **Collaborative Inquiry.** It illustrates the many benefits gained from the midsemester evaluation process over a four-year period. It also illustrates the inevitable difficulties that organizational inquiry systems encounter because their role is to surface unresolved issues and because most of the organizational participants are at personal stages of development which do not fully appreciate the value of inquiry and restructuring in order to increase effectiveness and legitimacy.

Probably the central point is that, although they can have routine, bureaucratized features such as the regular timing and the regular questions of the MBA midsemester evaluation, *the purpose of organizational inquiry systems is to break through the routine and the preconceived to the unique reality of the present situation that is not being adequately addressed by participants' personal and institutional routines.* A paradoxical corollary to this central point is that *there is no way to guarantee the safety, efficacy, and justice of organizational inquiry systems ahead of time. The best one can do ahead of time is to construct a mutually reinforcing network of such systems.* But even such a network cannot guarantee appropriate and efficacious change ahead of time. All this network can do is to provide more opportunities for individuals to exercise their action skills once the net catches an undigested chunk of reality.

In other words, *the safety and efficacy of organizational inquiry systems are totally dependent on the present alertness, commitment, and action skills of the individual participants.* Thus, the turn back from the moment of "TOTAL MUTUAL ALIENATION!!!" in the foregoing case was due, first and foremost, to the very risky on-the-spot intervention by several students just as the instructor was attempting to avoid discussion of the evaluation data. It was due, secondly, to the risks that other faculty members took in the days following to work differently with students on the data about their courses.

Such risky and dramatic events are inevitable when an organization begins moving, however partially, toward the **Collaborative Inquiry** stage of development, but middle managers and top executives are rarely prepared for them. Whether they approach managing as **Diplomats,** as **Technicians,** or as **Achievers,** most managers react to conflict by trying to smooth it over, suppress it, or win against it, rather than viewing it as an opportunity for personal and organizational self-education.

From a conventional point of view, it will appear that these comments amount to saying that in fact we cannot institutional-ize inquiry. And certainly, in the common way that we tend to think about what "institutionalizing" anything means, we can-not institutionalize organizational inquiry systems. We com-monly think of "institutionalizing" something as developing a "routine" for it that remains unaffected by particular events or people. Formal rituals, job descriptions, organizational charts, bureaucratic procedures, bodies of law, theories in the reflective sciences, and algorithms in artificial intelligence research are all examples of such "routines." The particular is subordinated to, and organized by, the universal—"the rule of law, not of men," we say with pride (except when we think of Eichman). The movement toward this kind of institutionalization has been the wonder and the horror of the past five centuries.

Explicit and public organizational inquiry systems can oper-ate helpfully only in conditions where relatively well-functioning goal-oriented systems, reflecting the **Systematic Productivity** stage of organizing, already exist. If goal-oriented systems do not ex-ist, or are not functioning well, explicit and public organizational inquiry systems will reveal an undigestible number of anoma-lies. Considering how difficult it was for the MBA program de-scribed above to digest the anomaly that its midsemester evalu-ation process revealed, one can imagine how short-lived the entire experiment would have been had not the goal-oriented systems of the program been strengthened during the restructuring pro-cess, and had not the overwhelming majority of the feedback about this program over the previous several years been posi-tive.

NOTES

1. N. Odebrecht, (Foguel, E., trans.), *Survival, Growth and Perpetuity* (Sal-vador, Brazil: Odebrecht Foundation, 1985).

2. Ibid., p. 113.

3. Ibid., p. 153.

4. C. Lindblom, *Politics and Markets: The World's Political-Economic Systems* (New York: Basic Books, 1977), p. 211.

5. For more extended discussions of why contemporary science cannot, in principle, generate more effective action, see W. Torbert, "Why Educational Research Has Been So Uneducational: The Case for a New Model of Social Science Based on Collaborative Inquiry," in P. Reason and J. Rowan, eds.,

Human Inquiry: A Sourcebook of New Paradigm Research (London: Wiley, 1981), and "Executive Mind, Timely Action," *ReVision* 4, no. 1 (1983), pp. 3–21.

6. This brief illustration is drawn from an extensive, unpublished analysis of P.A.C., Inc., by its former vice president, Humberto Gonzalez. I appreciate his permission to draw from his paper.

7. Chris Argyris illustrates this problem in some depth in "Skilled Incompetence," *Harvard Business Review* (Sep.–Oct. 1986), pp. 74–79.

8. On self-study within organizations, see S. Bruyn, "The Community Self-Study: Worker Self-Management versus the New Class," *Review of Social Economy*, 1984, pp. 388–413; and W. Torbert, "The Role of Self-Study in Improving Managerial and Institutional Effectiveness," *Human Systems Management* 2 (1981), pp. 72–82.

9. See Torbert, "The Role of Self-Study," for details of this two-year process.

The Strategist

Managers at the **Strategist** stage of development make sense of their world and take actions in a manner analogous to organizations at the **Collaborative Inquiry** stage. Such managers find delight in paradoxes, anomalies, and unique events. They respond flexibly to the historical process as it generates events, not just to goal-related outcomes and measures. They develop a commitment to an explicit theoretical structure that helps them to interpret events creatively and to generate new order and organization. This theory seems to them the key, simultaneously, to their ability to learn and to their power.

In the course of earlier chapters, we have already referred to the **Strategist** stage several times. The movement from the **Achiever** stage toward the **Strategist** stage includes a process of becoming aware that different persons, organizations, and cultures are not just different from one another in visible ways but also in terms of the frames through which they interpret events. The evolving **Strategist** begins to realize that all frames, including his or her own, are relative. No frame is easily demonstrable as superior to another because there are no objective criteria outside all frames. Frames are constructed through human interaction, not given by nature. These sorts of realizations, experienced not just as intellectual statements but as emotional truths, attune the evolving **Strategist** more deeply than managers at any prior stage to the uniqueness of persons and situations. But they also leave the evolving **Strategist** radically unanchored in any particular, taken-for-granted frame. This person may feel virtually paralyzed at moments in terms of taking action. Hence, the deep concern on his or her part to develop an explicit theory or frame that makes order out of the chaos. The easiest way to resolve this dilemma is to adopt an existing frame from one of the earlier developmental stages, or from some philosophy or religion or political ideology, gaining a sense of enhanced control because you now control the frame rather than the frame controlling you. This seemed to be the tone of "Mercury's" story about his adventures with "Nicky No-Mind" at The Bank in Chapter 4 on the **Opportunist.** One wonders whether David Stockman, whose approach we glanced at in Chapter 8 on the **Technician,** is not an evolving **Strategist** dressed in **Technician's** clothing. We also mentioned earlier that Henry Kissinger might represent the **Strategist** perspective. Let us examine his way of managing more closely.

Listen to Kissinger's voice, as he writes about his years in the White House. Compare his preoccupations to those of Harold Geneen in the chapter on the **Achiever,** and get an initial taste for some of the differences between the **Achiever's** managerial style and that of the **Strategist.** The first excerpt focuses on Kissinger's relationship to Melvin Laird, Nixon's secretary of defense. The second excerpt describes early moves in relation to mainland China that eventually led to Nixon's visit.

> Provided he was allowed some reasonable range for saving face by maneuvering to a new position without embarrassment, [Secretary of Defense] Laird accepted bureaucratic setbacks without rancor. But he insisted on his day in court. In working with him, intellectual arguments were only marginally useful and direct orders were suicidal. I eventually learned that it was safest to begin a battle with Laird by closing off insofar as possible all his bureaucratic or Congressional escape routes, provided I could figure them out, which was not always easy. Only then would I broach substance. But even with such tactics I lost as often as I won.

> * * * * *

> On November 26 I authorized an additional signal, proposed by the State Department, by which the decision to end the destroyer

patrol would be leaked to Chinese officials in Hong Kong. Thus began an intricate minuet between us and the Chinese so delicately arranged that both sides could always maintain that they were not in contact, so stylized that neither side needed to bear the onus of an initiative, so elliptical that existing relationships on both sides were not jeopardized.[1]

Remember Geneen's hatred of office politics and his overriding concern with "unshakable facts." Compare Geneen's bent with Kissinger's attentiveness to subtle political minuets and the qualitative symbolism of unique actions, such as leaking the decision to end the destroyer patrol to Chinese officials. Compare Geneen's obsession with objectivity and substance, with Kissinger's easy movement between substance and process (in the case of Laird's low tolerance for intellectual arguments)—and this despite the fact that Kissinger came from an academic background and might have been expected to be especially identified with the virtue of intellectual substance.

The following excerpt continues these themes and adds to them a clear delight in paradox. Kissinger evidently senses that a paradoxical understanding of situations is likely to come closer to their essence than an "objective" description based on quantitative measures, such as that on which Geneen bases his confidence.

> During [a] period of crisis the elements from which policy is shaped suddenly become fluid. In the resulting upheaval the statesman must act under constant pressure. Paradoxically, this confers an unusual capacity for creative action; everything suddenly depends on the ability to dominate and impose coherence on confused and seemingly random occurrences. Ideally this should occur without the use of force; however, sometimes one can avoid the use of force only by threatening it.
>
> Some may visualize crisis management as a frenzied affair in which key policymakers converge on the White House in their limousines, when harrassed officials are bombarded by nervous aides rushing in and out with the latest flash cables. Oddly enough, I have found this not to be accurate; periods of crisis, to be sure, involve great tension but they are also characterized by a strange tranquillity. All the petty day-to-day details are stripped away; they are either ignored, postponed, or handled by subordinates. Personality clashes are reduced, too much is usually at stake for nor-

mal jealousies to operate. In a crisis only the strongest strive for responsibility; the rest are intimidated by the knowledge that failure will demand a scapegoat. Many hide behind a consensus they will be reluctant to shape; others concentrate on registering objections that will provide alibis after the event. The few prepared to grapple with circumstances are usually undisturbed in the eye of the hurricane.

* * * * *

Of course, Chou [En-lai] and I used each other; that is on one level the purpose of diplomacy. But another of its purposes is to bring about a compatibility of aims; only the amateur or the insecure thinks he can permanently outmaneuver his opposite number. In foreign policy one must never forget that one deals in recurring cycles and on consecutive issues with the same people; trickery sacrifices structure to temporary benefit. Reliability is the cement of international order even among opponents; pettiness is the foe of permanence. This Chou En-lai grasped, and it enabled us to achieve not identical aims but comparable analyses of what was needed to use the international equilibrium to our mutual benefit at this particular moment in history.[2]

Compared to Geneen's overriding concern with clearly *quantifiable outcome measures*, Kissinger focuses on *qualitatively unique moments of history* when *creative action* is possible. He is vividly aware of the multiplicity of perspectives that the different participants in a situation bring to it and also, therefore, of the constant and inevitable interplay of substance and process in human affairs. And precisely because he is witnessing the interplay of fluidity and solidity through which new meanings are created, Kissinger cannot rely on a taken-for-granted set of categories that grants things their "objective" meaning. Instead, he emphasizes the importance of an *explicit theory* (in this case, balance of power issues which link all other apparently unrelated matters) for generating meaning and consistency. He champions this theory, since it is by no means accepted by all and since it is for him the foundation of order:

> The management of a balance of power is a permanent undertaking, not an exertion that has a foreseeable end. To a great extent it is a psychological phenomenon; if an equality of power is per-

ceived it will not be tested. Calculations must include potential as well as actual power, not only the possession of power but the will to bring it to bear. . . .

In foreign policy there is no escaping the need for an integrating conceptual framework. . . . The most important initiatives require painstaking preparation; results take months or years to emerge. Success requires a sense of history, an understanding of manifold forces not within our control and a broad view of the fabric of events. . . . A conceptual framework—which "links" events . . . in a firm conception of the national interest . . .—is an essential tool. The absence of linkage produces exactly the opposite of freedom of action; policymakers are forced to respond to parochial interests, buffeted by pressures without a fixed compass.[3]

The sense of having the intellectual key to interpreting reality and at the same time of being in a position of social power in which one is creating meaning—creating social reality—stimulates arrogance. The Hegelian view that one lives at the end of history, that one *is* the end of history, that the future emanates from one's own actions, comes naturally to the **Strategist.** The line between good and evil becomes fluid, too, under pressure, and the **Strategist** can easily persuade himself that he is the arbiter of good and evil, the Lone Ranger, masked but benign. Listen to the following excerpt of an interview between Oriana Fallaci and Kissinger in 1972:

O.F.: Dr. Kissinger, how do you explain the incredible moviestar status you enjoy? . . . Have you a theory on this matter?

H.K.: Yes, but I won't tell you. . . . Why should I as long as I'm still in the middle of my work? Rather, you tell me yours.

O.F.: I'm not sure, Dr. Kissinger. I'm looking for one through this interview. And I don't find it. I suppose that at the root of everything there's your success. I mean, like a chess player, you've made two or three good moves. China, first of all. People like chess players who checkmate the king.

H.K.: Yes, China has been a very important element in the mechanics of my success. And yet that's not the main point. The main point . . . Well yes, I'll tell you. What do I care? The main point arises from the fact that I've always acted alone. Americans like that immensely. Americans like the cowboy who leads the wagon train by riding ahead alone on his horse, the cowboy who rides all alone into the town, the village, with his horse and nothing else. Maybe even without a pistol, since he doesn't shoot. He acts, that's all, by being in the right place at the right time. In short, a Western.[4]

Of course, the contrast between Geneen and Kissinger is heightened by the fact that the one is operating in the realm of business and the other is operating in the realm of international relations. But a business manager can express the same appreciation as Kissinger of reality as a fluid dance and of the power of the heroic individual to mold it through timely action. Lee Iacocca puts it this way:

> If I had to sum up in one word the qualities that make a good manager, I'd say that it all comes down to decisiveness. You can use the fanciest computers in the world and you can gather all the charts and numbers, but in the end you have to bring all your information together, set up a timetable, and *act*.
>
> That's what life is all about—timing. . . . Nothing stands still in this world. I like to go duck hunting, where constant movement and change are facts of life. You can aim at a duck and get it in your sights, but the duck is always moving. *In order to hit the duck, you have to move your gun* [italics in original].
>
> But a committee faced with a major decision can't always move as quickly as the events it's trying to respond to. By the time the committee is ready to shoot, the duck has flown away. . . . My policy has always been to be democratic all the way to the point of decision. Then I become the ruthless comander. "Okay, I've heard everybody," I say. "Now here's what we're going to do."[5]

Here, once again but in a very different voice, we have the awareness of the paradoxical political minuet (this time integrating democratic and autocratic leadership styles). And here, once again, we have the vivid awareness of movement and change, this time dressed in the homespun metaphor of duck hunting. Moreover, if Kissinger was our early 1970s apotheosis of the heroic individual, Iacocca is certainly our early 1980s version. The Chrysler television ads featuring Iacocca symbolized the appeal of this kind of heroism, especially when the individual can be seen as individualizing the company he represents and challenging consumers to individualize themselves and become **Strategic** managers in their decision about what car to buy:

At the time, these ads were pretty unusual. But given our situation, we needed something dramatic. Due to circumstances beyond our control, Chrysler already had an identity all its own. We were already perceived as being very different from the rest of the American auto industry.

In marketing terms, the choice we faced was simple—either we could try to join the crowd and become one of the boys, or we could accept our separate identity and try to make it work to our advantage. By featuring the chairman in our ads, we chose the second course.

In the television ads, as in the print ads that preceded them, we decided to deal directly with the public's reservations and doubts. It was no secret that American consumers had a low opinion of American cars. Most people believed that German and Japanese cars were inherently better than anything Detroit was turning out.

We let them know right off the bat that was no longer the case. And we backed up our claim with an offer of $50 to any customer who compared one of our cars with anyone else's—even if they ended up buying from the competition.

At the same time, we were careful not to be *too* bold. We wanted to project a spirit of confidence but not arrogance. Given the perception of Chrysler products, we didn't want to claim directly that Chrysler made the best cars—although that's what we believed.

Instead, we wanted the customer to come to that decision on his own. And so we maintained that anyone who was looking for a new car ought to at least *consider* one of ours. We believed that the quality of our cars would be apparent to anyone who checked them out. If we could only get enough customers into the showrooms, our sales would increase accordingly. And that's what happened.[6]

Elements of the Strategist's Managerial Style

Awareness of paradox and contradiction	Recognizes importance of principle, contract, theory, and judgment—
Process oriented as well as goal oriented	not just rules and customs—for making good decisions
High value on individuality, unique market niches, particular historical moments	Fascinated by complex interweaving of emotional dependence and independence in relationships
Aware that what one sees depends upon one's world view, relativistic	Creative conflict resolution
Enjoys playing a variety of roles	Aware of dark side, of profundity of evil, and tempted by its power
Witty, good-natured humor	

How common is the **Strategist** style among managers today? The three studies of managers found the **Strategist** comprised 14 percent of the senior manager sample, 3 percent of the junior manager sample, and none the supervisory sample. (No managers at all were found at any later developmental stage.) In his study of consumer values, Mitchell estimated that 14 percent were "Inner-directed," his comparable category. He described this market segment as the most heterogeneous of all the segments—as bimodal in income and age, as individualistic, experiential and active, with global perspective. Its buying behavior is oriented toward durable, repairable, aesthetically satisfying, one-of-a-kind goods, and toward activities that invite active participation. Mitchell projected this segment as the fastest growing of all the segments, predicting that it would more than double in size between 1978 and 1988.

EVOLVING TOWARD THE STRATEGIST STAGE

How does a manager based in the **Achieving** style begin to move toward the **Strategic** managerial style? And what are the possible rewards to the organization in supporting such development?

One motivating event for this developmental move is a manager's transition from middle management to top management—from the relatively well-ordered world of following organizational policies to the more fluid and fiery world of creating organizational policies and helping the organization make its way in its never completely defined environment. But the reverse can happen just as well: a manager's personal development toward the **Strategist** style may make him or her more interested in, and more appealing for, a senior executive role. Or the two factors can be thoroughly interwoven as in the following case:

> Megan—a successful middle manager for Sears in Chicago, with several advanced degrees, a family, and a part-time teaching position, as well as her full-time career—entered a prestigious advanced management program, seeking, as she put it, "yet another merit badge."
>
> To her surprise, she found herself the target of a great deal of sharp but not hostile criticism at this program. Based on her own descriptions of her handling of managerial situations, the instruc-

tor and other participants raised questions about whether her "antiseptic" style would ever motivate subordinates. They also wondered why she was collecting so many "merit badges," but not making the move to senior management.

She decided to leave Sears and find a senior management role in a smaller company. In typically efficient **Achiever** style, she found just the right opening and made the move within 90 days. Deciding that she needed to explore alternatives to her "antiseptic" style, she also signed up for an intensive training program on the West Coast recommended to her by one of her colleagues. The program consisted of two four-day sessions among executives, with six months in between the sessions. Participants analyzed tapes of their interactions with one another and wrote autobiographies (exploring whether the developmental theory presented in this book helped illuminate events). In addition, they carefully monitored their own attempts to experiment with their own style back on the job.

In writing her autobiography during the intensive training program, Megan became aware that she had adopted her "antiseptic" style in her late teenage years after she gave up a promising career in musical theater because of the abrupt ending of a passionate love affair with one of her fellow actors. This revivified and reinterpreted memory seemed to reopen her emotional life.

At the same time, in analyzing the tapes of her interactions with the other executives at the training sessions, Megan became aware of a whole set of "distancing" tricks that she habitually played with others to protect the stability of her own world:

> In considering my cross-examining style, my mind sought similar behavior in other contexts. It was apparent why at work several employees had had a negative view of my leadership style. I was usually perceived as task oriented, emotionless, aloof. In counseling, the focus was always on facts and documented events leading toward logical conclusions that were often unpersuasive.

Megan decided to try a more "inquiring" mode of management at work in her new company, even though she was very skeptical of its likely efficacy:

> I had always preferred very explicit goals and timetables, a structured organization, and guided discussion leading to issue resolution. The collaborative process, of course, focuses more on inquiry, constructing shared meanings from experience, and building implicit consensus through responsible in-

teraction. It struck me that the resulting silence or passiveness within the leadership role would somehow diminish the effectiveness of the role. As the role collapsed in importance, so would problem solving or planning. I was therefore ready to dismiss collaborative inquiry as academic, metaphysical, and as largely impractical. Being a practitioner, however, I decided to take it into the business context for a trial.

She later documented a series of on-the-job action inquiry experiments such as the following two:

Critical Incident #1: I received information on a morale problem in a particular group. I met with one of the supervisors there to better understand the problems. In the course of this discussion, I rendered no advice. Instead I posed a dozen or so inquiries. To my astonishment the conversation lasted three and a half hours. Here are the specific results:

1. The supervisor stated that I had been the first executive ever to really listen to and understand the difficulties there.
2. I learned about the causes of those problems in far greater depth than would have been the case otherwise.
3. A warm rapport developed devoid of any destructive defensiveness.
4. The inquiries led the supervisor toward better definitions of the problems, and, therefore, toward workable solutions.
5. Word of this interaction spread like wildfire down into the ranks raising hope.

Critical Incident #2: I arrived at a meeting involving Administration, Finance, Purchasing, and an outside vendor. Upon surveying the scene it became quickly apparent that there was no meeting chairman. Everyone looked to me as the senior manager to direct the proceedings. I accepted the reins, but made no opening statement on agenda, specified no personal positions on the issues, and began the meeting with an inquiry. This was followed by other strategically placed inquiries. What evolved was a very clear sense of the needs of the business, a suitable program to meet those needs, procedures agreed upon by all parties present, and commitments from the vendor. All of this transpired in less than one hour in an amicable and orderly exchange of views. I was also startled at how completely satisfactory the outcome had been to me personally.

Upon entry to the West Coast training program, Megan was measured as exercising the **Achiever** style of management. Hence, her move to upper management appears to have preceded developmental change. The stage had evidently been set by the feedback she received at the advanced management program, but the action of transformation toward the **Strategist** style was induced by the inquiry systems built into the West Coast program—the autobiographical reflection guided by theory, the close analysis of tapes of one's own behavior, and the documentation of on-the-job experiments.

When the objective structures and categories of the **Achiever's** world begin to disintegrate, the natural fear is that only a chaotic vacuum—a state of entropy—will remain. Megan reflects this fear in her initial skepticism about what she calls "collaborative inquiry." She imagines this to be a vague, undefined, passive process ("silence or passiveness within the leadership role," "as the role collapsed in importance . . ."). This is because what is crisp and active about this type of management is both too large and too small for the **Achiever** to see. Collaborative inquiry does demand giving up control of others' moment-to-moment behavior, but it also requires that the manager work actively to develop a frame for, and a shared vision within, a meeting. The manager must also pay a very active kind of attention during the meeting itself so as to be able to surface key issues in a timely fashion. The vice president mentioned in the previous chapter, who described his practice of treating meetings as octaves, offers one impression of this close attention. What is so difficult to imagine, for persons who have not yet themselves experimented repeatedly with this sort of approach, is how active one's awareness can become, how many voices one can begin to hear within the silence of one's inner and outer listening, how pointed the question of what it is really timely to say can be, and finally, how the experience of guiding collaborative inquiry can contribute to a greater power and ability to take timely action.

The focus on inquiry sounds "academic, metaphysical, and impractical" until one actually undertakes it in a particular, practical, on-the-job situation. Then, like Megan, one is likely to be astonished and startled by the qualitatively new kinds of results one achieves. Thus, Megan enters a meeting, discovers it has no structure and leadership, wastes no time seeking to identify scapegoats, and wastes no energy by imposing a structure that may not fit or may engender resistance. She simply discovers with the others what is necessary and what they wish to do about it. There is no obtrusive ideology of leadership here, just actual leadership. Megan's confidence is not based on her prior knowledge of the meeting and the fulfillment of her expectations but rather on her ability to diagnose the situation as she enters the room and to manage whatever presents itself.

The case of Megan's development was introduced in response to the questions of how development to the **Strategist** stage can be promoted and what benefits such development provides for an organization. As the case implies, the problems of supporting development *beyond* the **Achiever** stage are distinct from the problems associated with supporting development *to* the **Achiever** stage. Managers at the early stages tend to be unreceptive to feedback and may respond to it inappropriately. This is no longer the issue with a manager like Megan. So interested in feedback and experimenting is Megan that she is even willing to try out modes of managing that are initially counterintuitive to her. ("I was ready to dismiss collaborative inquiry. . . . Being a practitioner, however, I decided to take it into the business context for a trial.") Now, the principal problems concern the nature of the organization. Are there mentors within the organization who are themselves at later stages of development and can help a manager like Megan work through the issues she is facing? Are there inquiry systems within the organization that promote the kinds of learning that Megan discovered through the West Coast training program? Few organizations today can confidently and validly answer "Yes."

As suggested by the case about Megan, the most obvious benefits to an organization of supporting development beyond the **Achiever** stage will come in relation to its senior management. For senior management is charged with the responsibility for developing the organization's vision, mission, strategy, and structure. Senior management is also responsible for rethinking the corporate strategy and reforming the structure as appropriate. And senior management is responsible for making sense out of the chaos that is the continually changing economic and political environment. These responsibilities require the abilities that the **Strategist** is beginning to develop. Indeed, they require abilities that demand managerial development beyond the **Strategist** style.

TRANSITION

In the previous two chapters, we have been examining the **Collaborative Inquiry** stage of organizing and the **Strategist** stage of managing. At this relatively rare stage of development, the system becomes capable of restructuring in intended, appropriate, and timely ways.

The final section of this book examines more cases of intentional restructuring on different scales. The first chapter examines the internal self-study and restructuring of an individual manager. The second chapter examines the restructuring of a business conversation between a banker and a potential client. The third chapter examines the restructuring of a small, early stage software company from the **Investments** stage to the **Incorporation** stage. The fourth chapter examines the restructuring of a large, late stage manufacturing company from the **Systematic Productivity** stage to the **Collaborative Inquiry** stage.

The principal focus throughout the upcoming chapters is on action inquiry—the leadership process that we have seen Megan beginning to discover in this chapter. The claim is that action inquiry simultaneously encourages task performance and developmental restructuring. The reader will have repeated opportunities to test whether action inquiry is simply another **Strategist**'s theory, or whether it opens to still later stages of development.

NOTES

1. H. Kissinger, *White House Years* (Boston: Little, Brown, 1979), pp. 33, 187.

2. Ibid., pp. 597–98, 746–47.

3. Ibid., pp. 114, 130.

4. O. Fallaci, *Interview with History* (Boston: Houghton Mifflin, 1976), pp. 40–41.

5. L. Iacocca (with W. Novak), *Iacocca: An Autobiography* (Toronto: Bantam, 1984), pp. 50–52.

6. Ibid., pp. 270–71.

Action Inquiry: An Approach to Transforming Managers and Organizations

CHAPTER THIRTEEN

A Self-Transforming Manager

Managing the corporate dream, we can now begin to see, requires leading individual managers and whole organizations through a series of developmental stages and, thus, through repeated restructurings from each stage to the next. Each stage is necessary at a certain time and for a certain purpose, so each stage is to be celebrated and supported. No stage is synonymous with the dream itself, however, so each stage is also to be challenged and confronted. Moreover, every situation represents an interplay of developmental processes—with different individuals, projects, and organizational units at different stages of development. Hence, the organization's leadership and systems must somehow "speak" to all stages yet focus attention on current organizational priorities.

As if all these demands were not enough, leaders must accept that their own understanding of the corporate dream and their own managerial style may require restructuring.

Managing the corporate dream is, in short, an awesome and paradoxical task. The leadership must provide continuity while generating basic transformation, must be simultaneously supportive and challenging, must speak many languages while generating a shared, common language, and must convey the strength to survive and grow through transformation, yet also possess a genuine vulnerability to self-transformation.

What kind of leadership approach integrates all the opposites? In the previous two chapters on **Collaborative Inquiry** and the **Strategist,** we began to see organizational systems and managerial styles that are simultaneously inquiring and productive. The term *action inquiry* is used to describe this kind of leadership—that simultaneously learns about the developing situation, accomplishes whatever task appears to have priority, and invites a reframing or restructuring of the task if necessary.

When truly practiced, action inquiry simultaneously enhances your own and the organization's *efficiency, effectiveness,* and *legitimacy.* By weaving together action and inquiry rather than separating them as does most managerial action and most academic inquiry, action inquiry can save you time and thus increase *efficiency.* By making explicit and testing the appropriateness of your dream, strategy, actions and outcomes, action inquiry results in early correction of errors, increasing the *immediate effectiveness* of outcomes. By testing and potentially restructuring your own or an organization's strategy, action inquiry generates *long-term effectiveness.*

By making explicit and testing your own and others' dreams, action inquiry develops an increasingly shared corporate dream. Then, by restructuring when current strategies are shown to contradict the dream or when the time appears propitious for transformation to the next stage of development, action inquiry increases the *legitimacy* and *integrity* of the enterprise to its members and clients. In this way, you also guard directly against being seduced into illegitimate enterprises, since a good test of legitimacy is whether you can make your dream or purpose explicit to other participants without hurting the chance to achieve it.

To enact action inquiry requires a high awareness of your own purposes, strategies, and actions, an extraordinarily fluid and instantaneous ability to translate awareness into words, and a continuing willingness to sacrifice your illusions about yourself, others, and situations as you receive new information. How do you achieve this awareness, this ability, and this willingness.

"Slowly," is one answer. Action inquiry requires a commitment to the continuing, moment-to-moment exercise of awareness, a commitment to continuing detachment in the midst of activity, that only comes to make sense to persons at later stages of development. Before that, managers may be interested in action inquiry because of its short-term promise of increased efficiency or because of its middle-term promise of effectiveness. They will see action inquiry, at best, as a necessary means to some other end, an exercise to end when the other end is achieved.

To treat action inquiry as a means initially, and as a means of questionable efficacy that deserves to be put to the test, is perfectly appropriate. If your commitment to action inquiry as an approach to managing is to develop at all, it will develop through multiple transformations, just as individual lives and organizations do.

A second answer to the question of how to develop the awareness, ability, and willingness to enact action inquiry is, paradoxically, "through action inquiry." Of course, efforts at action inquiry will necessarily be awkward, incomplete, and at best occasional at the outset, just as your first efforts to ride a bike were. But there is no easier way to learn.

To gain a more concrete acquaintance with this fluid leadership approach called action inquiry, we will examine four cases in the next four chapters. The first case, presented in this chapter, illustrates action inquiry as it can operate within an individual manager, opening him or her to developmental transformation. The second case shows how action inquiry in the midst of a business deal can transform a deteriorating situation into a productive one. The third case shows a consultant exercising action inquiry over a two-day period to help a small, early-stage software company complete a transformation to the **Incorporation** stage and generate net revenues for the first time. The fourth case shows how two managers at different organizational levels worked together for a year to help the manufacturing division of a *Fortune* 100 company to transform beyond the **Systematic Productivity** stage.

THE UNDERWATER PIPELINE PROJECT MANAGER

Let us listen in as one manager begins the process of examining actions he has taken of which he is less than completely proud. Steve Thompson is by normal measures a successful, $60,000 per year project manager for an underwater pipeline construction firm. As a form of self-study, he writes the following description of a critical incident between himself and his boss, Ron Cedrick. Taking the trouble to write about critical managerial incidents and to document carefully what actually occurred before making judgments is a useful discipline in beginning to detach oneself from one's automatic, everyday habits of action.

Thompson first describes the North Sea setting, then his own behavior with Cedrick during the incident, then the inner feelings that were molding his strategy at the time. At the end of Thompson's story, we trace how he proceeded to experiment with new kinds of action that more closely approximate action inquiry. Finally, we look at the later consequences for Steve Thompson's career development.

STEVE THOMPSON'S STORY

The Setting

Ron Cedrick was a unique man. His appearance was not unlike George C. Scott's Patton. Minus the .45 caliber pistols, but wearing a shiny gold colored metal hard hat, Ron Cedrick was aloof and distant. He was famous. He had singlehandedly tamed the seven seas through engineering/construction feats. He worked for himself in constant demand from oil companies. He was to the offshore contruction industry as Red Adair was to oil field fires. They traveled in the same circles, working for oil companies and commanding huge fees. The reason for this notoriety was simple. Ron Cedrick produced. No matter how difficult, the project always came in ahead of schedule.

British National Oil Company (BNOC) had contracted with him to manage the construction and installation of their "single anchor leg mooring (SALM) system." This system removed the need for flowing oil through hundreds of miles of pipeline from the offshore oil field to shore. Instead, this system enabled BNOC to fill oil tankers at sea in the oil field. The initial underwater construction had been completed in a deep, protected Norwegian fjord that was surrounded by majestic snow-capped mountains.

The calm of the picturesque fjord was behind us. It was February in the North Sea, gray, cold, wet, and rough. At that time of year, the North Sea could be unpredictably violent. We were onboard a 600-foot derrick ship, saturation diving to 540 feet below the surface of the North Sea. Saturation diving is a deep sea diving procedure which enables two to six man diving teams to work at great depths without lost time for decompression. The divers, two per dive, work tethered from a diving submersible (bell) in a light-less, weightless, and hostile environment for periods of between 8 and 12 hours per dive. Once the dive has been completed, the bell is winched back to the surface where it is mated to pressurized living chambers. The two divers then transfer under pressure from the bell to the dry living chambers on the deck of the ship. They remained pressurized until required to dive again.

The most critical part of this dangerous procedure is the launch and recovery of the bell through the interface. The interface is that area between the deck of the ship and 25 feet below the surface of the water—the wave-affected region. This is the area where the bell is most vulnerable to the surface condition of seas. Rough seas have separated more than one diving bell from its winch cable. When this happens, there is usually little hope of returning the divers alive.

The work had been challenging and different. The saturation divers and topside crew were doing an outstanding job. Ron Cedrick was extremely pleased with our performance. This was of particular importance to me because it was my first job as project manager.

My Behavior

The wind had changed directions and was coming at us from abeam, the same direction as the moderate swell. I did not like the looks of the sea. "It looks like it does before it really blows," I thought. The bell had just gone into the water for an anticipated 12-hour run.

After alerting the shift supervisor to "keep an eye on the weather," I went up to the ship's bridge to have a look at the most recent weather forecast and facsimile. While I was reading the forecast that confirmed my suspicions, Ron Cedrick came up to me. "You and your boys have done a real fine job. I personally appreciate that and I know it will continue." He went on to explain that we had to complete the flowline connection today in order to be ahead of schedule. He said, "I know that the weather's gettin' up a bit, but those boys respect and will do what you ask—I've seen it. We need to keep that bell in the water just as long as we can before we let a little ole weather shut us down."

"Yes, sir," I responded confidently.

The outcome was all too predictable. I kept the bell in the water too long. The weather blew a gale. I pushed the diving operation beyond its safe limit. The recovery of the bell through 20-foot seas was perilous. In the process, I not only compromised the safety of the divers, but also set a poor precedent for the permissible operating parameters.

Feelings during the Event

I had an overwhelming desire to succeed. That desire was manifested by hard work, industriousness, and total task orientation. In defining or framing "success," I identified not only successful completion of the installation, but also the satisfaction of Ron Cedrick as being synonymous with my success. After receiving positive reward from Ron Cedrick for the work we had completed in the fjord, I felt in conflict between my responsibility to my fellow workers and fulfilling the expectations that Ron Cedrick had for our performance.

The moment I reviewed the weather forecast and facsimile, I became tense with fear. I was afraid that I would not have the strength of character to tell Ron Cedrick that I would have to shut down the operation. I was afraid that I would have to deceive the people who worked for me into thinking that pushing our safe operational limits was justified.

Finally, the awareness that I had manipulated my fellow workers and jeopardized the safety of the divers due to a weakness in my character destroyed my illusion that I was an honest, ethical man. I received none of the satisfaction from the reward given me by Ron Cedrick for "pulling it off"—we had completed the flow-line connection.

The foregoing story shows how the careful description of your own behavior and feelings in an actual situation can bring to light incongruities between self-image and actual experience. After the emergency described in the above story was over, with the mission successfully accomplished, Steve Thompson could simply have congratulated himself for getting the job done and winning the praise of his superior.

Instead, Thompson recognized a serious weakness of character in himself, a weakness which many, if not most, people share, but which few have the strength of character to face. This paradox—that integrity is developed by the unsparing, unceasing observation of one's lack of integrity—is at the heart of action inquiry. A precondition for becoming genuinely more responsible is courageously facing one's initial lack of responsibility.

But why bother with this kind of painful self-examination? Thompson was already quite successful in terms of annual income. Moreover, he in fact completed the immediate operation successfully, from the point of view both of its *efficiency* ("ahead of schedule") and its *effectiveness* ("completed flowline connection," no injuries, Cedrick satisfied). His concern centers on the rather intangible possibility that his actions may have reduced the *legitimacy* of the operation as a whole ("jeopardized the safety of the divers," "set a poor precedent for the permissible operation parameters").

Thompson also says that the experience in effect reduced his legitimacy with himself ("destroyed my illusion that I was an honest, ethical man"). His personal dream evidently includes being an honest, ethical man—a man of integrity. Prior to his examination of this incident, he evidently believed that his strategies and actions were consistent with this dream. Now he experiences a serious discrepancy between dream and actuality. But one wonders whether the exercise of writing this story may not itself be at least partially responsible for his self-criticism. Why not leave well enough alone? Why bother with this form of self-study?

The answer that Thompson himself gives is that a series of self-study exercises helped him recognize his responsibility, not just for the technical effects of his managerial actions, but also for the less tangible interpersonal, political, or ethical effects of his actions. Increasingly, he began to consider the broadly "political" effects of his and others' actions in determining how to act in ongoing projects rather than merely regretting afterwards that he had allowed himself to be pressured into acting illegitimately.

Very high-minded, the reader may reply, but is this self-study activity *practical*? What is its "return on investment"?

Nine months after Thompson wrote about the incident with Cedrick and began experimenting with action inquiry, his colleagues said that he was a changed man. No longer merely a brittle, macho "technical ace" who pushed himself and everyone else to the limit on particular jobs, he was now seen as a concerned, trustworthy, broad-visioned leader. Three months later, he received an offer to join top management and the board of directors of the company at an annual salary more than double his previous salary.

Three years later, he became president of a competing company. His first major action as president was to try action inquiry on a corporate scale. The company had recently lost a major client. Rather than accepting this fait accompli and perhaps feeling superior to his predecessor, Thompson personally called this client and determined specifically how the company had failed to meet his expectations. He then engaged members of his own company in analyzing and restructuring the systems and relationships responsible for poor performance. Finally, he made a new contract with the client, which bound Thompson's company to an unusual proportion of the financial responsibility for any failure in timely performance. This time, the company met its obligations and thus regained a significant customer.

Returning to the beginning of the story, what were Thompson's actual experiments with action inquiry? How might he have responded differently to Cedrick? What Thompson came to realize, through rehearsing different ways he might have responded to Ron Cedrick that day on the ship's bridge, is that there are always a galaxy of responses to any situation, not just the one or two that occur to any of us immediately.

The two obvious responses in this case were either to cave in to the pressure and say, "Yes, sir" confidently to Cedrick, as Thompson did in the original situation, or, at the other extreme, to confront Cedrick and insist on bringing the bell back up. But in fact, *neither* of these responses feels right. The first response lacks integrity and makes us the victims of a superior's manipulation. The second response also lacks integrity, but in a more subtle way, by too quickly polarizing the situation and obscuring whatever uncertainty we may still feel about the proper course of action. The second response is also risky in a political sense—too risky for most of us. For Cedrick is a superior, and superiors (not to mention ordinary mortals) often do not like to be taken by surprise, especially by a statement that "crosses" them.

Usually, discussions about what to do in situations like this run back and forth between these two unsatisfactory responses, with "idealists" favoring the second (confrontation) and "realists" insisting that the first (caving in), however unpalatable, is "the way it is."

What Thompson learned through rehearsal was that there were many other aspects of the situation of which he was *implicitly* aware at the time but which he had not made fully *explicit* to himself, much less to Cedrick. Had he been able to listen to the various stirrings and voices within himself, with more confidence that they deserved attention, he would have found material enough for any number of other responses.

The simplest third alternative would have been to respond exactly as he did but then to bring the bell out of the water earlier than he actually did. To accomplish this, he would have had to remember, throughout the exchange with Cedrick, his suspicions (now confirmed) about the likely weather. He would also have had to listen to Cedrick's very real compliment about how respected he (Thompson) was, rather than being influenced by the manipulative context of that compliment. And finally, he would have had to feel clearly that others' respect for him was based on his independent and professional good judgment, not on being a daredevil, and certainly not on being a servile, easily manipulated conformist.

Or a fourth alternative: Thompson might say, "I'm not sure how much is at stake for you or the company in completing this ahead of schedule." If Cedrick does not offer an answer during a brief pause, Thompson could continue, "We can certainly leave her down a while, but I'm not sure we'll be able to finish. It looks like it's about to blow a gale. The boys know I'll push them, but they also know I won't endanger lives. Do you want to stay up here with me to monitor the situation, or do you want me to continue on my own judgment?" In these comments, Thompson is honest about his various uncertainties, is appropriately deferential to nis superior, and invites further consideration of the complicated developmental threads weaving through this moment. At the same time, the tone is strong, the words are clear, and he shows that he cannot be covertly manipulated.

Again, however, Thompson can exercise this alternative only if he cultivates an awareness of the many factors influencing the moment. Such awareness does not demand a simple clarity or certainty. Instead, it actively uses the tensions among different developmental threads to create a pattern of speech that does them justice.

Paradoxically, then, the method by which a manager expands his or her sense of responsibility to include long-run issues of legitimacy and integrity, as well as short-run issues of efficiency and middle-run issues of effectiveness, is to pay more attention to the many influences operating at the immediate moment of decision. The very sense of being stuck between two uncomfortable alternatives—the proverbial "rock and a hard place"—comes to be taken as a sign to listen more carefully for other voices. The manager then molds an original solution that does justice to the complex of influences, both implementing and testing the solution through action inquiry.

Most forms of professional knowledge result in *conditional confidence*—confidence that you will act well so long as the situation does not violate your assumptions about it. The active, awakening attention described here results in *unconditional confidence*—confidence that you can meet any situation that arises because you are capable of discarding inaccurate assumptions and ineffective strategies in the midst of ongoing action.

There is only one major hitch. Developing an active attention and the ability to mold creative speech, tone, and movement in the midst of ongoing pressures is the hardest work in the world. And it never ends. The better you become at it, the more moments you will remember to try this creative work. Moreover, the better you become at it, the more you become aware of how frequently you are in fact acting automatically and passively, manipulated by forces of which you are at best only peripherally or belatedly aware.

Action inquiry ultimately costs all our illusions. We like to think we are independent. Yet active study of ourselves in business or family settings shows us how automatic and easily manipulated we ordinarily are—how we are encased within the **Diplomat**'s assumptions, or the **Technician**'s, or the **Achiever**'s. We like to believe that in most cases we know what we are doing. Yet our own action inquiry cannot even begin until we give up this illusion and struggle to learn what is really at stake for us in the midst of each situation.

CHAPTER FOURTEEN

Transforming a Conversation

Let us turn to a second example of the costs and benefits of action inquiry—this time focusing on a real-time business situation.

Jane Dixon emerges from her bank training program and is invited to join one of the bank's commercial lending groups. As is common, Dixon is initially assigned to visit 10 small companies where there is little business potential. In this way, the neophyte lender can practice her presentation skills and begin to learn what questions to ask, at virtually no risk to the bank's business. This procedure also permits the bank to test the new lender's ability to persevere through a considerable string of frustratingly ambiguous and unrewarding experiences.

Dixon aggressively calls all 10 potential accounts the first day. Even this step is by no means easy, for phones and addresses have sometimes changed, and the first person to answer the phone is sometimes less than courteous and cooperative. From the very first instant, Dixon finds herself faced with a choice between giving up on a potential account, persevering unimaginatively, or inventing some ingenious way of gaining information about, and better access to, any given company.

Because self-study exercises have shown her that she too easily gives up on relationships when she hears the first hint of a no, and because she has also learned that simple doggedness frequently courts further rejection, Dixon now makes use of a variety of resources (such as customers of the companies and other officers at the bank) to seek access to her potential clients.

Most bank training programs advocate creative selling of this kind. However, the lesson often does not take because the training program has not helped individual trainees to see what blocks them from creative selling and what commitments must be made to overcome that block.

Ultimately, Dixon visits 9 of the 10 companies, and 8 are "dry wells." But to her surprise, the ninth is considering borrowing a million dollars for a major expansion. However, the company is already negotiating with another bank and expects to hear its terms within the week. Undaunted, Dixon uses her bank's sophisticated new financial computer package (with the enthusiastic support of the MIS staff because she is the first lender to approach rather than to avoid them), and delivers her analysis, proposal, and terms to the company on the same day as her competitor.

When she calls the next day, she learns that both banks have offered exactly the same terms on the loan, leaving the company president in a quandary. He explains that he feels a prior commitment to the other bank but is impressed by her turn-around time and the possible implications that may have for the future quality of her service. On the other hand, he is not so naive that he cannot imagine a change in motivation once the sale is made. Dixon asks whether the president would like to meet to discuss these issues, but he says that he must make up his own mind.

Two days later, Dixon calls again to learn the president's final decision. He says that he remains uncertain about all the legal implications of the loan. At this point, she strongly urges him to meet with her at the bank, where she can call in one of the bank's lawyers to help them if necessary.

The meeting at the bank is a prolonged one. The president anxiously asks for clarification of each legal term in the bank's standard agreement. After consulting with the lawyer for some time, without achieving any sense of resolution, Dixon begins to doubt whether the president will take either loan. The increasing frustration of circling and recircling through the morass of technicalities reminds her of similar situations in previous group projects when she learned that one can sometimes break the vicious circle by disclosing one's perception of what is happening, in a nonaccusatory, inquiring way.

At this point, action inquiry ceases to be an exercise done on paper or with a supportive mentor and becomes, suddenly, a risk she can choose to take now. Heart very much in mouth, Dixon interrupts the flow of conversation to say, "Can we stop and change tracks for just a minute? I'm feeling increasingly frustrated by our conversation because I sense it's not resolving your real concerns. Instead, we both seem to be growing increasingly anxious. This is the bank's standard agreement form. It's important for our ongoing relationships with our clients, as well as our general reputation in the community, that we write the agreement in a way that maximally protects both parties. It is in my interest to make sure that you are satisfied and not deceived, so that we feel that we are working together and can possibly develop an ongoing business relationship. But it seems that you don't believe any of that right now, or don't trust me. Is this true? Am I doing something that blocks your confidence in me? Or, if not, can you tell me what you are seeing as the real issue right now?"

With this, the president confesses that he has never before taken a major bank loan, and that the legal language highlights his fear that he will lose the business he has founded and nurtured to forces that are beyond his capacity to control.

The two discuss the dangers, difficulties, and opportunities that always attend the moment when an enterprise grows beyond the singlehanded control of the founder. They also explicitly discuss their shared purpose for the first time—how doing the loan benefits both of them.

The costs of this process are obvious. Dixon has committed a great deal of time and energy to this potential client with no guaranteed return. Furthermore, she took the risk of possibly heightening the tensions when she interrupted the flow of the meeting as she did. She also took the risk of hearing something unpleasant about herself.

Or are these costs so obvious? From one perspective, they can all be written off as training in this case—still a cost, to be sure, but a necessary one rather than an avoidable one. Furthermore, the risk Dixon took in interrupting may in fact have been smaller than the risk of continuing the conversation without interruption. (Most managers who go very far in self-study find that they systematically *overestimate* the risks of acting differently in situations, computing all the possible costs but not the benefits. Conversely, they systematically *underestimate* the risks of acting habitually, computing all the possible benefits and blaming others for any costs.)

Another less visible cost in this case—but one which will be too high for many managers and will prevent them from emulating Dixon—is that she had to give up some basic assumptions she held in order to interrupt the legal conversation with the president as she did. Dixon describes her most basic assumption as having been that "the deal hinges on reason alone." From this assumption flow a series of corollaries, such as "trust is irrelevant," "the legalese will be accepted as soon as it's explained," and "negotiating an agreement is a deductive process of finding the correct path to the desired solution." In retrospect, these basic assumptions all appear to have been illusions.

So much for the costs. The benefits? The president decided to do business with Dixon the next day. She thereby gained the visibility of having made a large commercial loan even before being appointed a company officer. Eighteen months later, one of the eight "dry wells" took the initiative to contact her and shortly transformed itself into a "gusher." Another six months later, she became the first member of the group of commercial lenders who had joined the bank at the same time as she to receive a major promotion. She also won the most desirable sales territory in her area of the bank.

In this case, we see a manager seeking to act *efficiently*, *effectively*, and *legitimately* all at once, ultimately resorting to action inquiry to restructure a degenerating situation and achieve her aims. Initially, familiarity with computer software along with plain hard work enables Dixon to produce an analysis and proposal of loan terms more *efficiently* (i.e., in less time) than her competitor. Her recognition that she is marketing a service to a client, not merely offering an internally consistent financial analysis, results next in an *effective* series of initiatives toward the client after submission of the proposal. At this stage, she is also helped enormously by having an *effective* definition of *efficiency*. That is, instead of defining efficiency as spending the least possible amount of time on this activity, she evidently defines efficiency as gaining the most useful possible rehearsal or training for her new lending role.

Finally, we see in Dixon's comments to the company president, in the midst of their meeting about the legal implications of the loan agreement, how deeply she is attuned to generating long-term success and *legitimacy*. In the first place, she defines her own and the bank's entire interest in terms of establishing mutually beneficial, long-term, trusting relationships with clients. In the second place, she convincingly demonstrates that this is not mere rhetoric by interrupting her own attempt to persuade the president that the legal language is technically appropriate, in order to ask him whether he in fact has doubts about the ultimate legitimacy or wisdom of the loan. By engaging in a shared inquiry into the purpose and possible effects of the loan, Dixon and the president in fact create the very sense of mutual dream, mutual investment, mutual trust, and mutual benefit that was missing earlier. In general, a business negotiation becomes increasingly legitimate to all the parties involved as the negotiation itself is shown to be open to inspection, controllable, and aimed at benefiting all the parties.

Obviously, not every business transaction requires such a fundamental and explicit exploration of legitimacy. The manager must sense when the issue of legitimacy is really at stake and must learn how to address it when it does arise so that the very actions taken in addressing it themselves generate legitimacy. The problem is that too few American managers today appreciate the practical importance of the issue of legitimacy, and too few schools of management and corporations generate the kinds of rehearsals that teach aspiring managers how to address the issue of legitimacy effectively in everyday business transactions.

ACTION INQUIRY AS SIMULTANEOUS REHEARSAL AND PERFORMANCE

Our first illustration of action inquiry—the case of Steve Thompson, the underwater-oil-exploration project manager—involved rehearsals of the incident after the fact. The second illustration—of Jane Dixon, the neophyte commercial lender—implicitly involved numerous rehearsals before the critical meeting with the company president. Rehearsals in an atmosphere of inquiry, both before and after significant incidents at work, are essential to a lifelong professional commitment to becoming increasingly effective in action. The developmental theory presented in this book points particularly to the **Conception** stage and the **Experiments** stage of organizing as times for rehearsal. Organizations strongly committed to rehearsing generate the most sparkling and effective action—whether we think of the Boston Celtics, the New York City Ballet, Disney World, or Martin Luther King's nonviolent civil rights campaigns.

But the unique and essential feature of action inquiry is that "rehearsal" and "performance" blend into one another until they become simultaneous. The right kind of rehearsal does not replace questioning and uncertainty with answers and certainty. The ultimate performance at the conclusion of all one's rehearsals is not a polished answer but rather a more appropriate and more penetrating inquiry, as we see in the critical meeting between the commercial lender and the company president.

Rehearsal and performance of action inquiry blend into each other at the other end of the spectrum as well. Not even the earliest rehearsals can be entirely safe. Not even the earliest rehearsals can be entirely protected from real-life consequences. For at each rehearsal that is at all effectual, one's self-image is at stake. Illusions of which one was not even aware may be exposed.

Thus, there is a performance aspect even to Thompson's after-the-fact reflections. His very writing can be viewed as a performance. Thompson had to decide what particular incident to write about and who he could trust enough to ask for feedback. He took the risk of learning something less than complimentary about himself either from the writing itself or from the response of those reading the paper. Once he received feedback on the paper, he had to decide how to interpret that, and then had to take the risk of experimenting with new kinds of behavior, before he could really know what he had learned. Had Thompson chosen a "safer" incident in the first place, or not followed through with new kinds of behavior later—that is, had he merely *reflected* about the experience with Ron Cedrick—the inquiry process would almost certainly have been less effectual, less potent, and less meaningful.

Ultimately, the sense of simultaneous rehearsal and performance in action inquiry introduces the manager to a new quality of awareness—to a continuous, silent, impartial observing of your own performance amidst others. This silent observing is as different from an occasional, clamoring, judgmental self-consciousness as it is from arrogant or dreamy self-contentment.

The manager who takes on this moment-to-moment inquiry is committed more deeply than ever to performing effectively. For only a performance that is both literally and artistically effective honors action inquiry and encourages others to meet its demands. But complete identification with performing effectively would cut off that very quality of inquiry that alone can promote disillusionment and increased effectiveness in the midst of action. Hence, the manager experimenting with action inquiry simultaneously treats each performance as a rehearsal, primarily dedicated to cultivating this ongoing, impartial observing.

Each on-the-job dilemma comes to sound more and more like a call both to performance and to rehearsal, both to effectiveness and to inquiry.

CONCLUSION

The silent, inquiring observing that is the seed in the core of action inquiry determines *when* the time is right for *what type* of explicit inquiry. Even explicit inquiry, as our illustrations already show, need not end in a question mark. Its essential characteristic is that it invites and welcomes true information relevant to an ongoing situation, even if that information seems to violate the actor's preferences or initial assumptions about the situation.

This is what makes action inquiry a revolutionary process— so revolutionary that it revolutionizes revolution itself. In the past, revolutionaries have revolted against what they perceived as institutionalized inefficiency, ineffectiveness, or illegitimacy, with the assumption that they themselves are okay and "on the right side." Then they have typically established managerial styles and regimes just as closed and authoritarian as their predecessors, if not more so (think again about the aftermath of the French and Russian revolutions).

Action inquiry revolutionizes revolution by opening the "revolutionary" himself or herself to the possibility of transformation. Maybe the inquiry will reveal that what needs changing is something about the actor, not about (or not just about) the rest of the situation. The person committed to action inquiry draws strength, not primarily from any particular assumptions or opinions about the ongoing situation but rather from the action inquiry process itself—from this practical method for determining as the event unfolds what is really true, what is really valued, and what really works.

It is this self-overcoming quality of action inquiry that accounts for both its costs and its benefits. Because it treats no assumption or method as sacred, action inquiry ultimately costs all one's illusions. (And the learning process becomes no easier as one proceeds, for one tends to guard one's most precious illusions to the last.)

Because action inquiry aims at no narrow self-interest or self-protection and is ever alert to incongruities among dreams, strategies, actions, and outcomes, it can restructure situations for long-term success, simultaneously generating *efficiency*, *effectiveness*, and *legitimacy*.

TRANSITION

We have focused in these two chapters primarily on the inner side—the personal experience—of action inquiry. In the next two chapters, we will turn to the outer side—the organizational effects—of action inquiry.

CHAPTER FIFTEEN

Transforming a Small Early-Stage Organization: Action Inquiry as Economic Capital

Let us now examine the case of a small software company that has burned through its initial round of venture financing, with net revenues for its products not yet foreseeable on the horizon. The partners are seeking a second round of venture capital, and everybody at the company knows they must make a breakthrough in marketing and sales; yet, this "bottom-line" negative feedback alone, as stark as it is, is not propelling the company into a new operating pattern.

An organizational consultant who takes an action inquiry approach and who is familiar with developmental theory is invited to help the company over a two-day period. He approaches the assignment with the sense that he must discover what disharmonies among the corporate dream, the leadership's strategies, and the day-to-day operations account for the company's continuing losses. But more than this, he must discover a positive way to reframe or restructure the situation so that the leadership is motivated to correct the disharmonies.

The consultant interviews the top management (the president and the three vice presidents for production, marketing, and sales) of the computer software company, which numbers

35 employees in all. The president is a generation older than the three vice presidents, and the company is a partnership between the president and one of the vice presidents. Together, the two of them developed the initial product.

In the following three years, the company has produced a large number of high-quality products, but they are not selling well, and the company is nearing the end of its initial venture capital financing. The consultant discovers numerous problems that have remained unresolved for a long time. Neither mission nor market are well defined. Pricing is a subject of acrimonious controversy. Employee morale is fragile because it is unclear whether competence or cronyism is the basis for rewards. Decisions are not driven by any internal sense of mission; they are made only when situations deteriorate into external emergencies.

The bottleneck in decision making appears to be the relationship between the two partners. They respect one another and attempt to share responsibility as though equals. But they repeatedly fall prey to their differences in age, in formal role, and in managerial style. The president plays the role of optimistic, benign, absent-minded father. The vice president plays the role of pessimistic, sharp, rebellious son.

Having interviewed the senior managers individually during the first six hours of his two-day visit, the consultant is next slated to meet with the two partners to set the agenda for the next day's problem-solving retreat. But based on what he has heard, the consultant fears that the agenda-setting session may itself fall prey to the partners' well-intentioned wrangling. In his 10-minute walk around the outside of the building prior to the session, the consultant decides that the partners' pattern of behavior must change before any other productive decisions are likely.

Applying the developmental theory to his own two-day visit, the consultant interprets the initial interviews as the **Conception** stage of this intervention. In this light, the agenda-setting session with the two partners may represent the **Investments** stage. If so, the question is how to restructure his consulting style at this point from a more passive, receptive interviewing process to a more active, intervening process that highlights the new investment the partners must be willing to make if they are to achieve the major changes necessary in the organization as a whole. This reasoning convinces the consultant that he must attempt to reframe the partners' expectations and pattern of behavior from the outset of the agenda-setting session.

Applying the developmental theory to the company as a whole, the consultant sees the organization as spread-eagled across the fluid, decentralized **Investments** and **Experiments** stages, still living off venture capital on the one hand, while on the other hand experimenting with a whole line of products. At the same time, the company is failing to "bite the bullet" and meet the limiting, centralizing, differentiating demands of the **Incorporation** stage—the demand, in short, for net revenues.

In this context, the communal egalitarian aspects of the company's dream seem like an excuse for avoiding decisions. The communal, egalitarian ideology is evident in the partners' pattern of acting as though they are equal despite their different titles; in the fact that all four top officers are invited to attend the next day's retreat, even though the vice president for sales himself and the two partners have all mentioned the desirability of demoting the sales vice president because he is over his head in the vice presidential role; and in the fact that both partners wish to avoid any form of favoritism toward particular employees, yet have employed one partner's daughter and the other's best friend. However important and viable an aspect of the corporate dream this egalitarianism may ultimately be, the partners must show themselves capable of differentiating in an economically prudent and politically just way before their efforts to be egalitarian will become credible.

This analysis persuades the consultant that he himself must act in a decisive, differentiating manner throughout the next day and a half and encourage the two partners to do so as well. In particular, he decides to recommend at the agenda-setting session that only the partners and the consultant participate in the retreat and that whatever decisions the partners reach the next day be put in writing with definite implementation dates.

Applying the developmental theory to each of the partners as individuals, the consultant estimates that the vice president is in transition from the **Technician** stage to the **Achiever** stage of development, both itching for and resisting the true executive responsibility that a person at the **Achiever** stage relishes. The consultant estimates that the president is in transition from the **Achiever** stage to the **Strategist** stage, ready to give up day-to-day executive responsibility in favor of an elder statesman role of mentoring his junior partner and godfathering the company's research and development function.

In their initial interviews, both partners have used the image of ballots to describe their relative power within the company. The president, referring to their equal salaries and to his style of consulting his partner on all significant decisions, spoke of the partners as holding "ballots of the same size" in company decisions. The vice president saw the president as having the larger vote. The consultant now reasons that if the two switch their formal roles, the (erstwhile) president should still see their votes as equal, while the (erstwhile) vice president should see his vote as having become larger. Thus, the twosome should be more powerful. Moreover, the new roles will be more developmentally appropriate to each partner.

More immediately, the mere fact of having the two officers reverse roles for the agenda-setting meeting and the day-long retreat should alter their usual dynamics and put them into a posture of simultaneous rehearsal and performance conducive to action inquiry. Of course, the consultant himself will be in a similar posture as he makes this unexpected suggestion.

The consultant begins his feedback/agenda-setting session with the two partners by proposing that the vice president either resign or become president. This puts the vice president in the action-taking role right away, rather than his usual role of reacting to the president. Although quiet, the president seems ready to play this game. While the vice president considers these alternatives, the consultant proposes that the trio conduct the planning meeting with the vice president "rehearsing" as president. After considerable probing by the vice president to explore the consultant's reasoning, the two senior officers agree.

Now the vice president (in the role of president) acts decisively rather than reacting combatively. He and the consultant propose various changes, with the president (in the subordinate role) making constructive suggestions and raising questions. The two partners reach written agreement of six major organizational changes the next day. The first of these is implemented at lunch that day. The vice president for sales is invited to join them. The partners discuss the major changes they are considering, and ask him to accept a demotion. He agrees, expressing both his disappointment and his relief that his duties will be more circumscribed.

A month later, all the changes have been implemented. Two months later, the company completes, six months ahead of schedule, a first-of-its-kind product for a definite and large market. The company fails to get a second round of venture financing, but sales revenues begin to exceed costs for the first time in the company's history due to the new product.

In the meantime, the vice president decides *not* to become president. The president stipulates that henceforward he will draw a higher salary than his partner and exercise the managerial authority of president and CEO on a day-to-day basis, treating the vice president as a subordinate except at the monthly board meetings, where both of them sit in their roles as partners. Both agree that the six specific changes, along with the new clarity in roles, represent major improvements. And both agree that treating the planning meeting simultaneously as a role-playing rehearsal and as a for-real negotiation has prompted the changes.

Another three months later, the vice presidential partner decides he wishes to become president and negotiates the change with the older partner.

THE THEATER OF ACTION

In this case, the developmental theory evidently generated a convincing story about, and strategy for, the next steps that the partners and the company as a whole needed to take. But why was the developmental perspective so convincing? The mere fact that it helps to explain many of the phenomena the consultant encountered at the company is *not* why it was so convincing. Many theories that explain much never gain practitioners' attention.

The key to convincing the partners to take this theory/strategy seriously was the process of enacting the theory together rather than merely discussing it hypothetically—the process of action inquiry introduced by the consultant. Because the consultant himself acted on his developmental analysis and modeled action inquiry in his approach to the agenda-setting session, the partners saw that the approach could have practical consequences. By enacting different roles rather than merely discussing them, the partners directly experienced the value of differentiated roles during the next day and a half. By sharing their new decisions with the vice president for sales at lunch the second day, and by implementing one of the most sensitive of the decisions there and then (his demotion), the partners again directly experienced the value for the organization as a whole of making crisp decisions and of differentiating roles.

Each of these instances involved a process of simultaneous rehearsal and performance—a process of testing strategies that may be useful for future action by using them to guide present action. On the issue of the presidency of the company, the partners continued the process of simultaneous rehearsal and performance for four months, intervening to reframe their respective roles twice during that period.

The idea of rehearsal and performance is obviously drawn from the performing arts. During rehearsals for a theatrical performance, it is legitimate for the director to "break the frame of the play" at any moment, in order to give the actors feedback and possibly reset the scene altogether before the play continues. Such moments take "time out" from the ongoing action of the play. From another point of view, these moments represent a "time in" to the true perceptions of the different persons involved about what they are trying to do and what they are actually doing. Repeatedly taking these paradoxical "time out/time ins" ultimately generates a better performance.

Some other highly predefined social settings, like football games and courtrooms, also have "time out" procedures that interpolate feedback, rehearsal, and reframing right into the midst of the actual performance. Again, the purpose is to generate better performance.

Managerial settings are much more ambiguous and much less defined than football games and trials. Participants frequently bring conflicting agendas and assumptions to an occasion, yet there is no official procedure for "time outs." Consequently, when a manager believes one of these paradoxical "time out/time ins" will help improve performance, he or she must simultaneously "break the frame of the play" and legitimize the break. Action inquiry is the process of appropriately interpolating inquiry, feedback, and reframing into any conversation, meeting, negotiation, or institutional procedure, whenever such a break seems to serve the purpose of generating better performance.

Ordinarily, of course, critical organizational or family events are rehearsed "off-line," over coffee, with persons other than the main characters, before or after the event rather than "on-line" with the main characters during the event itself . The trouble with "off-line" rehearsals for relatively unstructured real life events is that they cease to be of use as soon as the actual event begins to take an unforeseen course.

To untangle the messes that frequently result when the inadequate order of our minds meet the unfathomed order of everyday business requires the practice of simultaneously rehearsing and performing, of simultaneously interrupting and continuing the action, of simultaneously offering negative feedback and a positive reframing of the setting. To realign corporate dream, strategy, operations, and outcomes requires the practice of action inquiry.

FIVE TYPES OF CAPITAL

The analogy between action inquiry and theater illuminates why and how action inquiry is effective at the moment of action. But now that we are studying its impact on an organization, we also need to study analogies that illuminate the longer term economic and political impact of action inquiry. In the following pages, we look back again at the case of the small software company, asking in what sense the consultant's action inquiry functioned as economic capital. In the next chapter, we will look at another case, asking in what sense action inquiry functions as political power.

It is obviously very difficult to quantify precisely how much action inquiry is exercised in a particular company and what its effect is on the economic performance of the company. But the case we have just studied shows that action inquiry can be the most crucial variable in the economic success of an organization. Action inquiry can, therefore, be considered a form of economic capital. We can understand its potential role and significance for organizations more clearly if we can show how it relates to other forms of capital.

Let us begin with Robert Heilbroner's simple definition and illustration of capital. He tells us that:

> Capital consists of anything that can enhance man's power to perform economically useful work. . . . A hoe is capital to a peasant; a road system is capital to the inhabitants of a modern industrial society. Knowledge is capital, too—indeed, perhaps the most precious part of society's stock of capital.[1]

If we look back at the computer software company, we can distinguish among five types of capital that enhanced the members' "power to perform useful work":

1. *Money*—the venture financing the partners initially arranged.
2. *Plant and equipment*—the company's offices and computers.
3. *Craft skill*—the software engineering skills of the company's young product development group.
4. *Applied science inventions*—the new type of software packages invented by the partners.
5. *Action inquiry*—not noticeably present at the company until the consultant's intervention.

These five kinds of capital represent five different degrees of human intelligence, ranging from money, which is dumb, to action inquiry, the highest form of practical human intelligence. They also represent five different degrees of power to multiply productivity. Money is only potential capital, is only capital insofar as it is used to purchase one of the other four types of capital. Each successive form of capital can multiply the productivity of all the prior forms, as will be discussed below. A short discussion of the differences among the types of capital will further clarify the particular economic role of action inquiry.

Looked at from a distance as a whole human institution, the international financial system, national monetary policies, and local banking industries represent one of the most interesting and mysterious manifestations of human intelligence one could study. But, contrary to the cliche, money itself is dumb. It does nothing apart from direct guidance by human intelligence. Insofar as its use "talks," it does so in the least interesting language imaginable. Of course, this is one reason why money seems so powerful: as the developmental theory presented in this book suggests, more people than we normally imagine have no higher language in common. In any event, unlike a hoe, money does not directly "enhance man's power to perform economically useful work." It does so only indirectly when it is used to purchase or hire one of the other four types of capital.

One of the most common steps that businesses take just prior to bankruptcy is to acquire a "working capital" loan which they proceed to spend on operating expenses. Used in this way, the money obviously does not function as capital, and the business merely becomes, to quote an old song, "another day older and deeper in debt." A second round of venture financing for our small software company might very well have had the same effect. Learning the developmental trick of **Incorporation**—to perform in a net-revenue-generating fashion consistent with making the corporate dream come true—has nothing directly to do with monetary capital. At best, a second round of financing would have bought the company time to learn the necessary trick.

Plant and Equipment as Capital

By contrast to monetary capital, plant and equipment have human intelligence built into them. Thus, they are "smarter" than money. They directly enhance human power to work in the physical realm. They can be privately owned and transferred for a price determined by the supply of and demand for such things, just like consumer goods. When economists and managers think of capital that multiplies the production of consumer goods or services, they are thinking in terms of plant and equipment. But the Industrial Era machinery we have known up until the present has significant limitations as capital. It does not, by and large, have the flexibility or decision-making power to start and stop itself, to fix itself, to improve itself, to supply itself with raw materials, to forecast demand for its work, or to market its product—all capabilities that multiply productivity. Although the small software company was housed in rather cramped, rented offices, additional plant and equipment was certainly not the form of capital it most needed at the time of the consultant's intervention.

Craft Skill as Capital

Craft skill has human intelligence *living* within it. Consequently, craft skills enhance man's power to work in a more flexible way than plant and equipment. Craft capital builds, starts, stops, fixes, improves, and directs inanimate machinery. Moreover, craft skill tends to improve with use for a long time rather than to deteriorate like machinery. Hence, craft skill is a qualitatively more powerful and more valuable (because more intelligent) type of capital than plant and equipment.

Craft capital cannot be bought and sold in the same way as consumer goods or capital equipment. Consequently, the market economic model does not do it justice. Craft capital can be hired at a market price but is transferred from one person to another on a master-apprentice basis. This is a primary reason why the labor market does not function like commodity markets (a related reason is that the labor market includes unskilled labor as well as the three types of human capital).[2] Wages are much "stickier" than other prices, much less susceptible to changes in supply and demand, and worker retention during layoffs is much more based on seniority than wage competition *because the senior workers generally represent the firm's craft capital.* Upon their satisfaction and cooperation depends the firm's capacity for maintaining, transferring, and increasing its craft capital. A company would, according to this perspective, appropriately offer these workers tenure or lifetime employment, treating their employment as a fixed capital expense. Current research suggests that many companies that do in fact operate in this way—and this includes cases as diverse as large Japanese businesses, the network of small worker-owned cooperatives in the Mondragon region of Spain, and certain American businesses like Lincoln Electric, Delta, and IBM—are more profitable more consistently than most companies.[3]

The small software company we have examined in this chapter had employed young software engineers with good craft skills in that area. The company was too young for issues of lifetime employment to have surfaced. As engineers themselves, the two partners seemed less attuned to the kinds of marketing craft skills they required. One partner's daughter and the vice president for sales who had not heretofore handled a managerial role (he had been an excellent salesman) were managing the marketing function. Appropriate marketing craft skills are relatively easy to acquire. The problem here is only superficially a matter of lacking certain craft skills. The deeper question is why the partners or the president had not been giving proper weight to marketing issues and had not succeeded in acquiring appropriate marketing skills.

Applied Science as Capital

Applied science, the fourth type of capital, is the type of capital with which the small software firm was probably best endowed. The two partners had together created a type of software that represented a major innovation, potentially introducing a new generation of more sophisticated software.

Applied science is a direct expression of the capacity of human intelligence to reflect in a logical, Aristotelian fashion about the world and thereby to deduce and test out the possibility of creating things never before seen on earth. Heilbroner speaks of knowledge as "the most precious part" of society's capital because applied science can create entirely new machines, new crafts, and new industries.[4] And today, applied science is generating an entirely new era in which the information content of machinery predominates over its energy consumption and transformation.[5] With the advent of robotics and of computer systems directed by artificial intelligence to perform both production and managerial functions, applied science is not only fundamentally increasing the cost effectiveness of machinery, but is in effect multiplying the very power of machinery as capital—endowing machinery with some of the craft skills and applied science capabilities heretofore reserved for human capital.[6]

Despite Heilbroner's view that knowledge or applied science is society's most precious type of capital, however, none of the types of capital so far discussed encompasses the full range of what is required to perform economically useful work. *The power to perform economically useful work ultimately consists of the ability to coordinate all the different types of capital so far mentioned, with the conditions of the market, in a timely fashion.* We do have a few words to point toward persons who are not simply good performers in one layer of reality—as a craftsman is with his hands or a scientist is with his mind—but who succeed in coordinating the different layers of reality at particular times. We speak in economic terms of *entrepreneurs* who coordinate the different types of capital, transforming scientific discoveries into commercial products for which they correctly anticipate a demand. We think of *consultants*, like the one described at the outset of this chapter, who sell their own time according to their record and reputation for providing not just general, expert knowledge, but advice that is timely for particular organizations. In political terms, we speak of *leaders* who make "dreams come true." In religious terms, we speak of *saints* who "justify" their visions with their moment-to-moment actions.

As the chapters on the organizational stages of development have shown, each organizational transformation represents a recalibration of the dream, strategy, operations, and market of the company or agency. Thus, *executives* also exercise this most precious and inclusive type of capital whenever they lead their group or company through a major transformation to a later stage of development.

Action Inquiry as Capital

Action inquiry is as different from formal, applied science as applied science is from manual craft. Action inquiry is not a type of knowledge but rather an ongoing aesthetic alertness that integrates intuition, knowledge, action, and outcomes, as these are occurring.[7] Whereas formal science works within a given framework or paradigm, action inquiry explicitly includes the possibility of questioning personal, situational, and organizational assumptions and restructuring if the data warrant.[8] Action inquiry capital does not become obsolete because its focus is, precisely, timely action. It is the creative source for all the less durable, less flexible, less intrinsically creative forms of capital.

As already demonstrated, action inquiry was the type of capital most obviously in short supply at the small software firm. If action inquiry is the most powerful type of capital, why were not the partners more aware of it? Why is everybody not already "into it"? First, the notion of action inquiry is only now beginning to be clarified and to be applied to economics. Second, each more powerful type of capital requires a correspondingly greater investment to develop in the first place. We can see these increasing investments externally in the amounts of time and money required to undergo the training and education necessary to develop craft skills or to become an applied scientist. Less visible is the personal commitment, discipline, and risk taking that makes the difference between a journeyman craftsman or engineer and a truly excellent and creative contributor.

We have begun to get a taste for the investments necessary to develop a capacity for action inquiry from the illustrations in the three previous chapters. The scale of these investments is awesome and includes disciplines not just of the mind but of the hand, the heart, and the mouth as well. For the present, we can simply assume that it requires a correspondingly greater investment than gaining a Ph.D. in an applied science. Thus, the commitment required to develop the capacity for action inquiry radically narrows the number of people seeking to develop this capacity.

Another reason why everybody is not already "into" action inquiry is that it is very difficult to recognize it, or its teachers. Consequently, it is difficult to know how to imitate the best present practice, as one would, at least implicitly, in beginning to learn a new sport or craft or musical instrument or a scientific discipline. Action inquiry is difficult to recognize partly because the reflective, deductive mode of scientific inquiry is so predominant in our civilization. It is difficult for us to imagine a more encompassing, more disciplined kind of inquiry than the empirical and theoretical sciences of the past five centuries, just as it must have been difficult for craftsmen or theologians in the Middle Ages to imagine a more encompassing, more disciplined inquiry than they practiced.

But it is important to understand that the difficulty of recognizing action inquiry exists *in principle* as well. Action inquiry leads one to act in increasingly timely, and therefore increasingly unique, ways.[9] The Coca-Cola Company's decision to introduce the new Coke formula and scrub "the real thing" illustrates this point. Was the decision in fact a case of action inquiry and exquisite timing, or a colossal blunder that betrayed the corporate dream?

It is not easy to tell. The decision was preceded by years of applied scientific marketing research which seems to have utterly missed the forest for the trees. People clearly preferred the sweeter Pepsi in blind taste tests. But they do not buy their soft drinks blindly. The helter-skelter reintroduction of Coca-Cola Classic when the new Coke fizzled and Classic's much larger market share today suggest that the Coca-Cola Company had inadvertently thrown out its corporate dream—its "real thing"— when it temporarily threw out its old formula.

But wait. Coke's market share against Pepsi had been declining since 1977. By withdrawing the old formula, the company gave the new formula and the new Cherry Coke center stage publicity they would not otherwise have received. By withdrawing the old formula, the company also gave the public as well as its own bottlers and distributors a chance to rediscover their commitment to "Classic." It is now selling more than when it was withdrawn from the market, despite its two new in-house competitors.

The intensive review process that began within the company when new Coke's sales dipped sharply shortly after its introduction was only marginally influenced by formal market survey data. The sudden review process was shaped, however unintentionally and fortuitously, more like an action inquiry process. Suddenly, the company found itself in a simultaneous rehearsal and performance mode. Could it interrupt its ongoing performance without ceasing to perform and without suffering further loss of legitimacy and market share? Could it follow up the initial laboriously arrived at but unsatisfactory reframing of its principal product, with a second much more spontaneous yet also more complex, more inclusive and unifying, and more satisfactory reframing?

It in fact did so.

The second decision, arrived at in weeks rather than years, was at once more subtle, more paradoxical, and more successful than the first decision. The company decided to reinvest in the new Coke by keeping it on the market with the company's flagship product name. Simultaneously, the company reintroduced the old product, but under a new name. Yet the new name emphasized the product's ancient heritage and unique standing in the industry.

When Coca-Cola or any other organization learns how to bottle the action inquiry process, it will have gained control of the ultimate kind of economic capital.

NOTES

1. R. Heilbroner, *The Making of Economic Society*, 6th ed. (Englewood Cliffs, N.J.: Prentice-Hall, 1980), p. 87.

2. See also Lester Thurow's discussion of the labor market for other related reasons, in *Dangerous Currents: The State of Economics* (New York: Vintage Books, 1984).

3. In this regard, see particularly the work of David Ellerman, including *Economics, Accounting, and Property Theory* (Lexington, Mass.: Lexington Books, 1982); "The Mondragon Cooperative Movement" (Boston: Harvard Business School Case # 1-384-270, 1984); and N. Fast, "The Lincoln Electric Company," in Christensen, Berg, and Salter, eds., *Policy Formulation and Administration* (Homewood, Ill.: Richard D. Irwin, 1980).

4. I am indebted to Eugen Loebl's provocative little book, *Humanomics* (New York: Random House, 1976) for originally highlighting the qualitative distinctiveness of applied science as a form of capital, in a way which pushed me toward the present fivefold typology of capital.

5. See S. Zuboff, "Technologies that Informate: Implications for Human Resource Management in the Computerized Industrial Workplace," in R. Walton and P. Lawrence, eds. *Human Resource Management Futures* (Boston: Harvard Business School, 1985).

6. Unfortunately for our understanding of our current economy, knowledge acts even less than craft skills like the economic commodities that economists' models assume (not that this has deterred economists from trying to treat knowledge as a commodity). Knowledge is not a discrete object at all and does not transact like objects. If I sell you my knowledge, I not only pocket the money after the sale, but I walk home with my knowledge undepleted as well. Indeed, economic transactions of knowledge always border on the fraudulent because even though you pay good money for it, you may very well not "get" it. Consequently, ownership of knowledge is rarely clear-cut, exclusive, or easily exchangeable in the way that ownership of tangible goods normally is.

The focus here is not on discrete bits of information such as hot market tips, but rather of theoretical knowledge, the basis for applied science. Theoretical knowledge is in some ways analogous to a road system or a telephone system: it is an infrastructure that enables communication, exchange, and new combinations; it provides the highest potential for economic growth when there is broad public access to it; and decisions to invest in this form of capital cannot be rigorously calculated by market logic, since it creates the structure within which market logic later works.

One of the keys to the economic predominance of the United States during the third quarter of the 20th century was the massive, national public investment in education and scientific research. Despite the difficulty of measuring the value of knowledge in quantitative terms, it has become evident during the 20th century that it is a key form of capital.

7. F. N. Brady, "Aesthetic Components of Management Ethics," *The Academy of Management Review* 11, no. 2, (1986), pp. 337–44.

8. For more extensive treatments of differences between formal, reflective science and action inquiry, see C. Argyris, R. Putnam, and D. Smith, *Action Science: Concepts, Methods, and Skills for Research and Intervention* (San Francisco: Jossey-Bass, 1985); D. Schon, *The Reflective Practitioner: How Professionals Think in Action* (New York: Basic Books, 1983); S. Shrivastva, *The Executive Mind* (San Francisco: Jossey-Bass, 1983); W. Torbert, three chapters in P. Reason and J. Rowan, *Human Inquiry: A Sourcebook of New Paradigm Research* (Chichester, England: Wiley, 1981), and "Executive Mind, Timely Action," *ReVision* 6, no. 1 (Spring, 1983). In brief: Whereas formal science collects data at one time, analyzes it at another time, and reaches conclusions at a third, action inquiry collects data, analyzes it, reaches conclusions, and acts anew all within the same time period. Whereas formal science creates theoretical maps of the external world, action inquiry collects data from the outside world, from one's own behavior, from one's ongoing thinking,and from one's intuitions. Action inquiry generates theoretical maps that connect these different layers and that change as the contents of the layers change. Whereas formal science aims to create theories generally valid at all times and places, action inquiry aims to generate attention and action maximally attuned to, illuminating of, and effective for the present time and place.

9. Actions become increasingly timely by successfully integrating increasing numbers of layers of reality and increasing numbers of temporal rhythms. An outside observer may very well not be aware of all the layers of reality and all the temporal rhythms that a particular action is working with. It is, therefore, increasingly difficult for anyone outside the actor to determine what the pattern of action is. Yet the actor cannot judge, alone, the effects of action. Hence, every judgment that a certain pattern of action represents action inquiry is, *in principle*, subject to controversy.

CHAPTER SIXTEEN

Transforming a Large Late-Stage Organization: Action Inquiry as Political Power

The previous chapter shows how action inquiry functions as one kind of economic capital and how, as such, it organizes the relationship among other, qualitatively different kinds of capital in an appropriate fashion. Yet in the example of the consultant influencing the two top executives of a small computer software company, it is evident that action inquiry is also a political influence process.

This chapter outlines four different kinds of political power: unilateral force, diplomacy, logistics, and action inquiry. The chapter also explores, through an extensive case and commentary, how action inquiry relates to the other three kinds of power, and how the exercise of action inquiry helps to transform a large manufacturing organization beyond the stage of **Systematic Productivity.**

Persons first exposed to the notion of action inquiry often raise questions about how realistic it is, politically speaking, as a strategy for managing. "What if the issue is your boss and he thinks any kind of inquiry is disloyal?" some people ask.[1] Others argue, "If the resources and the votes and the **media** are against you, and the powers-that-be aren't buying into this action inquiry business, what can it do for you?"[2]

These questions assume many things. They assume, first, that through some sort of valid inquiry process, the questioner has determined that the deck is stacked against action inquiry. If this assumption is correct, the questioner is likely to have used elements of action inquiry to make the determination.

Second, the questions assume away just the quality of power that is unique to action inquiry—namely, the power to reframe and restructure a situation. In other words, even if the deck is stacked against action inquiry, action inquiry may, in effect, reshuffle the deck or change the name of the game for which the deck is being used. Indeed, the sense that the deck is stacked is itself an indication that action inquiry is called for.

Third, the questions assume that action inquiry is necessarily an explicit, identifiable manner of acting. But as we have seen in the previous chapters, action inquiry also has an implicit component, internal to the actor. Moreover, the primary test of whether an actor is practicing action inquiry is whether the explicit behavior is uniquely timely for the current situation. Hence, action inquiry is not necessarily explicit or identifiable, and it legitimizes itself as timely as it is enacted.

Fourth, the questions also assume that to chose action inquiry as a strategy is to choose against conventional political strategies based on unilateral force, diplomacy, or logistical planning. This assumption is also untrue. *Implicit* action inquiry can determine what type of political power to use when. Implicit action inquiry plays with all types of political power—unilateral force, diplomacy, logistics, and explicit action inquiry—to generate the conditions for developmental transformation in individual managers, project groups, or large organizations.

FOUR TYPES OF POWER

Many so-called realists claim that the only real kind of power is **unilateral force** (and the threat of unilateral force). Certainly, it is the most visible form of power, just as plant and equipment is the most visible form of capital. When individuals or whole nations share little in the way of values, language, or customs, and are geographically distant from one another, they may still be able to understand one another's military might or wealth in resources. Even in organizations where the members share language and culture, and to a considerable degree values and customs as well, top management most unambiguously symbolizes its priorities for its members through its resource-allocation decisions. This is the form of power that the **Opportunist** understands and uses, treating it as the only form of power.

But is unilateral force the only or the ultimate form of power? By no means. Quite the contrary: it is the form of power closest to the very absence of power and control. It may succeed in creating minimal order from chaos and unconstrained violence, but it is the form of power that least knits together the actor and the acted-upon and that therefore least carries over beyond the moment of application.[3] Even in international relations it is not unilateral force itself that primarily determines the balance of power, but rather the diplomacy of the Metternichs, the Gromykos, the Chou En-lais, and the Kissingers. Indeed, Metternich first devised, articulated, and implemented the balance of power concept at the Congress of Vienna in 1815 on behalf of his Austro-Hungarian sovereign *in compensation for the empire's lack of military strength.*

Unlike unilateral force, diplomacy is not based on coercion and compliance but rather on attraction and identification. Diplomacy generates alliances, treaties, or contracts that promise to gratify the appetites of both parties, satisfy their sentiments, further their interests, or promote their ideals better than the use of unilateral power would. Diplomacy knits together the actors, at least through common forms of protocol. It can also generate common norms of conduct, sometimes even a sense of "playing on the same team." The influence of diplomacy extends through time, generating order and predictability, as long as the attraction and sense of identification lasts. The treaty that Metternich took the lead in so brilliantly negotiating at the Congress of Vienna prevented a major European war for the next century, until World War I.

Diplomatic power plays an important early role in the development of cooperation within all kinds of organizations. From their first day on the job, new members are usually very active in seeking out and enacting the norms of appropriate conduct as embodied by more senior, higher status members. If organizations could solicit desired conduct from their members only through external rewards and penalties wielded by unilateral force, the preponderance of organizational resources would have to go into the control function, as in a prisoner of war camp, with little remaining for productive work. All of the foregoing considerations establish diplomacy as fundamentally more powerful than unilateral force. It is, of course, the form of politics that the manager at the **Diplomatic** stage of development appreciates and employs. The difference between a manager at the **Diplomatic** stage of development and a professional diplomat is that the former *is*, and is therefore limited to, this kind of power, whereas the latter *has* this kind of power among others (unless he or she is also at the **Diplomatic** stage of development).

The trouble with diplomacy is that it does not necessarily generate conduct that is efficient, effective, and legitimate. Diplomats will frequently say within their own fraternity that their ultimate aim is not to achieve just results, nor to win negotiations, nor even to complete negotiations, but simply to keep their governments talking to one another rather than going to war. As shocking and cynical as this may at first sound to some readers, it can also be read as wise and idealistic; however unproductive talking may sometimes be, war is always counterproductive in the immediate sense that it destroys. In relations among nations that are virtual strangers and who prefer and can afford to remain so, ongoing diplomatic talks may indeed be the highest desirable aim.

But in a for-profit company, in a public agency, and in the growing interdependence of our "global village" in the Information Era, diplomacy as the single alternative to unilateral force is insufficient. *Logistics* is also necessary. Logistical power involves the exercise of instrumental, deductive rationality to accomplish objectives by making and implementing systematic plans. Logistics does not merely redistribute value, as unilateral force and diplomacy do, but generates things and services of value. The exercise of logistical power increases the self-esteem of those who exercise it because they experience themselves as the origins of value.

Logistics is less obtrusive and less visible than diplomacy and unilateral force for several reasons. First, it is relatively indirect and impersonal. Logistical power is frequently exercised through writing—a military strategy, a marketing plan, or a policies and procedures manual—rather than through barked orders or honeyed phrases. Second, the Industrial Era, with its focus on economic productivity, enshrines logistics in the bureaucratic mode of structuring organizations. This makes logistical power the invisible frame of activity at least as much as the visible content of particular tasks. For both reasons, the exercise of logistical power often does not feel to those influenced by it as though they are subject to someone else's power. In developmental terms, the **Technician** favors the use of logistical power. So does the **Achiever,** but the **Achiever** is willing to intertwine the three types of power so far discussed when necessary to achieve a goal.

Of course, no organization develops solely through the exercise of pure logistics. Even when people sincerely believe they are being purely rational, there are frequently incongruities among their objectives, their plans, and their modes of implementation. Also, not everyone by any means accepts the authority of reason as primary. Many are more immediately motivated by unilateral force and diplomacy. Consequently, senior management tends to exercise all three forms of power so far described. Then, because the resulting power equation is so complex, most members of the organization spend part of their time trying to interpret what kinds of power are being exercised when, and arguing about whether exercises of unilateral force and diplomacy serve to make their version of the corporate dream come true.

Almost all organizations—whether for-profit, not-for-profit, or public—suffer unproductive splits between what have come to be called the "formal" organization and the "informal" organization. The formal organization represents the rational superstructure of the organization—its supposed objective and its policies and lines of authority that supposedly support that objective—in short, logistical power. The informal organization represents the emotional substructure of the organization—members' reactions against what they perceive as the irrationalities and illegitimacies of the superstructure, along with the allegiances and alliances formed around persons who actually exercise power, whatever their formal position may be—in short, diplomatic power. In high-performing organizations, the informal structure for the most part supports and energizes the formal structure. But most organizations dissipate a significant proportion of their human resources in the friction between the two.

The friction between the formal and informal organizations increases under three conditions:

1. The more the formal organization is based on deductive reasoning apart from analogical reasoning.
2. The more the formal organization is supported by unilateral force and diplomacy apart from logistics and action inquiry.
3. The greater the proportion of organization members that hold the **Opportunistic, Diplomatic,** or **Technical** perspectives.

Action Inquiry as Political Power

None of the kinds of power so far described include the power to coordinate the formal and informal organization. None of them include the power to create corporate dreams, strategies, and organizational cultures that appropriately blend (rather than mix up) persons and sub groupings at different developmental stages. None of them include the power to confront and correct incongruities between intuitive dreams and rational strategies, or between strategies and actual implementation, or between actions and the political or economic effects of those actions (logistics comes closest in its ability to alter strategy based on undesirable effects). None of them include the power to transform individuals, groups, or whole organizations from primary reliance on one kind of power to primary reliance on another kind of power. None of them include the power to reframe and restructure situations. And none of the kinds of power already described legitimize themselves as they are being exercised. All these qualities of power, *not* characteristic of unilateral, diplomatic, and logistical power, inhere in a fourth kind of power here called action inquiry.[4]

Why is this fourth kind of power important in pragmatic terms? One answer is that frequently its exercise, and only its exercise, can increase productivity in a business or public agency. Efforts to increase productivity in mature organizations inevitably challenge the existing structures of power and many managers' basic assumptions about power. Since most managers—whether they be business managers, labor union managers, or government managers—are not familiar with the exercise of restructuring action inquiry power, they experience the restructuring of power as a threat to their power base and begin to resist. As we saw earlier, in Chapter 11 on **Collaborative Inquiry,** projects to increase productivity in mature organizations are condemned to remain fads that fail unless the entire initiative is propelled from the start by the action inquiry form of power and unless the education of an ever-increasing proportion of the participants in the theory and practice of action inquiry is understood as central to the projects' mission.

Capital, Power, and Developmental Stage

Types of Capital	Types of Power	Managerial Style	Stage of Organizing
Plant and equipment	Unilateral force	**Opportunistic**	**Investments**
Craft skill	Diplomacy	**Diplomatic**	**Incorporation**
Applied science	Logistics	**Technician**	**Experiments**
Interplay of all three types		**Achiever**	**Systematic Productivity**
Action inquiry		**Strategist Magician* Ironist***	**Collaborative Inquiry**

*See Postscript.

TRANSFORMING A LARGE ORGANIZATION

The following extended case shows how *implicit* action inquiry intertwines and appropriately sequences the different types of political power, including, ultimately, *explicit* action inquiry. The case concerns the effort to transform a *Fortune* 100 manufacturing company from a single-line-of-authority, functional organization structure, that had been appropriate during an era of product stability, to a matrix organization structure. A matrix organization structure divides authority between functional area managers and temporary project leaders who lead interarea teams in designing, manufacturing, and marketing new or fast-changing products. Thus, a matrix organization structure is *in principle* more flexible and more responsive to a turbulent market. But it also requires *in practice* that managers live with ambiguous and renegotiable power relationships and that they be capable of generating **Collaborative Inquiry.** Because they are unfamiliar with the very possibility of action inquiry and the **Collaborative Inquiry** stage of organizing, many managers today experience the potentially creative ambiguity as confusing and as threatening their power. Consequently, many companies have failed to complete the transition to matrix organizing.

The following case illustrates the kind of politics necessary to make such a transformation come true.

The key to success in this case appears to be the unusual set of implicit attitudes and skills that both Jane Dray and John Gordon—the two principal characters—had with regard to power (neither of them spoke of holding an explicit theory of power). Both seemed *willing to use the full range of types of power.* Both also seemed *aware of the costs and limited effectiveness of the earlier forms of power.* Dray seemed *to appreciate intuitively how to move fluidly up and down the stepladder of power without missing steps.* Gordon seemed *to appreciate the subtleties of using explicit action inquiry as a form of power.*

> The setting is a large division of a *Fortune* 100 company seeking to improve its ability to bring new products to market and later service them. In an attempt to shortcut interdepartmental rivalries and slow approval times, it is making the transition from total reliance on functional departments to a matrix structure. New product managers, responsible for product development, sales, and service, are authorized to negotiate with area heads in marketing, finance, personnel, manufacturing, and so forth, for product-team personnel. Each product-team member is to have dual reporting responsibilities for the life of the product-team, and organizational members may very well belong to more than one product-team at a time.
>
> The transition period to a matrix structure is often confusing and prone to conflict for organization members because of the loss of clarity as to "who's the boss" in particular situations. In this particular company, the initial period is unusually smooth, except with regard to the manufacturing area, where internal personnel prob-

lems lead the area as a whole to resist the transition. Openly negotiating personnel assignments within manufacturing would raise issues about different members' competence that the group is unwilling to face. Privately, members of the manufacturing area say they fear certain other members will be hurt. In small group discussions, they argue that the change is largely a ploy to decrease the power of department heads. In more public meetings, they argue that product quality will inevitably decline under a matrix structure.

The key players in the following events are Jane Dray, the division president, Don Keen, the manufacturing area head, Clyde Thomas, another senior manufacturing manager, and John Gordon, a junior manager in the marketing area who becomes one of the first new product team managers.

The division president, Jane Dray, is convinced that the matrix process can improve product quality in addition to its other advantages, *especially with regard to manufacturing itself,* but she is reluctant to use her budgetary power to bring manufacturing in line because she realizes that this action will seem to confirm the "power ploy" interpretation of the changes and will not model the more consultative matrix decision-making process she wishes to encourage. Cutting the other way, however, is the possibility that the area heads (all male) will interpret her reluctance to use her budgetary power as a sign of lack of real commitment to the structural change, or as a sign of "feminine weakness." Also, since manufacturing has chosen to interpret her every move as "power politics" from the outset, it seems virtually impossible not to confirm their interpretation no matter what she does. Furthermore, she judges (and other senior managers in the division agree) that for her to raise these very issues publicly at a manufacturing senior managers' meeting, in the absence of any commitment among the area managers to work through their own problems, will likely result only in their uniting against her.

After a period of private conversations with senior managers in the manufacturing area, resulting in no additional cooperation by the area with new product managers, Dray *does* make it clear to Don Keen, the manufacturing area head, that the price of failure to cooperate will be reduced budgetary expansion in manufacturing.

Sure enough, the area accedes to the formal change to matrix structure. A public meeting of area heads unanimously endorses the new structure. But then, as soon as John Gordon, a new product manager, returns to the process of negotiating for personnel, the manufacturing area attempts to assign a member to the team unilaterally, on the grounds that no other member is available or willing.

At this point in the case, we see that the division president, Jane Dray, who did not want to play "power politics" (i.e., to win by using unilateral force and diplomacy), ironically ended up doing so early in this decision-making sequence. Notice, though, that Dray in effect considered or actually tried all other three types of politics before making her unilateral budgetary threat. Although she rejected action inquiry as an *explicit* strategy to be used in a meeting with manufacturing, she *implicitly* used action inquiry in determining what "language of power" manufacturing could hear. The unilateral threat was effective in terms of achieving the immediate formal organizational change desired, but was apparently ineffective beyond that initial moment in that it did not change the decision-making behavior of the manufacturing group in regard to assigning a member to Gordon's new product team. Before the manufacturing group's own unilateral action, however, Dray exercised diplomatic power in arranging a formal public occasion at which area heads committed themselves to the new structure.

Let us return to the case:

> After consultation with Dray, John Gordon responds politely in writing to the manufacturing area that he has received its "proposal" and will be glad to continue discussions. In the meantime, Dray privately admonishes Don Keen (intentionally expressing, rather than masking, her real anger). She charges Keen with disloyalty to the company and direct betrayal of the spirit of the change that had just been publicly and unanimously ratified. Shortly thereafter, Keen contacts Gordon to "continue discussions," inviting him for the first time to a meeting of the senior manufacturing managers.

Note that during this sequence, Dray has in effect succeeded both in gaining greater compliance to the new structure and in raising the level of this power play from unilateral force to diplomacy. The actions she now choreographs for herself and the new product manager, John Gordon, are appeals to good form, to face saving, and to loyalty. Gordon's polite but vague note, written as though no gauntlet had been thrown, permits the manufacturing area head, Don Keen, to step back from someone hierarchically subordinate to him without losing face. By expressing her anger to Keen, Dray makes it clear that her "face" is "on the line," so her subordinate must back down.

All this is the language of diplomatic power, bodied forth with the grace of ballet. Had the president *not* taken the two diplomatic steps of gaining area heads' public commitment to the matrix structure and then admonishing the first deviant, noncompliance with the matrix process could easily have become the norm in other areas as well.

Let us again return to the case:

> Now a peculiar incident occurs, characteristic of times of organizational tension and distrust. Not trusting the manufacturing area's earlier claim that only one manager was willing to work on his team, Gordon has met with a junior manufacturing manager to explore his willingness to participate (and the junior manager says he *is* willing to join the team). A week later, Keen, in an apparent effort to flex his diminishing organizational muscle, asks Gordon not to approach his junior managers directly in the future. Gordon agrees (without mentioning his recent meeting). Still later, a senior manufacturing manager reports having seen the junior manager enter Gordon's office (without specifying when). Keen concludes that Gordon has broken his word.
>
> As his meeting between the senior manufacturing managers approaches, Gordon learns of these latest developments when one of the senior manufacturing managers, Clyde Thomas, reproves him for further poisoning the atmosphere by lying. During the same conversation, Thomas explains that at the forthcoming meeting Keen will ask for volunteers for the new product team, as well as for one other project. Thomas himself will volunteer and so probably will the man originally assigned by the area to this project. After this scenario, the way will be open for the second man to be assigned to the *other* project without loss of face.
>
> The foregoing script is duly enacted at the meeting.

Why was the carefully scripted meeting a success despite the new poison of the alleged lie? One explanation is that Keen, Dray, and Gordon all intuitively recognized that Dray had now won two successive "hands" of this power game, once playing unilateral force, once playing diplomacy. Thus, she appeared able to coordinate at least two types of power, perhaps more. In addition, she had not sacrificed any of her resources or allies in winning. So, Keen might be pardoned for concluding that he was not about to win by opposing her. He had better try to win by cooperating with her and her ally/protege, Gordon. That Gordon had lied (in Keen's version of the story) diminished Gordon's personal credibility but did not affect his symbolic position as Dray's protege. Hence, the poison did not affect the immediate outcome. Instead, a series of diplomatic initiatives allowed the various participants to rehearse for a third type of power game—the cooperative logistics enacted at the meeting.

But Gordon wishes to test whether it is possible to go still further—to penetrate beyond this sequence of distrusting, grudging, time-consuming, temporary, back-room accommodations to a more fluid and harmonious relationship with the manufacturing area.

> After the agenda for the meeting is announced at its outset, Gordon says that he would like to review recent history in the hope of beginning anew. He believes that the only way to "exorcise" (a word he used) the existing frame of distrust, which is poisoning and distorting participants' perceptions of one another's actions, is:
>
> 1. To name what is going on .
> 2. For all parties to accept responsibility for the existing state of affairs.
> 3. For all parties to commit publicly to a more open and collaborative mode of interacting in the future.
>
> He acknowledges the frustration that he and Dray have felt with the manufacturing area, leading to their decision to use a unilateral power strategy a few months before. He also acknowledges his own distrust of the area as indicated by his conversation with the junior manager. He then points to the damaging distortions that have resulted from mutual distrust, such as the area's mistaken belief that he has broken his word in speaking to the junior manager.
>
> Four members of the manufacturing group speak after him. Keen begins by denying that words like *power* and *distrust* are relevant. Gordon holds his tongue, judging that argument will polarize him and the area managers. The three subsequent speakers, starting with Thomas, all describe ways in which the manufacturing area has contributed to the negative atmosphere, acknowledge (for the first time in an area meeting) the difficulties that the area has had

in discussing its own internal problems, and join in the hope of creating more open and productive modes of operating.

In the 18 months following this meeting, Dray experiences no more "insoluble" problems with the manufacturing area. Personnel assignments are made easily and informally through conversations among the relevant parties. Morale within the manufacturing area improves dramatically. By several indices, the manufacturing area becomes the most productive in the division. During the same time period, the particular new product team under dispute becomes the most successful in the division's history. Also, overall customer satisfaction with company products improves markedly.

Still another 18 months later, the manufacturing area itself (rather than R&D or engineering) develops a major new product for the company.

All these outcomes required additional actions, of course, but in retrospect, the events described here appear to have been the turning point. It is noteworthy that the division's upswing occurred during a recessionary period, bucking an industrywide downturn, so external economic trends do not seem to explain the outcomes.

One key to success in this case appears to have been Dray's *implicit* action inquiry as she moved, first downward through the types of power until she arrived at a common power language with manufacturing (unilateral force), then back up through the types of power until she set the stage for Gordon's use of logistics and *explicit* action inquiry. A second key to success in this case appears to have been Gordon's timely and adroit exercise of *explicit* action inquiry in his meeting with the manufacturing area. The successful outcomes include: a fundamental and lasting transformation in his relationship to manufacturing; a fundamental and lasting transformation within the manufacturing area itself; and the completion of the division's transformation to a matrix structure.

The case shows how *implicit* action inquiry determines when *explicit* action inquiry can be exercised successfully. But even though this case ends with success, readers may feel that, in general, explicit action inquiry leaves you too vulnerable.

Let us conclude by examining this concern more closely. The first point to make is that the actor is in fact much less vulnerable than he or she may at first appear. The actor is protected by

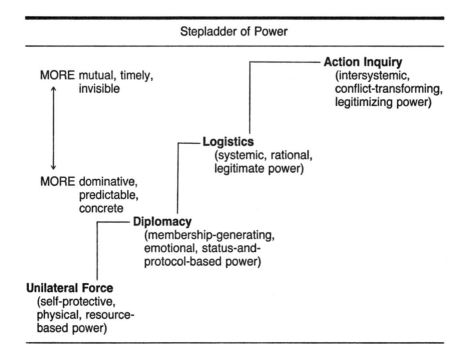

Stepladder of Power

MORE mutual, timely,
invisible

Action Inquiry
(intersystemic,
conflict-transforming,
legitimizing power)

Logistics
(systemic, rational,
legitimate power)

MORE dominative,
predictable,
concrete

Diplomacy
(membership-generating,
emotional, status-and-
protocol-based power)

Unilateral Force
(self-protective,
physical, resource-
based power)

the vigilance that action inquiry requires. Note that in the case, Jane Dray decided *against explicit* action inquiry early on because her *implicit* action inquiry judged the risk of vulnerability too high.

The second point to make about the vulnerability of *explicit* action inquiry is that this vulnerability represents the essence of its creative power. In a social-emotional sense, the point of vulnerability is the equalizing point—the point from which people can begin working together rather than holding themselves off because of the perceived differences among them. In a scientific-intellectual sense, the point of vulnerability is the point where the known and the unknown meet—the point from which people can discover something truly new rather than retreading old and inadequate solutions to the dilemma. In a pragmatic sense, the point of vulnerability is the point from which genuine action inquiry emanates, the point from which the "disciplined stabs in the dark" that characterize significant experiments begin.

No one can be forced to this creative point, so action inquiry in never guaranteed to influence a situation successfully. But, if other actors in the situation accept the challenge of coming to this point as well—to the point of creative vulnerability relevant to the work they are trying to do together—then they have the possibility of intentionally sculpting a timely, new solution together.

It is true that the direction proposed by the person who initiates *explicit* action inquiry may be reversed in the subsequent action or transformed into something unrecognizable. To those who believe that "winning" for that person would have been achieving the initial objective, it will appear that the voluntary vulnerability contributed to losing. But if you are committed enough to action inquiry to use it, you will not compute winning and losing in this way, once an action inquiry process is underway. You know (because you are determined to exercise the vigilance necessary) that any changes in yourself or in your objectives or in the eventual outcomes will represent improvements over the starting point.

Nietzche claimed that the most difficult thing in the world is to transform oneself. This, he said, requires the greatest power of all, the power of self-overcoming. As the previous paragraph indicates, action inquiry opens toward this power. What appears as a shortcoming from the point of view of the more self-protective forms of power is the very heart of this self-transcending form of power.

This capacity for, and commitment to, self-transcendence is what makes this the self-legitimizing form of power. As others recognize and participate in a process of action inquiry that is not limited by anyone's preexisting self-interests, they (at least implicitly) experience the justice of the process and become internally committed to its outcomes.

NOTES

1. The analysis of Steve Thompson's story in Chapter 13 represents one answer to this question. Thompson's boss is the issue there, and he gives the impression that he might well view inquiry as disloyal; hence the effort to construct a hypothetical inquiry that legitimizes itself as loyal.

2. In a dissertation that documents his efforts to introduce a Quality of Working Life type of project into a tempestuous shark-like city government environment, Robert Krim addresses this question: *The Challenge of Creating*

Organizational Effectiveness: Labor-Management Cooperation and Learning Strategies in the Public Sector (Sociology Department, Boston College, 1986).

3. Political theorist Hannah Arendt in *On Violence* (New York: Harcourt Brace Jovanovich, 1970) makes a similar point, strongly emphasizing that violence is the opposite of power. In that essay and in *The Human Condition* (Garden City, N.J.: Doubleday, 1959), Arendt conceived of action and power in ways that led toward the notion of action inquiry presented here.

4. As one indication of how rare is the exercise of "action inquiry" power (and even the notion of such power), it is noteworthy that many theorists of power do not even recognize it in their typologies of power. For example, one of the most cited typologies of power in the management literature (J. French and B. Raven, "The Bases of Social Power," in D. Cartwright, ed., *Studies in Social Power* [Ann Arbor: University of Michigan Institute for Social Research, 1959]) delineates five types of power, none of which approximate action inquiry. Their five types are:

1. Coercive (related to unilateral force).
2. Referent (related to diplomacy).
3. Legitimate (related to logistics).
4. Expert (also related to logistics).
5. Reward (potentially related to any of the four types presented here).

One political theorist who has highlighted the distinction between the more familiar types of power and something approaching action inquiry is James MacGregor Burns. In his book, *Leadership* (New York: Harper & Row, 1978), he distinguishes between *transactional* power, which accomplishes trades without influencing the players' values, and *transforming* power, which influences people more deeply, potentially changing their very definition of their own needs, purposes, and values rather than just satisfying their current needs. [See also B. Bass, *Leadership and Performance Beyond Expectations* (New York: Free Press, 1985).]

Peters and Waterman (*In Search of Excellence* [New York: Harper & Row, 1982], p. 82) describe the relevance of *transforming* power to managerial leadership as follows:

> Leadership is many things. It is patient, usually boring coalition building. . . . It is meticulously shifting the attention of the institution through the mundane language of management systems. . . . It is being visible when things are going awry, and invisible when they are working well. It's building a loyal team at the top that speaks more or less with one voice. . . . It's being tough when necessary, and it's the occasional use of naked power. . . . Most of these actions are what . . . Burns . . . calls "transactional leadership."
>
> But Burns has posited another, less frequently occurring form of leadership, something which he calls "transforming leadership"—leadership that builds on man's need for meaning, leadership that creates institutional purpose. We are fairly sure that the culture of almost every excellent company . . . can be traced to transforming leadership somewhere in its history. . . .
>
> The transforming leader is concerned with minutiae, as well. But he is concerned with a different kind of minutiae; he is concerned with the tricks of the pedagogue, the mentor, the linguist—the more successfully to be-

come the value shaper, the exemplar, the maker of meanings. His job is much tougher than that of the transactional leader, for he is the true artist, the true pathfinder.

There is one major difference between what Peters and Waterman say about the transforming leader and what this book describes as the transforming power of action inquiry. In Peters and Waterman's version of transformation, the leader transforms others. Action inquiry is self-transforming as well.

Postscript

Management today by and large does not even approach the threshold of the challenge of managing corporate dreams. As we have seen, managers at the **Opportunistic, Diplomatic,** and **Technician** stages of development are preoccupied with much narrower realities than making a corporate dream come true. Managers at the **Achiever** stage are typically concerned with achieving tangible goals, not as one expression of a corporate dream but rather to the exclusion of anything so intangible as a dream.

Managing the corporate dream requires leading an organization through multiple, fundamental restructurings. As we have seen, the dream must first be dreamed, at the **Conception** stage. Next, it must be brought down to earth through **Investments** and **Incorporation.** Chance, a changing environment, and inattention will generate disharmonies among the organization's dream, its strategies, its daily operations, and its outcomes. Managing the corporate dream requires identifying and correcting these incongruities, first through various **Experiments,** later through **Systematic Productivity.**

The developmental restructurings of managers and organizations lead not to a single determinate way of managing and organizing but rather to increasingly subtle, increasingly systematic, and increasingly timely inquiry processes. The chapters on the **Strategist,** on **Collaborative Inquiry** and on action inquiry illustrate actions that are simultaneously productive, inquiring, and restructuring—actions that are simultaneously efficient, effective, and legitimate.

This book, along with virtually all examples of managing in the contemporary world, ends here.

But the developmental process does not end here.

Indeed, the chapters in Section III on action inquiry point beyond the **Strategist** stage of development. Action inquiry can become an explicit theory or frame held and championed by the **Strategist,** and he or she can on occasion act with restructuring power. But the **Strategist**'s sense of power comes more from having the right theory or frame to begin with than from the capacity for reframing or restructuring itself. A person at the **Strategist** stage might well find the developmental theory of repeated restructurings presented in this book appealing. To have a theory about restructuring gives you a strategic advantage over all those who inadvertently resist necessary restructurings. Having such a theory also cunningly protects you from having to restructure (since your theory accounts for restructuring, you don't have to restructure it when restructuring is apropos). With a theory that "sees" the need for restructuring, you can "be right" more often than others. You may even be able to fool others some of the time, and yourself for a long time, that you have all the answers. But at some point history will object to the **Strategist**'s claim to be right, the **Strategist** will fail to restructure theory and action, and the claim's credibility will disintegrate.

The following few pages point briefly to later stages of managerial development already implicit in the chapters on action inquiry. Even more briefly, this Postscript also points toward later stages of organizational development. The empirical rarity of these late stages makes these comments tentative and largely speculative.

FROM STRATEGIST TO MAGICIAN

The transformation from the **Strategist** stage, like all other transformations to later stages, is a movement from *being* something to *having* that kind of thing. This time the transformation is from being *in the right frame of mind* to having a *reframing mind*. In the previous chapter on action inquiry as political power, the ultimate power of action inquiry is described as the power of self-overcoming. A reframing mind continually overcomes itself, divesting itself of its own presuppositions. A reframing mind assumes only the dynamic stillness of action inquiry. It attunes itself to the frames of reference held by other actors in a situation, and to underlying organizational and historical developmental rhythms, seeking the common sense of the situation, seeking the motivating challenge of the situation.

Discovering the motivating challenge can create a social ju-jitsu effect: just as total disintegration is threatening, the person or organization or nation suddenly coalesces and acts with unforeseeable vigor and resolve. For this reason, the person exercising this form of power is often experienced as a **Magician.**

A mild version of this principle is found in one manager, among the fifty described in Chapter 6, who took the role of general manager of the Bradford Consolidated Fund. This manager was the only one who was scored at the **Magician** stage of development.[1] Referring to his approach to the 34-item In-Basket Test, he later described himself as "searching for some key to the whole thing, some key that would let *me* in and turn the whole (campaign) into a challenge for us all." (Note that he did not assume he held this key to begin with, as a **Strategist** like Henry Kissinger would.) This manager decided to propose an immediate increase of the campaign fundraising goal by 25 percent. In so doing, he became the only one of the fifty managers to propose such a total reframing of the debilitated effort. In his written communications he incited staff and board members to consider how such a change might help to resolve the various particular issues they were raising. He explained that he was not certain that this frame-change in the midst of an on-going campaign was the right move. He was proposing it in part to test everybody else's response, and he planned to listen very closely to their responses. But he sensed that the organization was out of focus, both internally and in relation to the community at large, and he believed that some challenge on this scale was necessary.

The vice president of the *Fortune* 100 electronics firm, who was quoted in Chapter 11 on **Collaborative Inquiry** about his method of running meetings, is one of the very few managers this researcher has been able to find who measures at the **Magician** stage of development. More than a decade prior to joining his present company, this man's life disintegrated. He had recognized himself as an alcoholic and as gay, and he had lost a job and switched careers. In the process of reframing who he was and what his career was to become, this man discovered the Pythagorean theory of octaves. He later applied this theory to many different situations, including the leadership of meetings. Significantly, however, his approach was not that of the **Strategist** who would treat the theory as the "right frame" or "answer" to particular dilemmas. Indeed, this vice president reports that he intentionally did *not* use the theory for five years after discovering it, for fear of being trapped by it. Instead, he tried to listen anew to each situation without preconceptions. Gradually, he found that the octave theory could help him listen.

The traumatic character of the vice president's transformation toward the **Magician** stage may be a regular feature of such transformations. Another version of a "right frame" disintegrating traumatically and being replaced by a passion for reframing is the story, now so well known, of Lee Iacocca's firing from the presidency of Ford. In describing his feelings at the time, Iacocca speaks of having been "on top of the world" at Ford and of his fall as a "final humiliation." His language for this period of his life is uniformly apocalyptic. He speaks of "suicide," "murder," "coming apart at the seams," "mess," "death," and "ris(ing) from the ashes."[2] To rise from the ashes, Iacocca chose not private therapy, not some low-risk job, but public, reframing action, raising the Chrysler Corporation from the ashes with him. We have been celebrating his magicianship ever since.

The transformation to the **Magician** managerial style requires facing and learning how to transform the entire dark side of the human condition as that manifests itself in oneself and one's surroundings. Unlike the **Strategist,** who may believe that he or she is on the side of good and can beat evil or at least keep it at bay, the **Magician** recognizes that the polarization between good and evil—between victory and defeat, between the sacred and the profane, between classes, races, or sexes, between I and Thou—is recreated at each moment by our relatively fixed and one-sided perspectives on the world. Evil emanates from the character of our own fallen, passive attention; it cannot be permanently defeated. Indeed, to fight against it as though it were only outside ourselves is merely to reinforce it. Action inquiry becomes, for the **Magician,** not so much a theory of managing as an ongoing jousting, at one and the same time, with one's own attention and with the outside world.

The **Magician** requires no official social role. His or her power and authority derive from listening to developmental rhythms—

from active attention—from action inquiry addressed both within and without. By virtue of this listening, he or she takes "the executive role," a sense of responsibility for the whole that is open to anyone, regardless of official role.[3]

Listening in this way, with a sense of wonder constantly re-awakening in the body, heart, and mind, the **Magician** experiences the rhythm of a particular conversation, the life of each individual conversing, the particular organization within which the conversation is occurring, and the nation within which the organization is located—as radiating from the past and the future into the only time when awareness and action is possible—this inclusive present.

Elements of the Magician's Managerial Style

Disintegration of ego-identity, near-death experience	Shamanistic body/mind integration
Impression of spirit rising from ashes	Exercises own attention, researches interplay of thought, feeling, action, and effects on outside world
Seeks participation in historical/spiritual transformations	Treats time and events as symbolic, analogical, metaphorical (not merely linear, digital, literal)
Creator of mythical events that reframe situations	
Anchoring in inclusive present, seeing light and dark, order and mess	
Blends opposites, creating "positive-sum games"	

FOUNDATIONAL COMMUNITY

Just as the **Strategist**'s interest in a *theory* to guide restructuring can deepen and transform into the **Magician**'s *experience* of continual restructuring, so an organization's commitment to *structures* that facilitate **Collaborative Inquiry** can deepen and transform into a **Foundational Community**'s *historical process* of continual restructuring.

Just such a transformation occurred at IBM in the early 1960s after it had achieved the decentralized **Collaborative Inquiry** stage in the 1950s under Thomas Watson, Jr. In a massive $5 billion gamble that put the entire company at stake, a management committee that brought together all five divisions developed the

System/360 family of computers that made all competitive lines and all of IBM's own previous lines obsolete. The struggles within top management and the programming and production challenges of bringing out six computer models of entirely new design at once were unprecedented within the industry (and quite possibly within business in general up to that time).[4] The outcome was to destroy the projected return on investment for IBM's existing computer lines, but simultaneously to capture a still larger share of the business market than ever before (indeed, to greatly expand the market) and thus to create a far greater return on investment than it destroyed.

A completely different example of **Foundational Community** organizing is the Beatles in the late 1960s. Starting with the *Sergeant Pepper* and *Magical Mystery Tour* albums, they entered their most creative and commercially successful period. Each album represented a total reframing of the band (e.g., "Sgt. Pepper's Lonely Hearts Club Band"), as well as a new musical genre and a new social consciousness. At the heart of this process was a foundation-shaking action inquiry process on the part of the band's members, including spiritual journeys to India, the death of Brian Epstein (the "invisible" Beatle who managed the band), the creation of a new corporate entity (Apple Records), growing unresolved discord, and ultimately, disbandment. The band did not survive the upending transformation toward the **Foundational Community** stage.

Still a third completely different example of development toward the **Foundational Community** stage can be located in the history of the Chinese Communists. A Chinese Communist state developed in southern China in the early 1920s. Then Chiang Kai-shek, with his American artillery and planes, surrounded and wiped out that structure. Mao Ze-dong and 100,000 people set out on what became known as the Long March, a year-long migration under continual attack. Only 10,000 of the original 100,000 survived. But along the way to Shensi in the northwest, the revolutionary cause of the Red Army and its mode of conduct in relation to the civilian populations, not to mention its mythic fortitude and sheer survival, attracted the allegiance of swelling numbers. The experience of the Long March so thoroughly refounded the lives of members of the Red Army—granting them heroic meaning in place of their prior experience of chaos and victimization—that many could later literally not remember their lives before the Long March. [5]

These briefest of glances at three widely diverse organizations—IBM, the Beatles, and the Chinese Communists—suggest that the **Foundational Community** stage of organizing is the fire in which fundamentally new economic, political, aesthetic, and spiritual possibilities are actualized. At this stage, the organization not only reframes itself but also the wider culture within which it is lodged. A kind of social alchemy is temporarily achieved when opposites blend—IBM simultaneously destroys and creates ROI, the criminal Chinese Communists create a new basis for law and order, the Beatles celebrate alienation and community. Organizational members participate in a personally and socially foundation-shaking-and-regenerating action inquiry process. They "bet" their careers, their organizations, and even their lives—not just their money—on their corporate dream. Their action together, if it is successful (and there can in principle be no predetermined criterion of success), is necessarily heroic, humorful, and impeccably timely. It becomes the basis of legend and myth. Their relationship to one another is one of covenanting—and of struggling over the meaning of that covenant—not merely that of contracting.

BEYOND MAGICIANSHIP AND FOUNDATIONAL COMMUNITY

It is not clear that any historical events fully embody the **Foundational Community** stage of organizing. Nevertheless, it is possible to glimpse the outlines of yet another stage of managing and of organizing beyond the **Magician** and the **Foundational Community** stage.

When the **Magician** begins to mask his or her reframing powers, a transformation toward what might be called the **Ironic** style begins. Whereas the **Magician** *is* the authenticity and power of action inquiry, attuning self and situations, the **Ironic** leader detaches himself or herself yet again and *has* this authenticity and power. The **Ironic** leader is lower profile, more indirect and impersonal, focusing on how the developmental process can be socially institutionalized. The organization that would result would be characterized by **Liberating Disciplines**—structures that would simultaneously make sense to organizational members at various stages of development and invite developmental transformation.

THE IRONIC LEADER

Dag Hammarskjöld, the Swedish economist and secretary-general of the United Nations from 1953 until his death in a plane crash in Africa in 1961, took the entirety of his public life as an occasion, as a mask, for his efforts to subordinate himself spiritually to a higher order. This became known only after his death when his personal journal was published under the title *Markings*. [6] He had used the journal to help him stand outside himself throughout his years of 20-hour workdays.

Poems, like the following one from 1958, bear witness to his efforts to subordinate his actions, thoughts, and feelings to a clear, impartial light:

> The mine detector
> Weaves its old pattern
> Without end.
>
> Words without import
> Are lobbed to and fro
> Between us.
>
> Forgotten intrigues
> With their spider's web
> Snare our hands.
>
> Choked by its clown's mask
> And quite dry, my mind
> Is crumbling.

The reader may at first wonder how this poem illustrates Hammarskjöld's development toward the **Ironic** perspective. The poem may at first seem simply depressing. It seems to describe disintegration ("my mind/Is crumbling") rather than development. But, while the poem *describes* mental or structural disintegration, it *enacts* a higher commitment and a higher clarity, a dispassionate observing of the truly eternal fluctuations of attention ("The mine detector/Weaves its old pattern/Without end") that enables him to survive even the crumbling of a more contingent structure. Only an individual capable of seeing disintegration without flinching and without removing the constricting "clown's mask" can intentionally and constructively reframe and restructure an organization or a wider culture.

Hammarskjöld's outer efforts toward global integration obviously ended incomplete. Peaceful global integration is most likely a centuries-long project, and an improbable one at that. But he did make the project seem an urgent and honorable one, worthy of the attention and commitment of leaders around the world. His bearing momentarily made real the possibility and moral power of an "international civil servant." Since his death, the United Nations has neither exuded nor attracted this quality of vocation.

Ironies are, not surprisingly, a hallmark of the **Ironic** style. The distances and tensions between the ideal and the actual, between one's inner awareness and one's outer performance, between self and others are accepted as an essential condition of life, to be transformed in particular instances but never obliterated. The belief that all distances and tensions could be permanently obliterated in an effortless, classless utopia strikes the active attention as mere passive lunacy. Quite the contrary, the **Ironic** leader's responsibility is to cultivate a quality of awareness and action that highlights the dynamic tensions of the whole enterprise—not so starkly as to engender terror and hopelessness—but rather in just the tones that can make their significance visible to other members and will challenge them to higher performance and further development.

To help achieve this kind of super-vision, the **Ironic** leader often takes on an entire outer role as a mask—does the opposite of what would be "natural" for him or her—just as the monkish Hammarskjöld did in becoming the first global politician. In this way, the executive is exposed at every moment to just those realities to which, by inclination, he or she would remain blind.

Thus, Jean Riboud—long an avowed socialist and supporter of the Mitterrand government in France—served as CEO of Schlumberger, Ltd., by several measures the best-managed capitalist company in the world.[7]

Thus, Pericles of Athens—rich, from a distinguished family, with powerful friends, and with a charismatic voice—shunned politics altogether at first, then joined not the aristocrats, his "natural" party, but the democrats, the party of the many and the poor in Athens.[8] In this role, he concentrated Athens into the seed syllable of Western civilization.

Thus, the debonair Gandhi doffed his three-piece lawyer's suit and donned a primitive loin cloth, taking a lead role in transforming India from colony to nation.[9]

Thus, a saint at the stage of development corresponding to the **Ironic** style of managing could be expected to take the role of a devil in public. Among several of the Middle and Far Eastern religious traditions, this process of masking one's charisma—one's sacred caring—has a name: "the Path of Blame." As a way of combating the dependence of the student and helping it to become independence, the spiritual teacher who chooses this path acts in precisely ambiguous ways—in ways of questionable taste, devilishly—and attracts either questions or blame.

Recent research on President Eisenhower suggests that the image the public developed of him as an amiable golfer who was more a figurehead than an active decision maker is an image he deliberately cultivated.[10] Behind this mask, the former five-star general of the army and hero of World War II managed every threat to world peace during his eight-year presidency in ways that did not lead to warfare.

Shirley MacLaine is a striking example of the ironic interplay of mask and authenticity. The complete clown outwardly and inwardly—she impartially dons costumes, characters, expressions, steps, and all the other accoutrements of Hollywood stardom onstage—and, equally impartially, documents in her autobiographical writing offstage the many costumes her thoughts and feelings wear as she reaches out socially and spiritually.[11] All her masks are donned to convey a simple and sincere, spontaneously humorous and agonizing, authenticity. The marvel is how regularly she succeeds.

(It has been suggested that, if this is a media age, and if that means that actors are in fact particularly well qualified professionally to serve as politicians, then hopefully the public will eventually come to elect good actors. The best actors would wage campaigns characterized by irony and humor. Under such conditions, the most likely candidates would not be Ronald Reagan, Clint Eastwood, or Robert Redford, but the true greats like Shirley MacLaine or Meryl Streep.)

STEPPING ON AND OFF THE HISTORICAL STAGE

Unlike the **Magician,** the **Ironic** leader is no longer identified with his historical/spiritual role. Consequently, the **Ironic** leader characteristically steps on and off the historical stage deliberately and repeatedly, using the timing of appearance and disappearance as one more lever of power and awareness. Charles de Gaulle has played out perhaps the most historically significant, certainly the most precisely calculated, choreography of retirement and return in the past half century. In Section Three we examined numerous examples of managerial reframing—reframing that affects one's own behavior, reframing that transforms an interpersonal business relationship, reframing that transforms small and large organizations. De Gaulle twice reframed France as a whole through his carefully timed self-exile from power and carefully timed return to power.

De Gaulle exiled himself to Britain in June of 1940, at the age of 49, to proclaim the French resistance. By carefully remaining a member of the Reynaud government (though his first impulse had been to resign) as its intentions to surrender to the Germans became clear, de Gaulle arrived in London as a government official as well as an army general, with a significant claim to legitimacy in founding a government-in-exile.[12] (Roosevelt and the Americans refused governmental recognition to de Gaulle, gambling for a long time that the Vichy government in France would renounce its collaboration with the Germans, but it never did.)

De Gaulle re-entered France right on the heels of the Allied troops in June of 1944, establishing his administrative apparatus in each zone of France as it was liberated and before it could be put under Joint Allied Occupation command. So precisely timed, de Gaulle's retirement and return maintained the continuity of France's honor and of France's position as one of the great powers. No other scenario that was being considered at that time could have resulted in France resuming its role as a great power immediately after the Vichy period and becoming an occupying power in Germany and Austria, rather than itself becoming occupied.

Even before he came into full power and authority as president back in France, however, de Gaulle recognized that his peculiar role in the nation's history would soon require another retirement. In September of 1944, nearly a year and a half before he would resign the presidency, de Gaulle said, "I have a mission, and it is coming to an end. I must disappear. France may again one day have need of a pure image. That image must be left with her."[13] When he felt that the fragmentation of political parties prevented him from exercising coherent power, he resigned.

In 1958, with the war in Algeria lurching from brutality to brutality and with a military plot to take over the government on the brink of being implemented, President Coty of the Fourth Republic made secret contact with de Gaulle. Through a carefully calibrated series of initiatives and periods of waiting for events to develop, over the next 20 days de Gaulle received a mandate to draw up a new constitution for a Fifth Republic. In 1969, after the student riots of 1968, de Gaulle called for a national referendum and then resigned the presidency immediately when his proposals were defeated.

De Gaulle's precision of timing and choreography in his three "retirements" and his two "returns" is centrally responsible for the legitimacy of both republican government and executive power in France today. Because his focus was never on power for personal ends but rather on creating publicly legitimized institutions capable of exercising power, he was always prepared to step off the historical stage whenever the public decided to create institutions incapable of exercising power (the Fourth Republic) or more directly voted against his proposals (the 1969 national referendum). It is very likely that he could have become a dictator in 1945 and again in 1958 had he so wished. The possibility was publicly discussed. That he could have, and did not, conveyed a special plausibility, durability, prestige, legitimacy, and authority to Gaullist republicanism, a legitimacy which now, ironically, embraces a socialist government.

LIBERATING DISCIPLINES

What qualities of organizing parallel the **Ironist** stage of personal development and represent a transformation beyond the fiery **Foundational Community** stage of organizing?

Once a historically foundation-shaking period is over and an organization is externally at peace, relatively speaking, as the

Chinese Communists were in the 1950s and 1960s, the question can arise how to create the moral equivalent of the earlier foundation-shaking period in order to encourage developmental transformation on the part of later generations. This was, in effect, Mao's effort when he generated the Cultural Revolution. The result, however, was anything but disciplined or liberating.

IBM today, by contrast, is certainly a disciplined organization and claims that it is liberating as well: respect for the individual is its highest espoused value. How does an organization of over 400,000, whose founding father and son ended their tenure over 15 years ago, generate liberating disciplines that make their employees feel respected on an individual basis, that make their plants highly efficient, and that induce their executives to break from past practices at critical moments? One can cite the incredible array of interconnected inquiry and productivity systems at IBM—the rewards for individual and team performance, the commitment of over $2,000 per employee per year to education and training, the "Open Door" policy that lets workers bypass their immediate boss to have complaints investigated, the plant morale studies that are carefully reviewed, the "Speak Up" and "Suggestion Box" programs that result in bonus checks to workers for more than $60 million per year—and still feel mystified that so huge an organization can so frequently make major, appropriate changes in its own past practice (most recently, for example, entering the personal computer market by creating an autonomous unit in 1981; buying Rolm in 1983) with so little internal confusion or resistance. [14] One can also question whether IBM's liberating disciplines actually function in the way those of a **Liberating Disciplines** stage of organization theoretically would—namely, to promote development from stage to stage by organization members, groups, plants, and divisions. There is simply no research bearing on the question.

The Jesuit Order within the Catholic Church may represent a closer approximation to the **Liberating Disciplines** stage of organizing than either the Chinese Communist Cultural Revolution or IBM today. Aspiring Jesuits go through nearly a generation of intellectual and spiritual training. At the heart of this training are a series of meditational exercises developed by St. Ignatius of Loyola, the founder of the order, in the 16th century. [15] Certainly, this scale and depth of education corresponds in a general way to the challenge of supporting human development to the later stages, as well as to the challenge of developing a capacity for action inquiry. Moreover, these disciplines are liberating in the very specific sense that Jesuits do not graduate from them into an externally regulated monastic world. Instead, they travel, often alone, to all corners of the world, sometimes separated from the rest of the order for the remainder of their lives.

Jesuits frequently adopt leadership styles characteristic of the **Ironist.** They may mask their Christian mission for many years under a willingness to learn from, and adopt the customs of, the culture they enter. For example, in the early years of the order, Robert de Nobili succeeded in converting over 40,000 Indians to Christianity by presenting himself as a Brahmin in dress, language, observance of rituals, mastery of Sanskrit texts, and ability to compose ragas. So respected was his reputation as a Brahmin that when he much later explained how Christianity represented the development and perfection of the Brahmin faith, his explanation held authority because of his standing within the Brahmin community, and many Brahmins accepted baptism. [16]

An organization at the **Liberating Disciplines** stage should in theory develop many leaders capable of playing executive roles across different organizations and capable of starting new organizations. On this count, too, the Jesuit Order fits. By ones and twos, Jesuits have found their ways close to the seats of power of more nations than any other single organization in modern history. In addition, this remarkably small number of men have started many organizations over the past 400 years, ranging from the entire Republic of Paraguay in the 18th century to some 28 different colleges and universities in the United States in the 19th century.

An organization at the **Liberating Disciplines** stage of development should have vast cultural power and influence because of its continual, active attention to the many conundrums of managing the corporate dream. Few organizations in the West have stirred wider ambivalence about their influence than have the Jesuits over the past four centuries.

If partial illustrations of **Foundational Community** were difficult to offer, history to date may have provided us with only the merest shadows of **Liberating Disciplines.** (On the other hand, since organizations at these highest stages in theory engage in the study and choreography of all layers of experience—spiritual, strategic, behavioral, and external—and mask their inner workings from public view, merely external observation of them can yield no more than shadows of what is actually happening. Hence, the difficulty in discerning the **Liberating Disciplines** stage of organizing may result primarily from our own restricted research methodologies.)

In any event, the foregoing glances at the Chinese Communist Cultural Revolution, IBM, and the Jesuit Order should serve to warn us that, whatever the ethical and political implications may be of taking human and organizational development seriously, they are in no way clarified by reference to current political distinctions between left and right wing approaches, or between statist and market approaches, to action dilemmas.

IN CONCLUSION

In conclusion, these brief speculations and illustrations point to managerial development beyond the **Strategist** stage and to organizational development beyond the **Collaborative Inquiry** stage. These fleeting and shadowy images open toward a wide field beyond the scope of the research that underlies this book.

The challenge of promoting one another's development and greater social justice calls us toward this field.

The challenge of formulating, reinterpreting, and managing corporate dreams calls us toward this field.

Virtually everything else holds us back.

NOTES

1. This case is not reported in the study referenced in Chapter 6 because it was part of the pilot study prior to the creation of the formal scoring system.

2. L. Iacocca, *Iacocca: An Autobiography* (Toronto, Bantam: 1984), pp. xiii–xv.

3. This notion of "the executive role" is developed by T. Mills, *The Sociology of Small Groups* (Englewood Cliffs, N.J.: Prentice-Hall, 1965).

4. T. Wise, "IBM's $5,000,000,000 Gamble" and "The Rocky Road to the Marketplace," *Fortune*, September (p. 118 ff) and October (p. 137 ff), 1966.

5. E. Snow, *Red Star Over China* (New York: Evergreen Ed., Grove Press, 1973).

6. D. Hammarskjöld, *Markings* (New York: Alfred A. Knopf, 1964), p. 168.

7. K. Auletta, *The Art of Corporate Success: The Story of Schlumberger* (New York: Putnam, 1984).

8. Plutarch, "Pericles," in *The Rise and Fall of Athens,* trans. R. Warner (New York: Penguin Books, 1972).

9. E. Erickson, *Gandhi's Truth* (New York: W. W. Norton, 1969).

10. S. Ambrose, *Eisenhower: The President* (New York: Simon & Schuster, 1985).

11. For example, S. MacLaine, *Out on a Limb* (New York: Bantam, 1983).

12. D. Cook, *Charles de Gaulle: A Biography* (New York: Putnam, 1983), p. 67 ff .

13. Ibid., p. 257.

14. D. Kneale, "Working at IBM: Intense Loyalty in a Rigid Culture," *The Wall Street Journal,* April 7, 1986, p. 27.

15. Ignatius, of Loyola, *The Spiritual Exercises* (London: Burns and Oates, 1900).

16. R. Fulop-Miller, *The Power and Secret of the Jesuits* (New York: The Viking Press, 1930).

Theory and Method

Initially formulated by Jean Piaget in his research on children, developmental theory has been one of the most fruitful branches of psychological research of this century.[1] Only in the past decade, however, have a few researchers begun to explore whether the same developmental logic may apply, by analogy, to organizations.[2] Developmental theory makes a series of strong claims about how development occurs. It claims that:

1. Development consists of a series of *fundamental transfor mations*. Each transformation reduces the "worldview" in which one was embedded to a part of a more inclusive worldview. In each transformation, what has been *subject becomes object*: the worldview that the person *was* (controlled by) *becomes* a capacity that the person *has* (control of).
2. This series of transformations occurs in a *definite sequence*.
3. This sequence is *irreversible*—in other words, a person does not regress once having reached a given stage.
4. A person's *development can cease at any stage*—in other words, persons do not necessarily progress.
5. Persons at later stages of development can follow the logic of earlier stages, but *persons at earlier stages tend to reinterpret later stage actions and logics into their own terms.*

6. *Development is caused, neither by the person nor by the environment,* neither by "nature" or by "nurture," *but by an interaction between the two.*

If this theory is correct, persons literally operate in a number of different realities even when they are in the same room listening to the same words. This immediately explains why conflict is such a ubiquitous aspect of organizational life and why implementation of strategy is so difficult.

Of course, so strong and so elegant a theory is also controversial. The principal objection of other scholars is precisely that it is *too* strong and *too* elegant. Not all elements of the personality necessarily transform at once, they argue. A person may become conceptually more sophisticated while remaining emotionally or behaviorally less "mature." Or, even if all elements of the personality demonstrate later stage functioning at one time, regression to earlier stage functioning is still possible, say the critics, under conditions of stress, fatigue, or novelty.

Although these objections seem commonsensical, their validity is not easy to weigh. Developmental theorists will grant, for example, that a person measured as capable of late-stage functioning may behave in what appears to be an early-stage fashion at a given moment. But they will argue that the developmental question is not how the person behaves but how the person understands the behavior. Whereas an "early-stage" person will treat such behavior as natural, the "late-stage" person will be able to take a self-critical perspective on the behavior as a regrettable lapse or regression. Indeed, the person may be able to take two perspectives on the behavior at once, a self-critical perspective and a self-accepting perspective that forgives.

The issue of "regression under stress" has been an important concern for me since I first encountered developmental theory 20 years ago. I approached the theory as a practicing manager who operated under stress a great deal of the time. How persons understood things in sedentary reflection was of no interest to me unless it related clearly and strongly to how they (and I) behaved under stress. I also approached developmental theory with the question of whether it could explain organizational as well as individual development. I had just lived through some extraordinarily challenging organizational dilemmas that I knew

I had not fully understood, nor always handled well. I needed a theory that would make some sense of those events and could help me to do better next time.[3]

Approaching developmental theory from this pragmatic angle, I came to take a different perspective on the issue of "regression under stress" from either the developmentalists or their critics. First, I realized that each pragmatic situation in which we find ourselves must be the temporary focus for *many* developmental rhythms on *many* scales of size and time. A business meeting, for example, can be viewed as a developmental process. That particular meeting may be one of a series, perhaps representing a single stage in the longer developmental process. The stage of the company's development and of the meeting leader's development will also influence the quality of the meeting. Thus, what may appear, out of context, to be regressive behavior on the part of the leader may in fact be behavior attuned to an early developmental transformation of the meeting or of the group that has been newly brought together for this series of meetings.

On the other hand, it quickly became evident to me that neither I, nor any of the executives I knew, disciplined ourselves from moment to moment in the effort to distinguish these multiple rhythms and to sculpt timely, transforming actions. Even those with a reputation as magicians usually turned out to be magicians on one scale only—perhaps on the scale of interpersonal politics, perhaps on the scale of organizational strategy, perhaps on the scale of public symbolism. I wondered whether there might be later developmental stages than those thus far articulated—stages at which thinking, feeling, and acting would become integrated in an alertness to the multiple developmental rhythms impinging on each situation.[4] Of such persons, one would be able to say that neither their understanding nor their action regressed under conditions of stress, fatigue, and novelty. All of the data and theory presented in this book suggest that such persons are at best rare.

THE BOOK'S METHOD

Within this book, the organizational stage theory is itself still in an early stage of development. It has been tested in case study research by others in addition to this author.[5] But the impressionistic portrait of each stage represents quite accurately the low level of precision that currently exists in discriminating among the stages. For example, different eras in the century-long history of IBM are used to illustrate each of the stages. Although reasons are offered for the dates chosen to bound each stage, a more precise theoretical delineation of the stages, combined with stricter operational criteria for each proposition and a closer study of the company itself, could very conceivably result in relocating the stage boundaries.

When the organization case studies used in these stage-portraits do not derive directly from the author's research, the sources are cited. Some of these sources are scholarly. Some are not. When the source is not scholarly, the illustration is usually brief, intended only to suggest the significance of the topic, not to serve as an authoritative judgment about the instance.

As already noted earlier, the theory of personal development is at a relatively late stage in its development. Many researchers have developed and tested the well-known formulations of the theory, or their own. Interview coding techniques and questionnaire scoring systems have been developed and rigorously validated. The author's own research with colleagues, relating developmental stage to managerial style, is based on such systems and reports statistically significant findings.[6] This research underlies the anonymous case studies of managers that appear throughout the book. The case studies themselves are written either by the manager described or by this author (except where otherwise specified). When a case study is used to illustrate a particular stage of development, the manager has been scored at that stage by a carefully validated developmental test.[7] Also, the author has been able to observe the person's actual managerial behavior to explore whether it confirms the indications of the test score and written case. In many of these cases, the managers have received, and responded to, feedback on the developmental test. Overall, an increasing proportion of persons at each later stage asked for feedback, and this fact along with the differences by stage in their response to the feedback provided further confirmations of the original score. Finally, some 50 managers who participated in all the foregoing steps of the research also wrote soul-searching developmental autobiographies. So, as many as half a dozen independent sources of data underlie the assignment of each of the anonymous managerial cases to a particular stage of development.

The evidentiary status of the cases of managers in the public domain, like Geneen, Iacocca, Kissinger, and Stockman, is very different. Here, the author treats scholarly biographies and/or their own "work autobiographies" as data sources, with no test scores or other direct evidence to confirm or disconfirm interpretations. Some may object that autobiographical data is anything but objective, since the authors can beautify their own portraits as they wish. This is true, but from a developmental point of view the interest is precisely in what they think looks good and what they do not mention at all. For example, do they mention mistakes at all? Just small, insignificant, painless ones? Do they raise the question of whether the central thrust of their life's work is mistaken or demonic? Do they take the question seriously? Put differently, from a developmental point of view the interest is in what they argue about and how they argue, not in what conclusions they reach. In any event, these public portraits are meant to be suggestive of the concerns of a certain managerial style rather than proof that the person portrayed would be scored at that stage of development by the test referred to above.

Altogether, then, the data in this book are of various kinds and deserve varying degrees of confidence. Indeed, to ask whether the book proves anything is to miss its point. Its purpose is to outline and illustrate a kind of theory and a mode of practice that the author has tested and found edifying in his own practice as a professional manager—and to do so in such a way that others become committed to testing the theory and practice for themselves.

In other words, this book is not so much like a report on a finished piece of empirical science as it is an enactment of action inquiry. Insofar as this book's logic is representative of the Aristotelian, hypothetico-deductive paradigm of analytic science that logic is nested within a logic representative of the Anaxagorean, analogical approach of a more ancient action science.[8]

NOTES

1. Robert Kegan's *The Evolving Self* (Cambridge, Mass.: Harvard Univ. Press, 1982) reviews the history of developmental theory and emphasizes the dy-

namic process of development in a way that comes closest to the spirit of this book. Five years of research on managers using Jane Loevinger's measure of ego development and relating developmental stage to managerial style serves as background to the present work. J. Loevinger and E. Wessler, *Measuring Ego Development*, vols. 1, 2 (San Francisco: Jossey-Bass, 1970); K. Merron, "The Relationship between Ego Development and Managerial Effectiveness under Conditions of High Uncertainty" (doctoral thesis, Harvard Graduate School of Education, 1985).

2. W. Torbert, *Creating a Community of Inquiry* (London: Wiley, 1976); D. Lavoie and S. Culbert, "Stages of Organization and Development," *Human Relations* 31, no. 5 (1978), pp. 417–38; R. Quinn and K. Cameron, "Organizational Life Cycles and Shifting Criteria of Effectiveness: Some Preliminary Evidence," *Management Science* 29 (1983), pp. 33–51; K. Cameron and D.Whetten, "Models of the Organization Life Cycle: Applications to Higher Education," *Research in Higher Education*, 1983; W. Torbert, " 'Executive Mind,' Timely Action," *Re-Vision* 7, no. 1, (1983), pp. 3–21; J. Bartunek, "Changing Interpretive Schemes and Organizational Restructuring: The Example of a Religious Order," *Administrative Science Quarterly* 29 (1985), pp. 355–72; J. Bartunek and B. Betters-Reed, "The Stages of Organizational Creation," *American Journal of Community Psychology*, Fall 1986; D. Fisher, K. Merron, and W. Torbert, "Meaning Making and Managerial Effectiveness: A Developmental Perspective," paper presented at Academy of Management national meeting, Chicago, August 1986.

3. Torbert, *Creating a Community*.

4. Since that time, there has been additional theorizing about such later stages: L. Kohlberg, *Collected Paper on Moral Development* (Cambridge, Mass.: Center for Moral Education, 1976); K. Wilber, *The Atman Project: A Transpersonal View of Human Development* (Wheaton, Ill.: A Quest Book, 1980); E. Langer and C. Alexander, eds., *Beyond Formal Operations* (New York: Oxford University Press, 1984); S. Cook-Greuter, "Maps for Living: Ego-Development Theory from Symbiosis to Conscious Universal Embeddedness" (Cambridge, Mass.: Dare Institute, 1985).

5. See Note 2.

6. See Fisher, Merron, and Torbert, "Meaning Making"; also, W. Torbert and K. Merron, "Ego Development and Managerial Effectiveness" (Boston College School of Management, 1984).

7. Scorers were trained at Loevinger workshops at Washington University, St. Louis, and attained reliability ratings with other trained scorers of at least .80. The Loevinger Sentence Completion Test has been validated in a wide variety of ways by a wide variety of researchers. For example: C. Redmore, "Susceptibility to Faking of a Sentence Completion Test of Ego Development," *Journal of Personality Assessment* 40, no. 6 (1976), pp. 607–16, and J. Loevinger, "Construct Validity of the Sentence Completion Test of Ego Development," *Applied Psychological Measurement* 3, no. 3 (1979), pp. 281–311.

8. J. Needleman, *A Sense of the Cosmos: The Encounter of Modern Science and Ancient Tradition* (Garden City, N.Y.: Doubleday, 1975) and *The Heart of Philosophy* (New York: Alfred A. Knopf, 1982).

Identifying and Exercising
Action Inquiry

This appendix discusses one case that illustrates how to identify and exercise action inquiry, from moment to moment and sentence to sentence, in an ongoing business situation. A dilemma is described and the reader is invited to choose how you would act. Readers who choose to join in by making notes about how you would act can then test your responses to the dilemma against the four different responses offered and analyzed in the following pages.

The reader is invited to invest in this way because otherwise action inquiry will seem frustratingly incomplete. Taken either as a prepackaged technique or as a theory that can be learned first and then applied later, action inquiry *is* incomplete. It remains incomplete until each practitioner cultivates a quality of awareness for himself or herself, in the midst of action,that sculpts spontaneous action inquiry at each moment.

The case concerns a plant manager who has turned around three different plants for his company from decreasing profitability to increasing profitability, and who is now being considered for a new role as a corporate vice president to improve productivity and profitability of all plants showing shaky balance sheets. This manager seems to have the capacity to restructure plants. How can the president of the company determine whether this is so and whether the plant manager's style of restructuring is conducive to long-term success?

Here is the business situation.

Ed has been plant manager of three manufacturing plants for a large, multidivision corporation. In each case, the plant's profitability was declining when he arrived, in two of the cases showing losses in the years just prior to his becoming the plant's manager. In all three cases, he managed the plant so that it turned a profit in his first year. In the first two cases, profits were still larger in the following two years. He is at present nearing the end of his second year at the third plant.

Now he is being touted for promotion to a new corporate vice presidency to serve as a troubleshooter for the least profitable plants in all the divisions. But several of the board of directors are concerned about some events in the three plants Ed has managed that may or may not reflect negatively on Ed's managing:

1. The profitability of the first two plants began to decline precipitously as soon as Ed left.
2. Workers in one of the two plants have voted to unionize for the first time in its history.
3. Two of his six immediate subordinates at the third plant have recently resigned, protesting his "autocratic" management.

The board suggests that you, as corporate president, meet with Ed and test to decide for yourself whether he will be effective in the proposed role, not just in the short run but over time.

You know Ed from occasional meetings, and you know how hard he plays. You know he'll be prepared with a fast answer for anything you ask.

He enters your office for the interview.

Before we examine several alternative possible strategies and scenarios for this interview, let us establish what the overall significance of the interview is. What is at stake is whether Ed himself represents a rare form of capital and power—whether he is reliably capable of timely action that turns unprofitable plants into profitable settings once again. For every thousand of its employees, any company or agency today should consider itself fortunate if even one has developed such a capacity beyond the most rudimentary levels. Moreover, the company can congratulate itself if its organizational information systems are such that top management can identify such individuals, can further develop their capacity, and can place them in positions where their influence can have the greatest effect on the company as a whole. In short, this meeting between the president and Ed could easily rank among the top 20 actions the president is taking that year in terms of potential influence on the long-term profitability of the company. Thus, this event should be as worthy of sentence-by-sentence attention as, say, the document describing the financial terms of an acquisition that one is negotiating. The difference is that "reading" the meeting with Ed requires the skill of reading a living text in the language of action—as one participates in writing it!

ALTERNATIVE SOLUTIONS TO THE CASE

The reader may wish at this point to make some notes about a strategy for dealing with Ed as well as about what actually to say to Ed.

The following are three examples of strategies suggested and actual opening statements made in role plays by other managers who have responded to this case.

Strategy I: Try to put him (Ed) in my (the president's) position of judging and try to get his criteria for judging a troubleshooter.

Actual Exchange

President: Ed, one of the main responsibilities I see you having in this vice presidential spot is bringing along people who will be doing what you've been doing in the plants. Now tell me, what are some of the things you'll look for in choosing a troubleshooter, say, for the plant you are in now?

Ed: I think the first thing is the guy has got to be tough because the plant has been going downhill for two years or more and everybody's got a stake in what's going on. He is going to get baloney from people for every move he makes for the first year or so, so he has definitely got to not be turned by what he's told inside the plant. He's going to be perceived as a devil for a long period of time and he has to live with that.

President: Okay. Now let's look at him, say, five years down the line. We're looking at someone who's going in there to stay five years down the line, who's he going to have working for him?

Ed: Oh, well, I don't think it's something where a person should be thinking of staying for five years. Its the kind of thing you've got to get in and out. Once the thing is situated right you have to send in another management to consolidate things because he will have made a lot of enemies.

Strategy II: State the concern directly.

Actual Exchange

President: In evaluating you for your potential in the company, there's been some concern talked about that I share around some of the negative things that have happened in your plants, such as unionization and the resignations and the dips in the balance sheet as soon as you leave.

Ed: You are saying that you share that concern? That you think those things are my responsibility?

President: I do. I share in it and I want to understand it. Why did those things happen?

Ed: You want to understand it? Well, I know there's talk around the company about these things but I don't see how you can assign responsibility for the plants going downhill to me when in the time I was there they were going uphill and it's going downhill since I left. It seems to me if there had been a manager who could maintain what I started, there would be no problem today. The workers want consistent direction. When they get inconsistent management—first hands-off, then hands-on with me, then hands-off again—they unionize. As far as the two staff members resigning . . . it's the best thing that ever happened to me, saved me a year of grief trying to fire them or reassign them. They were the biggest part of this plant's problem.

Strategy III: Ask for specific analysis of what happened in the plants Ed managed.

Actual Exchange

President: Good morning, Ed. In discussing the new corporate vice presidency this morning, I'd like to get at what you've learned from these past experiences you've had. I'd like to hear your specific analysis of what's happened in your three tours as plant manager.

Ed: Yeah, I think I've learned a lot over the past eight years. You gotta remember that when I started out I'd never been a plant manager before and I had no sense of the rhythms of a given year. I was working my ass off, and I think in the first plant I was overlooking all kinds of ongoing processes as I was making all the changes I was making. And I had no idea until a year later when they came back to hit me in the face that I was going to have problems with them. By the time I got to the second plant, I knew a lot better how to use the budget to get things done, how to reassign people rather than telling them to act differently, how to wait.

The foregoing three strategies are quite different from one another in some ways. For example, Strategy II states the board's concern directly, whereas Strategies I and III approach the matter in relatively indirect ways. Strategies I and III also differ from one another. Strategy I is sculpted more obviously to test (to trap?) Ed. Strategy III seems less directive, more relaxing. Put a little differently, Strategy I seems tricky, Strategy II seems informative and information-seeking, and Strategy III seems conflict-avoiding.

As a first, very tentative guess, one can wonder whether the conflict avoidance of Strategy III indicates a **Diplomat**'s managerial style, whether the trickiness of Strategy I indicates a **Technician**'s style, and whether the goal-directedness and the openness about negative feedback in Strategy II indicates an **Achiever**'s style.

What is the relative effectiveness of each of the three strategies? What is it about the shape of the action that makes it more or less effective? Do any of these inquiry strategies more or less approximate what is meant here by action inquiry? Of course, the role-playing episodes quoted above are very brief, so they offer only limited evidence. But they are of interest nonetheless, because we are trying to learn how to judge *on a moment-to-mo-*

ment basis whether action is effective and whether it represents action inquiry.

About 50 percent of the more than 600 managers to whom this case has been presented agree that none of these strategies as implemented (nor the dozen or so other minor variations) help them to determine whether Ed is competent to take on the new role.

About 40 percent of the remaining participants initially believe that Ed is *not* competent for the job, as indicated primarily by what they refer to as Ed's defensiveness. (Many of these participants confess that they had already judged Ed as not competent for the job on the basis of the data presented in the case.) But when asked whether the president's behavior may have been responsible for Ed's defensiveness, most members of this subgroup agree. They note that Ed sounds more defensive in Strategy II, after the president questions his competence, than in Strategy III, where Ed acknowledges past mistakes quite openly. If the president's behavior is significantly responsible for Ed's defensiveness, then Ed's defensiveness serves less as data about *his* ineffectiveness than as data about *the president's* ineffectiveness. Indeed, Ed's responses to Strategies I through III are not necessarily inconsistent with the view that he is an intuitively great and courageous manager who is capable of action inquiry on an occasional basis (though he presumably knows nothing about the term "action inquiry"), who is used to being misunderstood, and who would respond well to a mentor capable of teaching him more about effective action.

What can become clear to participants in a discussion about this case, after having tried various role plays, is the degree to which we all tend to judge others based on incomplete, secondhand data, or on data biased by our method of inquiry.

Some will reply that such incompleteness and bias are inevitable in human interaction. True. But two related strategies can guard against, and significantly overcome, these limitations. First, one can treat the firsthand action in the current situation as data. Second, one can publicly state (and thereby test) one's initial interpretations about both firsthand and secondhand data.

Upon reflection, about 90 percent of the managers who have considered the "Ed case" presented in the foregoing pages conclude that all of the three strategies so far suggested are equally *ineffective* at this point in resolving the question of how effective Ed really is and whether he represents a source of action inquiry capital for the company.[1]

Is there a kind of truth that the president could tell Ed that more nearly approximates the notion of action inquiry and that can be shown to be more efficient, more effective, and more legitimate than any of the foregoing approaches?

Consider the following strategy and exchange:

Strategy IV: Begin by describing the dilemma that I (the president) face in attempting to conduct this conversation. Move to questions of Ed's managerial style and effects only as he either (1) acknowledges my dilemma, (2) describes his dilemma, or (3) illustrates the very questions about his style that others have raised by the way he acts during our conversation.

Actual Exchange

President: Hi, Ed. Glad you could come. In discussing this new vice presidency with you today, I would like to explore how you contribute to the long-term success of our company, since doing just that is the point of this new role. There are issues that are very personal in the sense that they concern your overall managerial style, and very nebulous in the sense that no one has hard data on the relationship between one manager's style and the company's long-term success. So, it's an area where it's easy to get defensive and just spin our wheels. I'm not at all confident that we can have the conversation I would like to have. I'm not sure how willing you are to get into this kind of exploration. I certainly know I can't make you get into it.

Ed: But of course you can. No problem. I'm perfectly willing to share with you anything you would like to discuss. Let's not beat around the bush. What's up?

President: I wonder if your immediate subordinates and the hourly workers at your plants feel as "dismissed" as I do now. I'm telling you that I have some problems here, and you respond by telling me that I don't. One of the questions on the larger scale is whether you're able to acknowledge and respond to other people's versions of reality.

However this conversation might continue, the reader will note that it differs qualitatively from all of the first three exchanges. Whereas the first three strategies are more or less direct about *Ed's past actions or present opinions,* the fourth strategy directly addresses the situation framing all the other discussions— namely, *the action dilemma that both men face together in this meeting.* Both of the president's actual comments are attempts to describe and manage the present dilemma. The president's first comment invites Ed to join in the managing process. His second comment responds to Ed's first comment, focusing not on the content of Ed's words so much as on the effect of his speech as action.

Since the president neither accuses Ed of anything in his first statement nor is indirect in a way that could make Ed feel he should protect all his flanks, it seems valid to treat the way Ed responds as data about *his* managerial style. In this particular scenario, Ed comes off sounding more hearty and dismissive than defensive, in the one short comment we hear. Whether this mini-action is representative of his general style is a question that the president immediately asks directly (rather than reaching a private, untested conclusion about it), while making it clear that this particular act of Ed is having a negative effect. This negative feedback should be highly credible, since the president is describing his own experience and not some secondhand information that could be distorted, and since Ed cannot afford to "dismiss" the president if he wishes the vice presidency.

The outstanding questions about Ed have been brought into sharp focus. Whether he is effective and whether he can engage in explicit action inquiry is testable by observing his (verbal) actions in the remainder of the conversation. Thus, although we can make no final determination of this strategy's effectiveness, it seems significantly more *efficient* and *effective* than the first three strategies at this point in the conversation. Moreover, it is the only strategy that is *legitimizing* the very questions the conversation is meant to answer as the conversation proceeds. As enacted, the primary effect of the other three strategies is to put Ed on the spot rather than to highlight the issue that puts both of them on the spot.

Both men are "on the spot" as we leave the exchange—both men are exposed and vulnerable. Moreover, the president's strategy is unfamiliar, and the rules of this game are still unclear. These aspects of the situation will undoubtedly leave many readers with the uncomfortable feeling that something is very much amiss. For some, the confrontation and potential for open conflict endemic to this approach feels dangerous and unacceptable. For others, the lack of clearly defined boundaries on what may be discussed over the next few minutes feels counterproductive. For the manager committed to the importance of identifying whether Ed can exercise action inquiry, however, these are the very conditions that can test for action inquiry.

Other readers may react even more negatively to Strategy IV. They may feel that Ed is here the target of misunderstanding or even manipulation. But if Ed is capable of action inquiry, he should be able to raise this issue and should wish to do so, both to test his own perception and to learn from the president's response whether Ed will want to work with him as closely as the new role would demand. If the president is, in turn, truly capable of recognizing and appreciating action inquiry, he would treat such an act by Ed as one indicator that he deserves the promotion.

Strategy IV makes explicit and knits together four basic elements of human speech. These four elements are:

1. **Framing**—the frame or purpose of the current endeavor, setting, or conversation—not just the speaker's goal, but the frame or purpose that underlies everyone's participation.
2. **Advocating**—what the speaker advocates be done within the frame.
3. **Illustrating**—a concrete example to clarify what the speaker is referring to.
4. **Inquiring**—a question about how others respond to the speaker's perspective and inititative.[2]

In order to make meaning out of any comment, listeners must make inferences about all four of these elements, even though a given comment may be explicit about only one. For example, Strategy III is explicit only about the *inquiry* the president wishes to make of Ed. Indeed, most comments in ordinary conversation are explicit about only one or at most two of these four elements. Of the four elements, the one most rarely made explicit is *framing*.

In his two comments in the role play of Strategy IV, the president makes all four elements explicit, although they are so tightly interwoven that they are difficult to separate out. Framing and advocating are most prominent in the first comment. Illustrating and inquiring are most prominent in the second comment. The president might have helped Ed and the conversation more if he had asked a straightforward question at the end of his first remark.

By making all four of these elements explicit, action inquiry increases the control of the speaker over the direction of the conversation while simultaneously inviting others to influence its direction as well. A second effect of making all four elements explicit is to reduce the likelihood that a listener will make a mistaken inference. Making all four of the elements explicit also makes it easier for the listener to disconfirm explicitly whatever elements do not make sense to him or her. If the listener disconfirms the original speaker's suggested framing of the situation, then reframing becomes a possibility for one person or the other, or for the situation itself.

Ed certainly seems comfortable disconfirming the president in Strategy IV. Insofar as Ed is disconfirming the president's concern that Ed may not be willing to hold the conversation, Ed is on strong ground. Until we have evidence to the contrary, we are probably willing to grant that Ed is in the best position to know what he is willing or not willing to do.

However, Ed throws out the baby with the bathwater: He also disconfirms the president's concern that it is objectively difficult, because there is no hard data, to assess Ed's contribution to the long-term success of the company. Ed's statement either neglects that part of what the president said altogether or else is referring to it when he says "Let's not beat around the bush." In either case, he has dismissed the president's effort to frame their joint dilemma.

Perhaps Ed is right. Perhaps there was no baby, only bathwater. Perhaps the president sees problems where there are none. Perhaps the president is one of this company's problems. If so, then Ed has the chance over the next few minutes of conversation to advocate and illustrate this perspective and inquire whether the president accepts it.

In role-playing Ed, the effort is to play him as easily edgy and abrasive but also as very responsive to the tone the president sets (note how willing to acknowledge errors Ed is in response to Strategy III). This role playing manner tests whether participants in the role play are simply put off by a tough exterior or will inquire to see whether there is real value beneath. This way of playing Ed demonstrates how much one's own behavior (the president's) can influence how others (in this case, Ed) present themselves. Seeing this emphasizes how important it is to use action inquiry to test what caused the behavior one observes, to guard against invalid generalizations about others, and to invite action inquiry in response. *Only an executive practicing action inquiry can validly determine whether another is capable of practicing it.*

Here, at the end of this extended illustration, we are not yet certain whether Ed is capable of action inquiry or whether he should be promoted. But, the point of the illustration was to help the reader gain a moment-to-moment sense of the challenge of identifying and exercising action inquiry. To exercise action inquiry, the manager must develop an awareness that listens critically to one's own speaking as well as to others, that attunes itself simultaneously to verbal messages and to action messages, that can translate the impact on oneself of others' actions instantaneously into words, and that feels strengthened by public testing and by learning truth rather than preserving illusion.

NOTES

1. The author is indebted to Chris Argyris for this general technique of managing action cases. Similar sorts of cases, with a different but closely related set of analytic categories, are to be found in C. Argyris and D. Schon, *Theory in Practice: Increasing Professional Effectiveness* (San Francisco: Jossey-Bass, 1974).

2. Again, Argyris and Schon have taken the lead in defining and illustrating these categories and showing their wider significance. See C. Argyris *Reason, Learning, and Action* (San Francisco: Jossey-Bass, 1981); D. Schon, *The Reflective Practitioner* (New York: Basic Books, 1983); C. Argyris, R. Putnam, and D. Smith, *Action Science* (San Francisco: Jossey-Bass, 1985). Also, W. Torbert, "Interpersonal Competence," chapter in A. Chickering, *The Modern American College* (San Francisco: Jossey-Bass, 1981).

INDEX